SECOND
NATURE

SECOND NATURE

Edited by Richard Mabey
with Susan Clifford & Angela King
for Common Ground

JONATHAN CAPE
THIRTY BEDFORD SQUARE LONDON

Jonathan Cape Ltd,
30 Bedford Square, London WC1B 3EL

Two of the essays published here have appeared
elsewhere previously: 'The Blinded Eye' by John
Fowles was first published in *Animals*, January 1971,
Vol. 13, No. 9; 'Animal World' by John Berger was
first published in *New Society* on 25 November, 1971.

British Library Cataloguing in Publication Data

Second nature.
1. Ecology – Great Britain
I. Mabey, Richard   II. Clifford, Susan
III. King, Angela   IV. Common Ground
574.5'0941   QH137

ISBN 0-224-02191-5

Printed in Great Britain by
Butler & Tanner Ltd
Frome and London

Contents

Preface by Susan Clifford & Angela King   vii
Introduction: Entitled to a View? by Richard Mabey   ix

Personal Landscapes

Ten-yard Panorama by Norman Nicholson   3
Sutton Mandeville – Walter's Path; *Westmere Evening*;
   September Daybreak (Crockey Hill) by Norman Ackroyd   12
Town, Bad: Country, Good by Edward Blishen   15
Lost Sheep; *In the Heat of May*; *Sheep at Upcott* by James Ravilious   25
Remedial Scenes by Ronald Blythe   28
Harry, St Peter's Allotment; *Kids with Collected Junk near*
   Byker Bridge by Sirkka-Liisa Konttinen   35
Knowing a Place by Peter Levi   36
Medicine Wheel by Chris Drury   44
Sheep Spaces; *Sod Swap*; *Wet Stones* by David Nash   46
The Demanding Landscape by Bel Mooney   49
Peak District, Derbyshire; *near Haystacks, Cumbria* by Fay Godwin   54
From Flint to Shale by Michael Berkeley   56
Revelation; *Isle of Arran*; *Vision* by John Hilliard   63
Letter to Laura by Fay Weldon   67
Abbotsbury Gardens by John Hubbard   74

Nature and Culture

The Blinded Eye by John Fowles   77
The Sunken Lane by John Hubbard   79
Bracken Leaves; *Sycamore Leaves*; *Ice Stacks*; *Ice Arch*; *Snowball in*
   Trees by Andy Goldsworthy   80

*Childhood Ground Abiding Places; Avon Gorge Water
Drawing; A Line in England, 1977; Low Water Circle
Walk, 1980* by Richard Long   90
Wind Series, Ambergate, Derbyshire by John Blakemore   94
Animal World by John Berger   96
Dog, 1980; Barn Owl by Elisabeth Frink   103
Closely-observed Creatures by David G. Measures   105
Sketchbooks, 1976–83; Hare; Lapwings on Stubble
by David G. Measures   105
Swallow Drinking; Carder Bee by Stephen Dalton   116
Night of Total Eclipse by David G. Measures   118
Possession by Kim Taplin   119
A Hollow Lane on the North Downs; No Horizons; Barking Dogs
by Hamish Fulton   132
The Time Things Take by David Pownall   136
Beginners' Way by Jamie McCullough   146
Sheep Grazing in Long Grass (No. 1); Henry Moore and Sheep Piece
by Henry Moore   148
Farndale; Grange, Cumbria; Lee Moor Variations
by Alexander Mackenzie   150
Plutonium Landscape by Conrad Atkinson   152
Laugharne by Dylan Thomas's House; Walter Scott's Tower
by Jorge Lewinski   153
Stone Staff and Triangle (No. 13) by Paul Hempton   154

Beyond the Golden Age

Home is Where the Heart is by Leonie Caldecott   157
England, Home and Beauty by Fraser Harrison   162
February; May; July; November by Paul Hill   173
The Golden Age of Labour by John Barrell   177
My Mother, Bolton Abbey, Yorkshire, November 1982
by David Hockney   187
Cloud Drawing by Roger Ackling   188
Badger Set; Frog Spawn by Paul Hill   196
A Place in the Country by Colin Ward   198
The Fritillary Fields; March by Robin Tanner   207
Between Country and City by Raymond Williams   209
Biographical Notes   220
Acknowledgments   234
Common Ground   235
Picture Credits   236

Preface

BY SUSAN CLIFFORD & ANGELA KING

Common Ground is a small charitable organisation which was established in 1983 with two main objectives: to promote the importance of common plants and animals, familiar and local places, local distinctiveness and our links with the past; and to explore the emotional value these things have for us by forging practical and philosophical links between the arts and the conservation of nature and landscapes.

One of our first concerns was to invite artists and writers to express their feelings about Britain's dwindling wild life and countryside. We had all heard a good deal about this from politicians and those professionally involved with the countryside and felt it was very important that we should be talking more about the conservation of our common cultural heritage and less about science, for example the current emphasis on the preservation of specific rare plants and animals and special 'protected' places. We approached Jonathan Cape and Richard Mabey in the autumn of 1982 with the idea of this anthology which, we hoped, would help to broaden the base of the conservation constituency and bring fresh ideas to the debate. With Richard Mabey's help and guidance the original theme has developed and his choice of writers has resulted in the exploration of many different approaches. The choice of artists is ours alone.

At their best the arts freshen our perception and the underlying and unifying reason behind our selection is that the artists chosen have enabled us to see nature and landscape in new and exciting ways.

The visual works do not 'illustrate' the essays, they are individual statements in another language. Our choice has been from living artists and includes new works for the book, previously unpublished works chosen by us or by the artist and a few earlier works. We have not tried to be comprehensive in our choice of styles, schools or approaches.

Many of the artists such as Richard Long, David Nash and Andy Goldsworthy, work in the countryside and make use of the natural materials which they find around them. Their work may be barely conspicuous and is often transient: a photograph of the work being the only concession to immortality. Hamish Fulton distils his experience of a walk into a single image, one photograph (with the addition of words). He does not touch or rearrange natural objects. Roger Ackling's inspiration comes perhaps more from the sky than the land, and he has chosen to express his notion of time and space by using the energy of the sun to burn natural materials such as card, wood and bone. The negative, burnt lines are the sun; the spaces in between them (positive) the clouds – an automatic photographic process.

Other artists we have chosen use more traditional methods. Some have used the medium of photography in fresh ways to explore familiar themes. David Hockney, unsatisfied with the photograph as a single image, uses a composite of photographs to construct what he considers to be a truer sense of time and place. John Hilliard splices positive and negative images to jog our perception. John Blakemore explores intimate knowledge of place and its dynamics by bringing movement into the still photograph.

Just as successive generations have redefined 'nature' so these artists make their own statements about their relationships with it, whether it be through the sumptuousness of a sunken lane in Dorset by John Hubbard, the magical and mysterious influence of Silbury Hill which preoccupies Paul Hempton, or the photographs of James Ravilious which record the continuity of life in rural north Devon.

People do not often feature in the images included, not because we or the artists favour wilderness to humanity, but because most of the British countryside is already so manifestly shaped by humans that it seems neither necessary nor appropriate to portray them. People in the picture often detract from our seeing the fundamentals of place and their omission allows us to have a more direct relationship with place and nature.

We hope that the essays and pictures will help others to see our surroundings with new eyes and will broaden our commitment and deepen our conviction to look after them.

Introduction:
Entitled to a View?

BY RICHARD MABEY

Sometime during 1983 I heard a distinguished scientist suggest that one answer to the problem of the picking of rare flowers might be for botanists to cut off the blooms first, so that other pickers – less scrupulous, no doubt – would be unable to find them. I imagine it was too mad and mean-spirited a proposition for anyone to take seriously. But it seemed to me to symbolise all the misanthropy and special pleading that has characterised the current debate about our relationships with nature and the land.

We have all become well-informed about the world's ecological crises, about the destruction of the tropical rain forests, the pollution of the oceans, the profligacy of agribusiness, and even about the economic connections between all these. Yet this knowledge has remained curiously remote, not connected in any obvious way with our ordinary, everyday experience. The fate of the natural world, which is also of course our fate, has been declared the province of specialists.

Even here in Britain, where the relationships between humankind and nature have been a central part of our cultural life (especially our painting and writing) we have begun to shy away from making personal, emotional responses. We have been persuaded of the overriding importance of rare organisms and scientifically defined special sites and conversely, of the disposability of the commonplace. We have been told that passion must be replaced by compromise and consensus, and that it is misguided to look for private political and economic interests behind the destruction of our last refuges. So we hold back (with relief, often) from making the links between, say, the destruction of our local copses and our foreign policy, between animals' rights and property interests. And as our worries grow, so the conventional wisdom increasingly reduces them to purely technical problems, for which the gathering of more scientific or economic evidence will, by itself, generate a solution. Moral arguments are now seen as, at their best, sentimental and impractical, and at their worst – it is a favourite phrase – 'purely subjective preferences'.

Somewhere along the line many deep and widely shared human feelings – an affection for native landscapes, a basic sympathy towards other living things, a feeling of respect for our rural history – have become regarded as a devalued currency.

This is the territory that is explored by *Second Nature*. It is not another book explicitly about the ecological crisis, and none of its contributors is a professional biologist or conservationist. Its origins lie in the need – widely felt, and focussed as the theme for this book by Common Ground – to bring the argument in a very literal sense back home, to the local landscapes that are most people's firsthand experience of nature and to the variety of personal meanings which they hold for us. An important part of that aim is an attempt to restore the links between the conservation movement and the arts, and the contributors are all working writers, teachers and artists for whom a relationship with nature and the land is both a matter of personal concern and a subject of their work. The responsibility for commissioning the essays and shaping the text has been mine and it will inevitably reflect some personal bias and preferences. (Angela King and Susan Clifford of Common Ground introduce the artists they commissioned separately in the Preface – though it is worth saying here that most share the same preoccupations as the writers). In the broadest sense the anthology is a radical one, though the individual contributors' positions may differ a good deal in emphasis. Some are from the political left, others more influenced by eastern philosophical ideas. Most would find at least some sympathy with the burgeoning green politics. But their contributions share two important common features. First, an insistence on relating the personal experience of nature and landscape to the larger issues of work, feminism, nuclear disarmament and the future of the countryside. Secondly, a perspective from backgrounds in teaching and the arts that are usually regarded as marginal to rural or ecological affairs. None of us – and I must begin to include myself here – is either a scientist or a thoroughbred countryperson. None of us works the land as a first occupation, though many of us live in rural surroundings. We are all observers, who will be regarded in some quarters as a species of tourist, beyond the pale because of *how* we look at the world, regardless of where we live.

Raymond Williams, whose book *The Country and the City* has been a source of inspiration to many contributors (and who has been given the last word in this book), has described there how strong but generalised associations have gathered around the actual settlements and inhabitants of the countryside.

On the country has gathered the idea of a natural way of life: of peace, innocence and simple virtue. On the city has gathered the idea of an achieved centre: of learning, communication, light. Powerful hostile associations have also developed: on the city as a place of noise, worldliness and ambition; on the country as a place of backwardness, ignorance, limitation. A contrast between country and city, as fundamental ways of life, reaches back into classical times ... Yet the real history, throughout, has been astonishingly varied. The 'country way of life' has included the very different practices of hunters, pastoralists, farmers and factory farmers, and its organisation has varied from the tribe and the manor to the feudal estate, from small peasantry and tenant farmers to the rural commune, from the *latifundia* and the plantation to the large capitalist enterprise and the state farm.

It has also included, one might add, the activities of itinerant labourers and wandering scholars, craftsmen, pedlars, scientists and visionaries.

Yet the myths and stereotypes are stubbornly persistent. I can remember being called a 'nature writer' for the first time, and flinching at the implication that this was different from simply being a writer; and at the hint of the same slight dottiness that Richard Jefferies's father saw when he referred disdainfully to 'our Dick poking about in them hedges'. Yet it was because I was also an outsider myself that I was able to see how narrowing these generalisations were, and how the fact that a distinctive place and way of life called the countryside still survived, against all odds, had very little to do with its imagined simplicity and immunity from the worldliness of the town.

The actual, detailed experience of life, work and play in the countryside simply will not be reduced to these categories. There is for instance a revival of many basic rural crafts, but only because wealthy urban emigrants are providing a market for their products; grassroots folk-music flourishes in all manner of eclectic mixtures of dance, song, oral ballads and grand choral extravagance; and intensively managed vineyards have revived acceptable home-grown wine for the first time for maybe a thousand years.

I suspect that much of what is generally regarded as the 'rural tradition' has this repeated blending of foreign and local, old and new, right through its history. It is what has kept it alive. This is especially true of one of the cornerstones of our popular involvement with nature − our passion for gardening and the mixture of ingenuity, generosity and sense of fellowship makes it one of the richest strands in our common culture. These leisure enthusiasms are merging with work, producing an exciting new traffic in ideas. The revival of traditional woodland management, for instance, has involved bringing to the oldest source of renewable energy the modern equipment and skills and labour of a largely urban workforce.

All of this is worlds away from the generalisations about rural and urban outlooks and achievements which Raymond Williams has exposed. Yet the belief in these fundamental contrasts still underpins many of our attitudes, and it is important to try to understand why they should be so tenacious.

One reason may be a root that goes deep into Western culture. The whole Judaeo-Christian tradition (especially after the intellectual revolutions of the Renaissance) rested on the assumption that humankind and nature were fundamentally separate and different. Humans were unique, it was believed, in possessing souls and a moral sense. Every new scientific discovery and cultural achievement reaffirmed their intellectual superiority. If there were still a few sensitive consciences unconvinced, there was always the scriptural edict that gave humans 'dominion' over the natural world and seemed to justify the idea that it was our property, to be used as we thought fit.

During the last two centuries we have seen at least two contrasting developments of this view, both, ironically, resulting from the growth of scientific knowledge. First, the realisation that we also are part of nature, as dependent on the efficient functioning of the ecosystem as whales or waterweeds. Secondly, an increasing understanding of the ways in which we are *different*, and of how we could further exploit nature to our own advantage. We are having a hard time reconciling the understanding of our dependence with the facts of our mastery, present and potential, and may be stuck with the existential giddiness that results.

What is especially revealing, however, is the way this basic dualistic view of the world worked its way through – and was to some extent used as a justification for – the long transformation of our society from a federation of relatively self-sufficient communities to a fully industrialised state, divided by work and location as well as class. One result was that a notion of 'the countryside' as a separate aspect of 'the country' became established, and it began to be seen as either a place of retreat or a centre of productivity. These different countrysides often co-exist in the same place – though they were not seen as related, and many landowners went to great pains to ensure no signs of labour marred their prospects.

In a different quarter was the growth of rural nostalgia amongst people who had never experienced rural life. This is a potent and vulnerable emotion, and has been exploited by the publishing and tourist industries for at least 200 years. Yet it is often felt with such force, almost as a personal loss, that it cannot simply be dismissed as a creation of the media. As Fraser Harrison suggests in his essay it may spring from a deep sense of estrangement from natural life.

All these movements of ideas, in the complex and often contradictory combinations they assume in the real world, have been reflected in the rural literature of the last century and a half. This is no place to try to précis what is an immensely complicated tradition; but it can perhaps be said that its rarest species is one in which writers explore their experiences of the rural and natural worlds (and, significantly, the two adjectives are often used synonymously) without assuming in advance that they must fit into a pattern of divided values and images – people and nature, town and country, emotion and intellect, native innocence and acquired learning. So there has been much writing of a chiefly descriptive kind, sometimes very fine, as in the later work of Richard Jefferies, but more often drained of emotional or moral content. There has been a parallel strand of 'Country Lore' which consists of falsified, often whimsical, accounts posing as revelations of inside knowledge. Through much of the writing there has been a reluctance to discuss moral or political ideas, as if in some way these broke the long dream of the countryside as a way of escape. As John Barrell writes in his essay, 'The Golden Age of Labour', the most potent myth in rural writing is of a 'natural' order, 'before politics, even before history; and as long as that remains our ideal, it seems as incapable of being realised by political action as of being realised without it'.

These strands in rural writing have been crucial in shaping our attitudes and many of them are discussed critically in the following essays. In one sense this anthology – especially those aspects that deal with firsthand experiences of place and nature – is part of that tradition, but it diverges from it in the shared concern of the contributors to make alternative experiences of rural and natural worlds *available* both to themselves and their audience. A major fault in English writing about the countryside is the way it has distanced its readers because the writers themselves felt distanced, by background, education or the process of writing itself, and have deliberately attempted to deny or hide their own viewpoint. It is as if they saw their learning and their capacity for reflection as barriers between them and the state of nature they wished to become. Edward Thomas, notoriously, said he wanted to write prose 'as near akin as possible to that of a Surrey peasant', with results that were often patronising to peasants, and fairly disastrous for Thomas's style. It was only when he turned to poetry and accepted his role as a displaced person, that his true – and, one might say, most *natural* – gifts became available.

H. J. Massingham, whose blend of documentary description and nostalgia can be seen as the precursor of 'modern' country writing, struggled continually to find an appropriate voice. Like Thomas, Massingham was an Oxford graduate, and regarded his background as something of an encumbrance. His aim was to commemorate the essence of rural life and challenge the fabric of what he called 'modernism'. He wished to become a 'genuine countryman' himself, and saw no contradiction in approaching this task by burying himself in the scholarly study of rural architecture, farming history, biology, dialect and literature. The results, as might be expected, were mixed: many accurate and sympathetic accounts of rural work and crafts; some of the earliest writing on landscape that implied it had a human history; and an urgent pleading of the importance of regionalism, decentralisation and ecology thirty years before these ideas came into real currency. Yet alongside this he built up an idealised portrait of the essence of the country, of all England and its history, in which the real variety is reduced to a formula. This is his description of a 'thinking countryman':

> He is far less pessimistic than is the intelligentsia of the town . . . he is patronised, ignored or despised. Legislation is continually against him; he is the victim of an urban economics built up without reference to him and, so far as his freedom of livelihood is concerned, is no more than a helot . . . Yet he lives not with despair but with nature. He is fortified against the depression imposed upon him because nature is cyclical and a perpetual fount of interest, a perpetual change and a perpetual stability . . . He has roots, he lives the organic life and so he can see our urban civilisation in a detachment denied to the urban mind.

There is so much that is good here – the making of the link with 'urban economics', the noting of the essential 'cyclical' nature of land work – that the reduction of all countrymen to a single emblematic figure, living (in *1948*) not even a, but *the* 'organic life' is almost forgivable. Yet the fostering of this idea of an exclusive kind of natural knowledge 'denied to the urban mind' is one of the most damaging of our myths of rural life. Used more generously, of course, the legend of 'the way we do things here' has been a powerful defence of the character of both local communities and landscapes; but it has to be said that it is also increasingly used by a small minority of the rural population as a justification of private (as distinct from communal) interest and privilege. As I write this our local paper is running the story of an unhappy collision of interests on the fringe of the Green Belt. A group of young children on a public footpath by a lake wandered into a large duck shoot, and were so distressed by the rafts of dead and wounded birds on the water that their parents complained to the local landowner and the press. He retorted that people who were upset by the shoot 'should be living in another country'. These clashes happen and are beyond any compromise. I have been in one myself, with the wild buckshot of a 'courtesy' shoot raining down on a group of junior children I was showing round a nature reserve. But what is inexcusable is that glib blurring of meanings, that appropriation not just of the whole country-side but the whole nation to a single point of view about our proper relationship with nature.

Second Nature, by contrast, is suggesting that the immense range of experiences of natural life and landscape reaching back through our history and often beyond any narrow definition of rural traditions, is part of a *common* culture.

I can only add, in conclusion, a personal note on the development of my own viewpoint. I can use the word quite literally here, since my attitudes towards the countryside in general have been reflected in my changes in feeling towards a particular stretch of landscape (which I have always known as the Top) that I have known intimately all my life. I find that I have been in at least four positions in respect of it, each adding to the former rather than replacing it, and none of them very proper in an area where such a high premium is put on knowing your place.

The first was as trespasser. I grew up inside a family which had left London just before the war to settle on the edge of a Chiltern commuter town, and I had what I suspect was a typical suburban boyhood. There was a bit of bird-watching (and birds'-nesting), a bit of paid work in the local orchards and harvest fields, and long summer holidays spent out of doors in camps under fallen trees, all contained within an area of not much more than two square miles and marked out territorially by widely agreed natural boundaries. Yet this was also the setting for a good deal of youthful business that had nothing particularly to do with being 'in the country' – assignations, summer parties, even the imposed hardship of school cross-country runs, the memories of which still make me shy away from the rutted, gorsy track they followed.

I cannot recall ever thinking that I lived at the edge of two sullenly opposed value systems, and I began slipping across the demarcation lines at an early age. It was simple physical intrusion at this stage and by my early teens I was quite resigned to being challenged by armed men in woods. At the time this seemed an entirely natural part of growing up – 'or growing out' and learning where one slipped into foreign territory. Exploring barricaded estates was no different from trespassing into other areas adults regarded as their preserve and was likely to be met with the same rebuff. It was only much later that I began to understand and resent the full implications of those confrontations on lonely paths.

The second view of exactly the same two square miles was as a romantic. The transition hadn't much to do with an extension of my boyhood interest in natural history. It was part of a general awakening that started when I was about fifteen. This was the time of *Look Back in Anger* and the beginning of C.N.D. and I can remember how *right* it felt to be taking the annual walk from Aldermaston across the edge of my Chiltern homeland in the spring sunshine. The dawnings of adult emotions – anxiety, exhilaration and outrage – somehow fused in the idea of nature as a refuge for life and feeling. The writers our little group of sixth form rebels worshipped were Blake, Shelley and above all Dylan Thomas, whose poem 'The force that through the green fuse drives the flower' seemed to sum up all we believed in. On the long bicycle rides up to cricket I used to gaze out in almost animistic rapture across the vast sweep of the Top, at its hazy ripples of chalky cornfields and steep woods and think: *that* is the model for the New Jerusalem.

A few years later I learned that the whole vista – woods, winter-bournes and all – had been bought by an insurance company, and might have been fatally disenchanted if I hadn't already lost most of my ingenuousness and moved into the third viewpoint, that of a rather scholarly objective observer.

The change had begun whilst I was at university during the black Cold War days of the mid-1960s, when it seemed improper to be concerned about anything other than human predicaments. That guilty sliver of doubt about the relevance of the natural world stayed with me until the late 1960s, when the growth of the conservation movement began to reveal the links between human politics and natural processes. Ironically, it was an essay by that most urban of writers, George Orwell, that was eventually most supportive. 'Thoughts on the Common Toad' is a celebration of spring and like much late Orwell is sharp, over-simplified and shrewish. It was published in 1946, only a couple of years before the Massingham passage quoted above, yet it gives a radically different view of the accessibility of nature, suggesting something closer to a commonwealth than a freemasonry. Added to a widened experience of countrysides (and countries) beyond my own parish and a less rose-tinted attitude towards the realities of landwork and owner-ship, it helped make the view from the Top not just an abstract vision, but a prospect of a whole people's history and inheritance. I began to make that crucial link between two different pasts: my own, half-remembered, half-imagined no doubt, and the land's. I learned that the woods I played in as a child had been there at least since medieval days, that paths I walked every week of my life were bounded by Saxon hedges and in all likelihood had been trodden out in neolithic times. I became fascinated by maps, and by the more palpable records of ditches and banks that had been scratched out of the land over the centuries. Above all I became enthralled by woods, and by the millennium of work by local people that had shaped and sustained them. The revelation that two of our best local copses were possibly thousands of years old came just in time to see them vanish under the insurance company's subsidised barley.

The fourth and final viewpoint was an inevitable result of this. A few years ago I bought a tiny ancient wood just beyond the rim of my home range and became a landowner myself. It has been a vertiginous crossing of many personal territorial boundaries; taking me into my first experience of regular labour on the land, and into a lineage that I had always instinctively distrusted. I still do not feel easy in ownership and find that in the wood I sometimes hide from strangers just as I did when I was a footloose child. Yet the experience is revealing much about the relationships that are possible between a community and its natural resources. The wood is now a parish plot again. Many people, locals and visitors of all ages and backgrounds, come to work in it, helping to redress the effects of forty years of mismanagement, cutting their own firewood, or simply walking and enjoying the bluebells that flood the ground in May. The children build camps and watch badgers and are gradually picking up some of the principles and skills of renewable cropping.

Scraps of the wood's long history are continually emerging, sometimes from old documents, sometimes from the ground itself. Only two centuries ago it was part of a huge tract of unbroken woodland nearly three miles across. Before that, a stretch of the enigmatic Chiltern earthwork known as Grim's Ditch was cut through it. The Ditch's origins are very obscure, and it acts like a psychologist's inkblot test, persuading observers that it is Saxon, Roman or Iron Age according to their preferences. There is an even chance it was built by slave labour.

Looking at landscapes in this way has become an ingrained habit. I find it hard to walk alongside hedgebanks without musing on their age, or to go through an ancient wood without grubbing about for signs of coppicing. But I am not at all sure how this new awareness of the human origins of landscapes affects the way I regard them. It has vastly increased the intellectual fascination they hold for me and the outrage I feel when they are gratuitously destroyed. But if I am honest it has not much altered the way they *appear* to me. In that I am still the romantic pantheist I was when I was a teenager. Whatever I find out about the origins of Grim's Ditch, its first meaning for me will always be a dark winter tunnel and a woodcock jinking away over the damp leaves; and in spring the bank where the first moschatel flowers, gothic and diminutive, glow palely amongst the twisted roots. The Ditch's history and the centuries of past makers and users are part of it, but they are always an aspect at which you look back, through that glittering confrontation with the present that nature will never let you escape.

More recently I have helped make a bit of landscape myself, a wide track across the steepest slope in the wood so that we can take out the firewood more easily. There were many heart-searching discussions before we even started. Then we felled the trees ourselves, and hired a contractor to grub out the stumps and grade the track with a huge excavator that was normally used (and the irony escaped no one) for agricultural drainage work. The driver had once worked making clock cases in London's East End, and had moved out to the Chilterns for his health. He made that track with an efficiency and sensitivity that has permanently changed my attitude towards the supposed contrast between craft and mechanisation. He could *nudge* trunks and trees into new positions, and he worked his way backwards down the track, pulling and smoothing a platform of earth with him. It reminded me – I could not help it – of the way a badger digs a sett. As the light faded robins would gather and follow the excavator up and down the track, like tiny gulls after a woodland plough.

I have, I realise, already begun to romanticise Len and his Wake-robin. It was only a routine job, after all, a functional timber track, and for all the democratic debates about its finer details it was an imposition by a small, opinionated minority on a larger community's landscape. It is now, for a few decades anyway, an ineradicable part of their view, and I have no idea whether a vestigial memory of how it was made will change its meaning for anyone other than those who were there at the time.

I find that I have much less certain feelings about landscapes now that I have a hand in changing one, and paradoxically am not so ready to dismiss those who judge them purely as visual scenery. I know this is treacherous ground. I have caught myself thrilling at the sight of a livid harvest moon in Wiltshire rising over stubble fires that stretched from one horizon to the other, and quite forgetting for a moment the full horror of what it is like to be inside a stubble burn, and the profligate waste of resources it represents. The mere look of a landscape can be dangerously deceptive. Yet 'a view', gathered in an untutored gaze, is for most of us the first experience we have of a natural prospect, and a reminder that the shape and mood of the land at least are still an immutable and fundamental part of our lives. It is nothing like a full response, but it is a straightforward and often a shared one, and I have been arguing that at this moment of critical change in the countryside we need above all else to embrace the richness and variety of response that nature and landscape can elicit.

At the moment the changes are pulling in different directions. The drift away from the countryside is ending, and the villages are filling up with working people again. Yet they are not farm-workers, and the progress of large-scale capitalist farming continues down a path of specialisation and profiteering that is taking it further and further away from the communities it once served. At the same time many areas on the urban fringes are beginning, both in their appearance and in their patterns of mixed, land-based economies, to look more like 'real' countryside than some intensively farmed rural areas.

Most of the current crises of industrial society seem, almost by definition, to be located in the urban areas. Yet increasingly the shape of the most promising alternatives – a more ingenious and frugal use of natural resources, a reverence for living systems (including our own), more flexible patterns of work and livelihood, smaller, more democratic communities with a respect for the character of their local environments – is emerging out of what we loosely call 'the rural tradition'. That movement, outwards from the personal, the commonplace, the local, is the movement of the argument in *Second Nature*. It may begin to succeed as a movement in the real world if we recognise that the experience of nature is not exclusive to a particular place or moment, a way of life or position of privilege, but is an aspect of all our individual lives and of our collective history.

Personal Landscapes

Ten-yard Panorama

BY NORMAN NICHOLSON

I suppose that the first I saw of the outdoor world was from my pram –
from the time, that is, that my eyes were able to distinguish anything
more than three feet away. They did not need to see much further, since
for me the outdoors was just our own back yard. I have no clear memory
from that earliest time. My memories come from a few years later and
even those are blurred. It is not easy to separate one visual image from
all the others which have been collected in the course of looking at that
particular scene on – at a rough calculation – nearly twenty-five
thousand days.

I know, however, almost exactly what it must have looked like.
Indeed, since I began writing this paragraph, I have walked out into the
yard to reassemble my recollections more precisely. The yard has not
changed much in seventy years. It is very narrow, to begin with, a little
canyon between steep walls. Sparrows that let on the irregular flag-
stones of its floor have to take off vertically, like helicopters, when
startled. One cliff of the canyon is formed by the outside wall of the
house, the lower end of which is a kind of lean-to of corrugated iron,
once painted dark green. This odd structure, which is rather like the
tin chapel of some nearly extinct fundamentalist sect, was built as a
dispensary by the pharmacist who owned the house in the 1880s. He
would leave his customer in the shop, and walk through to the back to
make up the prescription. My father, brought up in an even smaller
terrace house elsewhere in the town, firmly called that room The
Wash-house. My stepmother, in Edwardian avoidance of what she
thought was vulgar, called it The Studio.

Yet, though the yard is narrow, it is not dark, as there are no buildings
on the opposite side of the back street, which opens on to the playground of the old secondary school that I was to attend from my twelfth
to my seventeenth year. In my first term at the school, my stepmother,
to my great embarrassment, would watch me, in the playground, from

one of our upstairs windows. A few years earlier, before they built the wooden hut which served as our school gymnasium, she could have looked across the playground and over allotments and fields and the seven miles of the Duddon Sands, to the cranes, the church towers and the town hall of Barrow-in-Furness. My father used to say that, on a clear day, you could hear the town clock strike.

On the opposite side of the yard is the wall which divides it from the yard next door. This is still of the original brick, but so weathered and mildewed that it looks like the sandstone of a ruined abbey. Some time before 1914, my father had up-ended a row of black tiles, cemented them to the stone paving about a foot away from the wall, and filled the space between with soil. Here he planted a few cuttings of Virginia creeper, which, by the time of my boyhood, had already covered the whole of the dividing wall and part of the house. It is still growing today. In winter its black arteries give the wall the sinewy look of an old coal miner's arms. In summer, out of less soil than would be needed to fill a couple of beer barrels, it fountains out a huge tankage of sappy greenery. If we neglected it for two seasons, it would turn the yard into a jungle of tendril and sap. As I grew older, the month-by-month changes of the creeper became for me the signs of the seasons. The intense, startlingly red, and – as it seemed to me, later, after reading Lawrence – incredibly sexy, little nozzles that thrust out of the twigs in March; the great waterfall of green in June; the pattern of five-finger shadows thrown on the wall in July; the clinkering of autumn; the rare days in winter when the snow balanced itself, like an old-fashioned starched linen collar, along every horizontal curve of runner and twig – these made up my year.

Today the yard is greener than ever. There are window boxes with daffodils in spring and geraniums in summer; there are tubs and old chimney pots with roses, broom and clematis. There is now scarcely enough room to walk down the yard, let alone for a boy to play there. Today, too, unsolicited plants keep creeping in – dog's mercury, whose tough green buttonhooks, in the new year, are the first prior announcement of spring, Herb Robert, lesser periwinkle, lady's mantle, a primrose, a dog rose. There are those commoner weeds, greeted each year with pleasure, though not otherwise unduly encouraged – creeping buttercup, ivy-leaved toadflax, chickweed, pearlwort, and the willowherb which is so oddly named *montanum* though it grows in every crack of dirt in the back street. In the year of my wife's last illness, her occasional glimpses of the yard and my pluckings of leaf and flower were the last she saw of the world she had known.

I did not become much aware of what lay beyond the yard wall until I started school at the age of five. Millom, which I had, by now, come to realise was the place where I lived, is a small, nineteenth-century town divided by the railway, its two parts joined only by the railway bridge. The bridge, indeed, affords the only way, by road, from any direction, into the industrial side of the town where we lived. Newtown, as our side is called, is a grid of terraces and back streets built on a low peninsula that juts out into the Duddon estuary. Fields and salt-marsh surround it on three sides, so that, though we lived a mile and a half away from the main coast, the spring tide, curling round the peninsula reached to within two or three hundred yards of our house. This meant that two great wedges of open country or waste land were driven right into the middle of the town, one from either side, almost meeting at the railway bridge. My infant and elementary school lay just over that bridge, next to the cricket field. Westward there were only meadows and hedges, and, further away, the dunes, with not a brick between us and the Isle of Man.

I took this closeness to soil and sand entirely for granted. When I was six or seven, being brought up, at that time, by my grandmother – my mother having died a year or so before – we used to walk the mile or two to various spots on the shore, carrying bucket and spade, baskets and bags, and all that was necessary for the picnic. A jugful of boiling water, for making tea, could be obtained, price one penny, from one of the houses near by. It would never have occurred to my grandmother that you could drink anything but tea.

Yet I did not think of myself as living anywhere but in a town. I was in my own eyes, essentially a town boy, like the boys of Barrow-in-Furness, or, if it came to that, of London. The country was where the farmers lived. Admittedly, the farmers' sons came to our school, and one of them shared a desk with me. I remember that once we were told to draw a turnip from memory. Most of us, including me, drew a football with an aspidistra sprouting from the top, but I noticed that my neighbour had given *his* football a topping of crinkly leaves like the fronds of an arthritic fern. I had no great regard for his artistic abilities but it did strike me that he might know what a turnip looked like, so I rubbed out my leaves and copied his. Later in the lesson I was commended by the teacher for my powers of observation!

It was round about that time that certain plants must have impressed themselves upon my consciousness. They mostly belonged to high summer and August, and, even today, the sudden sight of one of them can bring back the brightness, the smell, the exhilaration of school holidays. For the most part I did not know their names, or, if I did, I had learnt them from cigarette cards – ragwort, tufted vetch, silverweed, and the harebell, which, like the Scots, we called 'bluebell'. With these I remember also the stalks of thistle growing in a parched brown pasture, with a doily of green around the base of the plant where the cattle had not been able to graze. The image is as clear as if I had seen it yesterday. In fact, as I write in August, I *did* see it yesterday.

A year or two later, my father remarried, and my stepmother was what was then known as a 'great walker' – though not, of course, a 'hiker', for I don't think the term had yet been invented. I now began to learn more of the country within two or three miles of Millom. On bank holidays we sometimes took the train from Foxfield to Coniston; on Ascension Day we climbed Black Combe, the great hill above Millom which can be seen from Scotland, Wales and the Isle of Man. Above all, every Sunday morning, my father and I went for a walk through the Hodbarrow Mines.

Hodbarrow, in its time, had been one of the most famous iron mines in the world, working a deposit of haematite which, until the end of the last century, was the richest ever exploited. By the 1920s, it was already in decline, though it continued to produce ore for another forty years. There were twenty or thirty abandoned shafts and about half a dozen still working – all spread over a huge acreage of limestone outcrop at the mouth of the Duddon. In the early part of this century, a mile-and-a-quarter-long sea wall had been thrown out, like the arch of a bow, enclosing a new parish of shingle, sand and sump. Gradually, as it was undermined, the land subsided, turning the enclosed hollow into a great sunken basin. It was out of bounds in my boyhood, but, since then, I have walked over every yard of it, searching for the sand and limestone flowers which hurried to colonise the new habitat in the sixty years between the high tides of yesterday and the permitted flooding of today. I could stand at the lowest point in Cumbria, seventy feet below sea level, and look up to Scafell Pike, the highest point in England.

Mining is really a rural industry – the harvesting of a crop which, unfortunately, does not renew itself. An iron ore mine, in particular, tends to look like rough, untidy farming on humpy and intractable land. For one thing, unlike coal, iron ore is not found in seams, spread flatly, like jam in a sandwich, between the rock strata. It lies in solid globules or blobs, which may contain many thousands of tons of metal and yet be encompassed within a surface area no bigger than a tennis court. In the old days, prospecting was such a hit-and-miss affair that they could drop boreholes all round a deposit, like a knife-thrower just missing his accomplice, and fail to probe to the spot where the iron lay.

All this meant that, in a large royalty like Hodbarrow, between all the pit-heads, the working and worked-out shafts, there was a scattering and jigsaw of broken ground where nature, from the beginning, had been fighting back. Again, unlike coal, iron ore mines are not dirty. The iron dust is red; old railway sleepers and wagons are stained a dark

cochineal. The rubble tips and spoil heaps – *never* call them 'slagbanks'!
– are like dark red tumuli, greening and weathering with grass and
horsetail. At Hodbarrow, the rock – a beautiful white limestone, tinged
with pink – could be seen breaking through the surface, quarried and
blasted into cliffs and chasms and potholes. Little mineral lines ran up
and down the hummocky ground like a roller-coaster at a fair. Where
the soil had lain undisturbed for long, there were rank thickets of
hawthorn and blackthorn, gorse and broom. On the old foreshore,
reclaimed by the sea-wall, there was heather and dwarf willow and
sea-holly. There were hares, foxes and badgers. The now rare natterjack
toad bred by the thousand. In that part of the hollow where the sand
was earthiest, the managers had grown a crop of mangels to give cover
to the partridge which they shot once a year. The men, too, had their
wildlife interests. A cuckoo's egg, laid in the nest of some small bird,
was watched and guarded till the young cuckoo was fledged and flew
away. My step-grandfather, who was in charge of one of the surface
engines that supplied power below ground, would come home, in
summer, with a sprig of centaury in his buttonhole. He died in 1931, but
the tansy which he planted outside his engine-house still grows on the
abandoned site.

Of course, when I was a boy, I did not give a thought to this now
seemingly remarkable closeness of wild nature to industry, of country
to town. I don't think I ever thought of the mines as being country at all.
I saw them as a place where men worked. For, even on a Sunday, there
would still be perhaps a single locomotive, fat and puffy as a pack mule,
dragging a few wagons up a pit-bank, and now and again the pit-head
wheels would start whirring to raise a couple of bogies or to lower two of
the bosses to inspect the underground levels. That a whole flora of
bushes and shrubs and weeds and mosses should be growing, often
within a few yards of the mine workings, was not a matter for surprise.

When I grew older, this closeness between wild nature and everyday
life took on a new meaning. Millom, I saw, came out of the rock, grew
on it like a tree and was entirely dependent on it. Physically, indeed, the
town is – or was, before the new housing of the 1930s – as much a
product of Cumbrian rock as any of the dale villages. The older houses,
the schools, the chapels, the town hall are all built of stone from two
nearby quarries; they are roofed with slates from the quarries of
Kirkby-in-Furness, on the other side of the Duddon. The town church is
of sandstone from St Bees, only twenty miles up the coast; the railway
station of Eskdale granite, from still nearer home. The limestone of
Hodbarrow, oddly enough, does not show itself in the town buildings
at all.

Yet it was from this limestone that the town came into being, and it was here that a kind of topographical emblem began to shape itself in my mind. Everywhere, and at all times, men are dependent on the physical world they live on. Here, in Millom of the mining days, you could see that pattern spread before you, you could read the history of the Industrial Revolution inscribed on the landscape. The ore came out of the rock; was shunted across to the ironworks; was smelted into pig-iron, sold and turned into money. The whole life of the town came from that first product of the rock. The ore was rightly called 'haematite' for it was the life-blood of the whole community. It is the same everywhere. Even if we feed on vitamin tablets and live in plastic houses, our life will still come from rock, wind, air and sun, though it is hard to remember this in a city. At Hodbarrow, you can't forget it.

It was when I was about fifteen that I first began to explore the hills. Of course, I had long known that they were there. In fine weather they were visible – whether I noticed them or not, I don't know – from the railway bridge on the way to my infant school. In fact, when my father introduced me to one of his customers, telling me that he came from Coniston, I asked if he were Coniston Old Man.

Now, at fifteen, with the guidance of a friend slightly older than me, I began to walk among the fells – Black Combe, Coniston Old Man, Wetherlam and, perhaps more important, the lower hills that lie along the slopes of the greater ones. On my bicycle I explored the whole course of the Duddon, beside which I had lived until then without knowing more than six miles of it. I pushed my bike over Wrynose Pass, along a road which was little more than a track through scree. It was all emptier and wilder in those days before the cars could tackle the passes, but my discovery is one that is still being made by thousands of visitors, especially by the young, and I need say no more about it.

For most of those visitors, the hills are an escape, a place to 'get away from it all'. For me, even in adolescence, this was only a half-truth. The hills had always been, and still are, the background to my everyday life – both the distant serrated skyline of Scafell, Scafell Pike, Bowfell, Crinkle Crags and Coniston, and the little scruffy outcrops that knuckle up close to the town. In fact, a very considerable proportion of the population of Great Britain still lives not far from, and often in sight of, the hills. In Manchester and Leeds they can look at the Pennines from their taller buildings. Practically the whole of industrial Yorkshire and much of Lancashire and Durham is huddled among the lower dales or tucked into clefts of the moors. The Iron-and-Steel Age of the twentieth century had its beginnings, over 250 years ago, beside the becks that flow into Morecambe Bay; the factory system evolved in the moorland valleys of East Lancashire. All Scotland is a hill or a declivity among hills; Edinburgh has a mountain within the city boundary.

The hills remind us of what we come from. They are not, of course, untouched by humans. The Cumbrian fells, which I can see from my bedroom window, look very different from what they must have been before people arrived there. Tree-felling, the clearance of scrub, quarrying, sheep-farming, the silting-up of tarns, the draining of the valley bottoms, enclosure and the making of pastures, the building of roads, walls and bridges, and, more recently, the planting of coniferous forests – all these have changed the landscape. But only on the surface. The underlying shapes are still the same. There is still the feeling that this is rock-bottom. This is what we have to live on and live with. This is the basic stuff of our world, and here the forces of sun, wind, rain, frost and ice are still at work. The slow process of geological change, the grinding down or building up of the landscape, is still going on, as it did millions of years before we came.

My delight in discovering the hills was short-lived. When I was sixteen I was, quite suddenly, snatched away from them, for I developed tuberculosis of the lungs and the larynx and was sent to a sanatorium in Hampshire. For fifteen months I was confined to bed, and it was then, paradoxically, that I began to become truly aware of the world around me. I lived in a chalet, screened from the main buildings of the sanatorium by a high hedge. From my wide and ever-open window, I could look down a gentle slope, over trees and copses, to the heather and plantations of the New Forest. Like most people in such institutions, I began to take an interest in the birds, and from my bed, or from a chair in the porch of my chalet, I was able to identify fifty to sixty species – including such comparatively uncommon ones as the lesser spotted woodpecker, the red-backed shrike and the nightjar. A goldcrest visited me regularly in winter, carefully scrutinising a spruce tree just outside my window; a pair of long-tailed tits nested within fifty yards of my chalet; and in June we were repeatedly kept awake by nightingales. The year was 1932 but, in this pocket of the South Country, England seemed still to lie in the golden afterglow of the era that ended in 1914.

In the autumn of that year, however, I had to return to Millom, to what seemed, then, to be a frighteningly harsh, cold and unsympathetic world – a world of rock and bare fell-sides, slate walls and threadbare pasture, of half-bankrupt farms, deserted mine-shafts, short-time working and the dole. Immediately, I ordered for myself a strict routine of rest and exercise, walking every morning, whatever the weather, out into the fields and lanes around the town. I kept up that routine for at least ten years, during which time I came to know every path, wall, hedge and very nearly every tree within walkable distance of my home. I could have taken you to within a couple of yards of any flower I wanted to show you. I still can, if it has not been obliterated by new buildings. For about a year after my return I went out only into the nearby fields, trying to pretend that the town and its industries did not exist. But I soon came to realise that the rarest flowers were to be found among the old mines and that the best place to see waterfowl was the reservoir of the ironworks. Before long, too, I learned that, if I wanted to observe the local slate in its full variety of colour and texture, I could not do better than examine the walls of the back streets which were built of it. With the aid, occasionally, of a bus or a train, my legs gave me the freedom of a little kingdom which, however isolated and confined, seemed to me wide enough and rich enough to typify the whole physical world.

Since then, marriage to a wife who drove a car enormously extended my range. I could not reach the tops of the fells, of course, but, from a more modest level, I got to know most of the Lake District and much of the North of England. Yet, apart from occasional excursions into such (for me!) foreign territories as the Home Counties, I seemed always to be exploring my own patch of South Cumberland. Wester Ross, Suther-land, Shetland, Norway – all these told me more about my own home, showed me more mountain flowers, more sea birds, and told me more about the Viking ancestry of the Nicholsons and Cornthwaites that I sprang from.

Ageing, and the inability to drive a car, have confined me, once again, to the smaller radius of my earlier days; but the even more familiar objects of field, farm, mine workings and so on are now enriched and, as it were, made more significant, more comprehensible, by my acquaintance with what I think of as the Greater Millom of the world beyond. The Old Man of Storr nods across to the Old Man of Coniston.

This experience of having lived the whole of my life, except for the years in the sanatorium, in one small community and in one house is now regarded as unusual and even odd. It was once common enough. Until the Industrial Revolution, probably most people in England lived and died within walking distance of the place where they were born, and this may still be true of millions living in the developing countries. To say that these people lived, or live, close to nature is so obvious as to be trite, yet I doubt if they would have felt 'close to nature' in the way in which we use the term today. Civilisation is, by definition, the society of the city, and the city has made all of us – including those who live in the country – self-conscious about nature. We have a kind of detachment, a feeling that, however knowledgeable and appreciative we may be, we are observers rather than participants. The conservationists approach their task with an enthusiasm and scientific understanding which was quite beyond the range of, say, an eighteenth-century farm labourer.

Moreover, for nearly all of us, our love of landscape is based, to a great extent, on the idea of the view. Now I don't think that the eighteenth-century farm labourer took much notice of the view, and I don't blame him for that. For a view is something which does not really exist. The hills and trees and fields may be there, but the view is merely a matter of geometrical relationship between the seer and the things seen. Move a couple of hundred yards and the view has changed – yet the hills, and trees and the fields obviously haven't.

I can enjoy a view as much as anybody. Wastwater, Stack Polly, Suilven, Staffa – I can pull them out of my mental filing cabinet like picture postcards. I should be sorry if any of these were to be defaced, but I still think that it is more important to regain something of the feeling that we are part of what we are looking at. To preserve rare species and 'Areas of Outstanding Beauty' is not enough. We must realise that we live in, belong to, the world we see and, indeed, the world we don't see – that we are one with sparrow and mouse, grass and weed, stone and water. Wordsworth says, in the *Intimations of Immortality Ode*:

> *But there's a Tree, of many, one,*
> *A single Field which I have looked upon,*
> *Both of them speak of something that is gone.*

A *single* field, it should be noted, not a landscape; and one tree, not a wood. Perhaps such things can still speak to us of something which is not quite gone yet.

NORMAN ACKROYD *Sutton Mandeville – Walter's Path*

NORMAN ACKROYD *Westmere Evening*

NORMAN ACKROYD *September Daybreak (Crockey Hill)*

Town, Bad: Country, Good

BY EDWARD BLISHEN

In June 1934, a fourteen-year-old schoolboy with a spirit like that of some wistful centenarian or Rip Van Winkle wrote in his diary of a walk he'd taken with his family. They'd crossed a suburb on the outskirts of London from the edge where they were now living to the opposite edge where they'd lived until the diarist was six years old. The effect was to make him lament:

> The old conglomeration of field and unpaved lane is gone and . . . new roads and houses jut into the splendid beauty of the old. Cat Hill, where the stream ran, down which we rushed each day, is still in its glory, but the corner where I remember standing with Father and Hilda Harding on the eve of a Sunday School treat, watching the stars – the corner, I say, is now covered in patently new shops which were – oh! so painful to me, as engines which secured the demolition of so many of my quaint childhood reminiscences.

This child with his ambitious but comically shaky prose was myself: and in the feelings he had about the destruction of the Village,* as that corner of the suburb was still called, he reflected, I think, not only his real sadness at the replacement of trees and fields with a network of stark drives and crescents, and random cottages with regiments of semi-detached houses, but also the reading he had been doing. I believe that, in what it says and also in what it seems to say, the literature to

---

* That end of the suburb continues, in 1983, to be spoken of as the Village by older residents. I sat recently in a local pub and listened to two elderly men as they set out to recover the map of the old place under the enormity of the new. They used a style of narrative that I recognised as one that thrilled me as a child. 'Remember Middle Street! And old Agnes! She had a moustache! I never liked *him* much! Him and his outside lav! Remember? Then there were them fields! Old Martin's! He was mean as they come! One of his bulls keeled over and died, once, and he never got over it!' Everything they said was an exclamation or a rhetorical question.

which as children we resort exerts a strong influence on our view of the countryside, and of the relative value of town and country. Indeed, our whole notion of locality is fed, in one way or another, by this reading: which has generated its own, often reach-me-down, responses to the British landscape. There is a small patch of Barnet, where I still live, that runs downhill behind the distraught High Street (with its feverish pattern of shops ever-changing, of one failed carpet store succeeding another, of building society offices remaining calm, blank and fixed where once were shops that on Saturday nights were busy bright caves of fruit and vegetables or coffee-smelling pallors of heaped hams and cheeses). This patch of the town is meadow, still, and incorrigible hedge, and when I walk through it I feel I'm in the world of much of my early reading. Here was fun: here was holiday: here was lying in the hay (like the children we read of, we used the hay to build prickly houses for ourselves and our sweethearts and best friends). Here was 'the stream down which we rushed each day', which we dammed and on which we launched entire navies of twigs and paper boats. I cannot walk here without thinking of the fiction: I cannot think of the fiction without remembering this still-green patch of the town. In this essay I shall attempt to recall my childhood reading as truly as possible; to distinguish in it a few of the ideas, prejudices, potent truths and half-truths (and perhaps some complete lies) it had to offer on the subject of the countryside, and the relation of town and country; and to try to judge how useful such ideas have been, with the attitudes they have fostered, in the increasingly complex matter of coming to conclusions about the fate of our environment.

I must begin with my father.

He and one of his brothers got on their bikes in Paddington, on a summer day shortly before the First World War, and cycled northwards. Their aim was to find a house for their widowed mother and themselves. The back streets of West London had always been their home: their knowledge of the countryside rested on memories of visits to an uncle in Tunbridge Wells, who was an ex-Hussar, ran a gymnasium, and would drill the boys (six of them) in his back garden before breakfast. Whatever the ultimate occupation of a child might be (and my father and his brothers all started work as vanboys in one or other of the Oxford Street department stores), the family aim was to instil the outlook of a soldier. I gathered from the way he spoke of it that my father thought of the English countryside at that time – the Common in Tunbridge Wells, for example, where Uncle Will took them for sharp and punishing runs – as a blueprint for a battlefield. Any actual battlefield, of course, that might lie in wait would be found, not in

England at all, but abroad. You trained in open country, here, in the expectation of fighting in open country, over there. Such a view of things must have become part of the outlook of multitudes of imperial Englishmen.

The house they found, that day in 1912 or 1913, was in New Barnet, ten miles out. My father remembered the enchanting sensation of leaving London behind, of the city thinning, of gaps between houses, of sudden open spaces and stiles: and glimpses, down side streets, of grassy slopes and horizons occupied by nothing but trees and an occasional aristocratic chimney-pot. The house, one of a pair called Norfolk Villas, had a garden and smelt of apples. (Its lavatory adjacent to the garden, as I discovered ten years or so later, smelt perpetually, deliciously of fruit. I remember, as if it were a graceful event in an idyllic setting, perching myself on the enormous lavatory seat, clutching the walls to save myself from drowning, and breathing air that was a mixture of perry and cider.) The two brothers agreed with the estate agent on the small rent, and felt they were about to carry their mother into the heart of the country. A few yards from their new home was Barnet Vale, a green groove that led to the top of a hill built by Telford in the early nineteenth century to take travellers along the Great North Road straight instead of in a rural loop. In another direction were Hadley Woods, a fragment of a once immense royal chase; you could lose yourself in there – and, better still, lose yourself *and* a girl. For my father and uncles the woods were a setting for what one of *their* uncles, writing home wistfully from the Crimea, described as a *'Sn-g-le'*. Within thirty years, large parts of the open space that first attracted my father were to vanish: but for the rest of his life his experience of that space coloured his view of the world around him, and *his* view – together with the surviving green stretches, including the woods – influenced my own picture of the world.

With, that is, the help of literature. Much of the reading I did as a child seems, when I look back, to have revolved, whatever the specific story it told, round the relationship between town and country. To the impression of the physical arrangement of the world that I derived from my experience as a small resident of Barnet, my reading gave a curious sense of system. Questions of being in, or of, the country and being in, or of, the town were not aesthetic or social questions merely. They became tightly related to various ideas of good and bad – sometimes of good and evil. Some of the first books I read came from a trunk, kept under a bed: the only books in the house. They formed a miscellany of largely Victorian novels, of small literary quality. I loved them deeply, and read them all – or pieced them together, in a child's fashion: weaving into them my own novice's vision of things. A child's reading of any text obviously cannot be an exercise in accurate absorption. To these books were added others that I borrowed from a Sunday School library: the accommodation here being a cupboard, so that until I joined the local library I thought the fate of books was to be incarcerated. In those days the only public library in the town was one created by a bequest from a nineteenth-century resident: and again, the result was a randomness of popular or once popular texts. There were many Victorian and Edwardian adventure and school stories. In my imagination, I lived, much of the time, thirty or forty years back: being, in a curious way, rather more at ease in the 1890s than in the 1920s. I suspect that this is a common effect of avid early reading: a child lags behind, encountering many books that take him back two, three or four decades. This may give him a strangely sensitive apprehension of the present in which he is living, and in which his awareness of the world is beginning to form. Persuaded though he is that the present is everlasting, he absorbs through reading a contrary notion – that it is constantly under threat: or is simply in a state of perpetual dissolution. The nineteenth-century schoolboys I read of were as real to me as my actual classmates: the Remove would never cease to occupy their studies (especially the Remove, who in any fictitious school were immortally fixed in their very transitoriness): but at the same time I knew they'd been swept away for ever by that busiest of schoolkeepers, time. And I acquired from my early reading just such a paradoxical sense of the landscape around me. Barnet would never vary from the idyllic perfection of its condition, *c.* 1928: but at the same time part of the very essence of unchangeable Barnet was the process of change in which it was involved. Of that process, mostly a matter of conflict between town and country, I can now see that my ragged reading appeared to offer a sort of diagram, a kind of account.

What were the ideas of town and country that I acquired from books? Largely, a set of notions that might be expressed as: town, on the whole, bad; country, in the main, good. Town, a setting for realistic misadventure: country, the scene for playful adventure. In the town, gangs: in the country, healthy tribes. The town was where you suffered and grew ill: the country was where you recuperated. The town was winter: the country was summer. The town was the setting for achievement: the country, an environment in which ambition came to a grateful halt or vanished altogether. When as a child I thought of the great division opened up by the Civil War, I thought of puritanism as belonging to the town: the country in its nature was cavalier. The town was brisk: the country took its time, and even yawned. It was not possible to have ideas about either that had no moral tinge to them. The division of the world between green leaf and red brick was a division of oneself, between a pleasanter and a less pleasant being. On the whole, one could be expected to behave more agreeably, certainly more relaxedly, in a field than in a street. In order merely to be educated, one had to step into the town: the country stood for half-term or free Wednesday afternoons. It is true that the great fictitious public schools about which, a first-generation grammar schoolboy, I read so much, were, almost without exception, set in the countryside. Greyfriars was on the edge of Courtfield Common, where Harry Wharton and Billy Bunter were as subject to rural mishap as Prince Hal and Falstaff on Gadshill. Talbot Baines Reed's St Dominic's was set amid 'the wooded banks and picturesque windings of the Shar'. But a school was in essence a town set down in the country. The anguishings, the strivings, the moral ferment of the school represented the town at its most characteristic, placed in the midst of countryside in which games were played and healthy extra-mural adventure occurred: a scene largely, though not totally, of moral intermission.

A few years ago, I re-read a book that at the age of eleven or twelve filled me with a dramatically enjoyable sense of personal doom: Thomas Hughes's *Tom Brown's Schooldays*, from which derived, of course, much of the boys' fiction that I read. Among its characters, most of them morally marred, I took it that I was myself to be found, perhaps a compound of all their weaknesses: so that I was resigned to the prospect of failing to reach even the fifth form undisgraced. (In childhood one reads as if having one's fortune told.) In the very first chapter, as I embarked on that re-reading, I recognised the essential voice of much of the early fiction that came my way. 'I pity people who were not born in a vale,' wrote Hughes. 'I don't mean a flat country, but a vale: that is, a flat country bounded by hills.' I knew nothing of the Wiltshire countryside he had in mind when he wrote that first chapter, or of the country gentleman's local patriotism he was promoting: but I thought Barnet must conform well enough to his requirements, so mysteriously tetchy in tone. There was, indeed, Barnet Hill: and, indeed, there was Barnet Vale. If, as he seemed to be saying, it was important to have rural origins, I had them. Of Hughes's outbursts against the new scientific element in education and the new technology of travel, and in favour of rootedness, I had, of course, no understanding: and yet I thought I understood them perfectly, in terms of the transformation that Barnet was undergoing, and of the whole bias of the fiction I read, which made the idea of the town horrid if thrilling and of the country wonderfully inviting. When I first read *Tom Brown's Schooldays*, much of Barnet Vale had begun to vanish under housing: including the stile between one field and the next on which my father was sitting when he proposed marriage to my mother. I did not care for what was happening to

Barnet, and yet I believe I understood it as a natural element in a process of change of which melancholy was an important product. Returning to the town from the country was always sad: and so the sorrow one felt when patches of the country were irretrievably replaced by patches of the town was not entirely unexpected.

The country was a victim: I think that is how I felt it. Because it was the home of the idyll and of the perfectly enjoyable, truly playful adventure, it was doomed. I remember, by way of illustration, the tremendous effect on me of reading Richard Jefferies's *Bevis*: which had, I believe, a greater influence on my imagination, in these matters, than anything else I read until I blundered early on H. G. Wells's *The New Machiavelli*. (I was lucky to belong to random libraries: if I had been confined to libraries more deliberately arranged I'd have been unlikely, in the 1920s or early 1930s, to come across a copy of *Bevis* at all.) I didn't, of course, at the time know that the fields and flooded quarries of Jefferies's Wiltshire were under a doom. But from his pages, which record more vividly than any others I know the equation between rural freedom and deep satisfaction in play, I received a sense of an openness that would not be allowed to remain. Perhaps I felt this because I read into the condition of Jefferies's world – which provided Bevis and his friends with a playground that could be felt to represent the entire surface of the earth, mountains and rivers and lakes and seas – the condition of the world actually around me during my own childhood: the fields on the edge of which the newest housing estates were obviously about to pup: the busy sense of greenness being overtaken and swallowed.

We were a family for Sunday evening walks: and our usual path was over the Totteridge fields, lying between the village of that name and the western edge of High Barnet, where we lived. The future in raw brick surrounded those fields: you could smell the mortar, the new wood, all the intruding odours introduced by the builder. (I loved those, too, as it happened, because they gave delight to my father: who, a meticulous workman himself, enjoyed being critical of anyone else's joinery, plastering or plumbing.) The fields were my shrunken, but perfectly adequate, equivalent of Richard Jefferies's wider acres, even though I hadn't the advantage of any expanse of water that could be thought of as a sea. The sense of greenness as what was constantly under threat sprang for me out of the coincidence of my little fields, so intimately known, and their Amazon of a stream (Pymm's Brook), with Richard Jefferies's fields and ponds that I knew with the intimacy that results from reading.

The nature of the interplay between the world of books, a young and inexperienced mind and the actual world, is particularly difficult to reconstruct in later life. But I recall another text that was vital to me, Edith Nesbit's *The Railway Children*, and the character of my response to the conclusion of the first chapter, in which the children, torn away from their totally satisfactory town life, find themselves in the country, apparently doomed to live there. I can still feel, as I read, my original sense of alarm at this transition – an alarm to which I was made sympathetic, although I did not share it, by the fashion in which it was epitomised. They arrive at their new home: there is no fire, the black grates contain cold, dead ashes.

> As the cart man turned to go out after he had brought in the boxes, there was a rustling, scampering sound that seemed to come from inside the walls of the house.
> 'Oh, what's that? cried the girls.
> 'It's only the rats,' said the cart man. And he went away and shut the door, and the sudden draught of it blew out the candle.
> 'Oh, dear,' said Phyllis, 'I wish we hadn't come!' and she knocked a chair over.
> '*Only* the rats!' said Peter, in the dark.

The country, I understood, was candles, darkness and rats. This was one of the reasons why it was doomed. Candles were outmoded, darkness was barbarous, and rats were unspeakable. To the doom that hung over the countryside because it was so beautiful and playful hung this other doom, which sprang from its being so out of step with the world of brisk good sense. It is a contrast I omitted from my earlier collection of them: the country had straws in its hair, but the town was level-headed and severely practical, and probably must prevail.

The more I attempt to think myself back into the frame of mind induced in me by early reading, the more I feel that what children's literature – today, as then – may appear to point to is the doom of the countryside. A child may feel deeply that play and retreat exist largely in order to give way, in the end, to work and the bright glare of town life: and that, by the same token, the green world is destined to be devoured by the red one. It strikes me that this may be one of several sets of false alternatives that our characteristic upbringing freely offers. So our school system succeeds in suggesting to most of us (though the last few years have given an ironic edge to it) that existence is divided between work, to be groaned at and endured, and excluding play: and play, to be welcomed (often hysterically), and excluding work. Perhaps it is not for nothing that Thomas Hughes's first chapter, that opening to one of the most famous of boys' stories, has its rural back to the wall. Children's literature discovers in the countryside an image for the happy adventurousness of childhood, and may therefore induce pessimism as to the hope of preserving the green spaces, precisely because they have come to stand for childhood which will not last. It may seem a matter of *either* the country, *or* the town. Oddly, teachers often compound this situation by inviting children to say whether they would rather live in the town or the country. (I think still with admiration of a boy I taught who responded to such an invitation, offered by one of my colleagues, by saying that as an ardent aeromodeller he was unable to give a coherent reply: the town being far better for buying aeromodels, and the country far better for flying them.) One effect of a children's literature that instinctively suggests such a profound opposition between the two, I suspect, is that we are less ready than we might be to consider questions of town and country in subtle terms of balance and fusion rather than in harsh terms of contrast and conflict.

There's a charming story by Juliana Horatia Ewing, whose work was much read to us when I was a small schoolchild, and whose name (with that of the poet, William Brighty Rands) proposed to me an ideal as to the kind of name writers ought to have that has rarely been satisfied since. The story is called 'Our Field', and is about the happiness a group of children derive from their discovery of 'a lovely field', rather bare at first glance, but full of grasses, flowers, seasons and opportunities. At the end the young narrator considers a question of the sort that wanders late into a child's mind. Who does the field belong to? 'Richard says he believes it belongs to the gentleman who lives at the big red house among the trees. But he must be wrong; for we see that gentleman at church every Sunday, but we never saw him in Our Field. And I don't believe anybody could have such a field of their very own, and never come to see it, from one end of Summer to the other.' I remember the feeling of reading *that*, too, and the way it united with other feelings: as to a great difference between the appraisal of things by children, and their appraisal by adults.

There are, of course, books for children that are concerned with urban life, and convey a town child's sense that, to some measure, he owns a street, an alley, a bus shelter: but the sense of ownership here is far more consciously make-believe than in the country. The countryside, in some general huge sense, may seem to emerge in children's stories as unowned. It is raw unclaimed world; and an essential feature of a field is the absence of any visible proprietor. Again, I am not sure whether actual experience determined the way books were read, or vice versa: but I do recall a double oddity in the view I and my small friends had of the Totteridge fields in which we played. We knew the owner was a farmer, indeed *the* farmer (thought of as so archetypal that I even

imagined him with a capital F), but he was never seen and we could not
have given him a name. But reflecting on this I see for the first time that
in fact I *did* know who the farmer was. He was a neighbour of mine: he
lived among his barns at the bottom of the road in which I lived. But
there was something about the essential nature of a little world of
meadows that meant it might have a generalised owner, but could not
have a particularised one. I think we suppressed our knowledge of its
ownership. One odd effect was that on an occasion when we'd set fire to
a tree (we'd established a home, complete with hearth, in one of its
forks), we ran for our lives in precisely that direction that, if he'd been
around, would have delivered us into the farmer's angry arms.

My attempt to recall, as faithfully as I can, the meanings I read into
this early literature has led to the surfacing, in my memory, of texts that
were out of the ordinary, highlights of reading. But the conclusions I
draw from these seem to chime in with my recollection of the general
effect of the mass of my reading, from which few titles now emerge. The
composite meaning of these books stirs me to this day with a sensation
that might be described as follows: that I am involved in an existence in
which thrilling dangers, some physical but many of them moral, await
me in the town, and will lead at some point to my going to the country to
recover: to enjoy, in every possible respect, a holiday from important
experience. These are the memories of a suburban child who lived on
the edge of London, and felt strongly the truth of Richard Jefferies's
remark: 'The inevitable end of every footpath round about London is
London. All paths go thither.' Though I was also aware that all paths
went thence: you could reverse the process and end up, after ten urban
miles, in Totteridge fields. I do not know what a country child would
have made of the same reading: though I'd be surprised if his sense of it
were vastly different. It is not likely that children's literature invented
these meanings for town and country: it may have deepened them,
since they relate so closely to certain images we have of childhood as
opposed to adulthood, but the ideas must spring originally from views
that are generated by an entire culture. It interests me greatly to reflect
that modern children's literature, much of it so much more sophisticated than the literature I read as a child, on the whole implies just the
differences between urban and rural life that I have discovered in my
own early reading. It reveals, I suspect, the condition of a people who
do not know how to make the ideas of town and country live com-
fortably together. Somehow, one seems to rebuke the other.

It can't have been long after I wrote in my diary of my sentimental
return to the Village that, having begun to read H. G. Wells's scientific
romances, I picked up what I didn't know was going to be quite
different, *The New Machiavelli*. It begins with one of the best of all

accounts of the destruction of a pleasant village by the activities of the speculative builder. Wells writes of it, fairly enough, in his own splendid, tetchy, schoolmaster's fashion. The world, which at best has struggled into the Second Form, is behaving messily as small boys do: all this mucking about with decent environments, this arranging that meadows should be 'slashed out into parallelograms of untidy road', and that 'more and more hoardings' should spring up, contributing 'more and more to the nomad tribes of filthy paper scraps that flew before the wind and overspread the country' — all this amounts, in Second Form fashion, to 'a hasty, trial experiment, a gigantic experiment of the most slovenly and wasteful kind.' 'I realised', reflects Wells's hero, 'that building was the enemy.' There is an account of *his* stream, *his* childhood brook, that I have never forgotten: it sang together with my own feelings about doomed parts of Barnet:

> The Ravensbrook of my earlier memories was a beautiful stream . . . On rare occasions of rapture one might see a rat cleaning his whiskers at the water's edge. The deep places were rich with tangled weeds, and in them fishes lurked — to me they were big fishes — waterboatmen and water-beetles traversed the calm surface of these still deeps . . . And after I was eleven, and before we left Bromstead, all the delight and beauty of it was destroyed.

For nearly fifty years I have remembered that passage, not for its own sake merely, but because when I first read it I felt (though I couldn't then have said what I felt) that much in all my earlier reading had been brought to a head. Of course, Barnet *was* like Bromstead: but it was more than that. It was a sensation about the balance of town and country: and for a long time, I believe, it seemed to clinch the impression I'd received, from so many children's books, that the country was all 'delight and beauty', that it coincided in some fashion with childhood itself, and that thereafter it must either be destroyed or, paradoxically, be for ever on the brink of destruction.

JAMES RAVILIOUS *Lost Sheep*

JAMES RAVILIOUS *In the Heat of May*

JAMES RAVILIOUS *Sheep at Upcott*

Remedial Scenes

BY RONALD BLYTHE

Does any doctor prescribe landscape nowadays? Until recently, for certain ailments of body and mind, tuberculosis or depression, it was all that could be prescribed. There are, wrote Richard Jefferies, 'three potent medicines of nature', the sea, the air and the sun. And he might have added the scenes which these elements both created and contain, for if anyone set out for a thorough, self-prescribed landscape cure, he did. A long time ago I read an essay of his called 'The Breeze on Beachy Head' and at once recognised in it a correct phrasing of what must be a common experience of perfect well-being. I am walking, climbing, or lying on grass, and not necessarily high up and filled with a great view, and suddenly all that I can see, hear and smell amalgamates and becomes a kind of landscape laser which passes right through me, healing me totally. Never having been ill, I must ask myself, of what? I suppose, in my case, of dullness, of that reduction of my senses brought on by not getting out. For Jefferies and all literary consumptives it was a very different matter, of course. They *had* to get out – doctor's orders! For a while the three potent medicines of sea, sun and air worked wonders, as a remarkable collection of poems and prose reveals. And then the healing had to stop. Some became reconciled to this fact; Jefferies did not. He turned on 'Nature' and said he hated it. Its indifference to whether he lived or died appalled him. Although what was really appalling him was that never again would there be such a fully alive day as that, for instance, which he spent on Beachy Head. 'Discover some excuse to be up there always . . . go without any pretext . . . it is the land of health.'

My initiatory heights of what we called 'High Suffolk' were little more than half a dozen steps upward in comparison with Beachy Head, but there the countryside would unroll, and any such tensions which I might be feeling with it. This release and revitalisation were not just the products of my native view, as I soon found out when I began to cycle further afield, or make long train journeys to Cornwall and Scotland. Or even, recently, when I walked the hilly outskirts of Sheffield. The landscape cure, originally discovered as a child in Suffolk, usually when I was sulkily in flight from the incessant tasks of goat-milking, brother-keeping, wood-chopping, errands to far-distant shops, etc. which hanging around the house entailed, worked anywhere. 'Where have you been?' they would ask, and I would give the classic answer, 'Out'. In the long run, perhaps, this could be the only answer to 'why does scenery do you good?' Because it takes you out of yourself into its out-ness. It can be a heady business, as Jefferies was to learn, but one which does not necessarily require a numinous vocabulary to describe it. Very much the reverse, in fact. I am transported by 'The Breeze on Beachy Head' because it is so brilliantly down to earth, and with not a yard of its natural geography smudged. Spray, jackdaws, brambles, plough-teams, the immense cliff, the liner *Orient*, Australia-bound, flaking chalk, bees on the furze are seen with intense clarity. It is an accurately recorded view which always reminds me of an incident in the life of the Victorian photographer P. H. Emerson, when the poverty-stricken Norfolk labourers saw their wetlands landscape miniaturised in a camera lens for the first time and were amazed that this beautiful place was just their poor old marsh!

High Suffolk was often similarly perplexing. Distant flint towers gave nothing away about the villages which they marked and the widely stretching scene was, for a boy, too broad to be local. And so the curative properties of landscape must have something to do with travel, and thus exertion. But I would personally put these things low on the list, for what toned me up all those years ago ('You need toning up,' my aunts would advise), tones me up still, and I need only to stare from the window to the steep Stour-side fields to set this desirable process in motion. Never having needed to test the healing quality of these familiar East Anglian scenes against disease, I can only say what they have done for me in terms of stimulus, hedonism and imagination, and while it isn't everything, it is a great deal. As landscape is the source of poetry's main imagery, as well as the limits of an individual's private association with a place, and a perpetual scientific delight, not to mention a larder, it is hardly surprising that it should frequently drug us – always, so far as I am concerned, for the best.

I realise now that my first scenery-seekings were deliberate excursions to find the drug. What I liked, and still like, is the way in which the panorama dominates me. The land is all view and I am all viewer, and soon the ecological patterns and colours not only spread before me but permeate me, and I become part of what I am seeing. I can see patches of medieval forest here and there among the corn, and although I know that 'the woods decay and fall', I also know that in comparison with human flesh they take ages to do so. Thus its ancientness must be one of the healing factors of landscape. High Suffolk tells me that the foundations of my view were laid in the Ice Age, and the shape of almost everything which covers its surface was fashioned centuries ago. But simultaneously with its antiquity it presents its very latest seasonal crop of flowers, birds, insects and sounds. And so I too, wandering on to Monk's Eleigh, always have a nice sense of just being born and everything before me. Landscape certainly provides most of us with a lift and although I know it won't keep me buoyant for ever, or maybe for very much longer, I shall go on absorbing all I can of it. When you think of the world's literature, what other cure-all (or at least make it possible to endure-all) medicine has received such thankful testimonials?

Once landscape had to be 'taken' quite literally as medicine. Both doctor and patient accepted that it was a gamble to go off in search of beneficial air or a change of surroundings, and it was a poignant moment when the sick in body or mind set off for the prescribed spring or climate: Naaman testily to a foreign holy river, the medieval hordes to their shrines and John Keats to the Mediterranean. And then there were those like the exiles in Robert Frost's poem 'New Hampshire' who knew that they would never get better until they got home –

> I met a Californian who would
> Talk California – a state so blessed
> He said, in climate, none had ever died there
> A natural death.

From Eden on we have been convinced that our Earth has a stratum of health running right through it, and that there are salubrious geographical spots where this healthiness can be tapped. Or so it was until yesterday and the dawn of antibiotics. One consulted the physician and he consulted the map. It did not necessarily mean going off into the wilds. Illness often demands good company, and the lady in Henry James's novel was right – 'She was all for scenery – yes, but she wanted it human and personal, and all she could say was that there would be more in London – wouldn't there? More of that kind than anywhere else?'

The history of the use of landscape and its elements as a cure is a mainly social history. One gets the recluses and the solitary searchers for healing, but the main pattern is of those in trouble following where those in trouble went before. Medicine, even landscape-medicine, has always been the practice of fairly rigid rules. Thus a scattering of attested health centres developed and were called 'resorts' because the sick and old and worried resorted to them, either for curative air or water, or for the re-creational activities which they offered. Anne Brontë resorted to Scarborough, not in any expectation of a cure but in all probability to save her poor father from seeing his third child in less than a year die in the house. Her illness, tuberculosis, right up until the last war, involved more people in landscape as a regime than any other, and her almost hour by hour account of her own illness gives an exact description of what must have happened to countless other men and women – and children – for whom the resort was the last resort.

Branwell, 't' Vicar's Pat', had died in September 1848. Three years before he had written a curious landscape poem entitled 'The Emigrant' in which he compares waking up on an Australia-bound ship, which is still in sight of the blue hills of England of which he has taken sad leave, to a loved one's voice distracting the journey which a dying man needs to make from time to eternity. Branwell signed his poem 'Northangerland'. No sooner was he in his grave, which was just a few yards from the parsonage, than the health of Emily and Anne began to decline with devastating speed. Emily, typically, refused to do a thing about it and, three months later, died lying on the downstairs sofa, sewing, and dressed as for an ordinary day. It was dreadfully cold and the moor winds filled the house the moment a door was opened. She had what was then called 'galloping consumption', a disease which made it pointless for her to take any notice of what was passing. Charlotte attempted to slow down the pace with books and love and flowers from the hillside, but it was all no use. Emily's last words were, 'No, no!' to attempts to get her to bed. A fortnight later, Dr Teale, a Leeds specialist, examined Anne, who immediately dealt with her shock in a poem, 'A dreadful darkness closes in/On my bewildered mind', although, unlike her sister, she had no intention of letting the consumption gallop off with her if she could prevent it. She did everything the doctor told her to, and this, of course, included seeking sea air. She also had a private reason for going to Scarborough, which was to spare Haworth a further association with death. Hers might be said to have been the classic death via landscape route, and one taken, in particular, by countless T.B. sufferers, before the advent of modern medicine. Anne Brontë decided to die in a boarding house, rather than a lodging house, because it would be livelier. She left home on 24 May, 1849 and died four days later. It was glorious spring weather and she behaved as though she were on holiday, sightseeing in York en route, buying clothes, hungrily taking in all the scenery she could on the hour's train journey from York to Scarborough, driving herself up and down the sands in a donkey-cart when she arrived there, appearing to be very happy, insisting on her companions, Charlotte and Ellen Nussey, seeing the elegant new spa saloon. On Monday morning Charlotte found her standing uncertainly at the top of the boarding house stairs, unable to descend them, and drew her back into their shared bedroom. Anne sat in the window while the doctor told her that she was about to die. After they had buried her within full view of the sea, Charlotte did not hurry back home to Haworth but drifted slowly through the countryside for a month, taking in Filey and Bridlington – and the enormity of her position. When at last she did reach the parsonage, she closed its doors on all that lay outside and used the writing of *Shirley*, the novel which three deaths had interrupted, as a therapy to help her come to terms with what had happened.

As the nineteenth century wore on, and indeed right up unto the 1930s, the custom of prescribing places for various illnesses intensified. The tubercular rich thronged the Mediterranean and the Alps, and the tubercular poor East Anglian sanitoria, where I often saw them lying outside in pram-beds in all weathers, sometimes with snow covering the mackintosh aprons which kept the blankets dry. Sea trips were also recommended and by the 1920s no great liner set sail without its quota of convalescents and the spiritually low. Much of the action in the novels and drama of the period is geared to the convention of people having to go somewhere special to get better, and much of the mood of this literature is created by a writer being able to invent a sick man's view of the world. But there were, of course, non-invented sick men's views of a natural scene dearly loved, and all the more so because it was fleeting. Bruce Cummings ('Barbellion'), a brilliant young naturalist who died in 1917 when he was in his late twenties, from disseminated sclerosis, wanted to 'swallow landscapes and swill down sunsets, or grapple the whole earth to me with ropes of steel', and in his *Journal of a Disappointed Man* the reader is made to watch the landscape of southern England being prised from him. Talking of London, he said, 'I live in a bigger, dirtier city – ill-health', and it was because of this that he constantly plunged himself into a cleansing countryside.

> It was fine to walk over the elastic turf with the wind bellowing into each ear and swirling all around me in a mighty sea of air until I was as clean-blown and resonant as a sea-shell. I moved along as easily as a disembodied spirit and felt free, almost transparent. The old earth seemed to have soaked me up into itself, I became dissolved into it, my separate body was melted away from me, and Nature received me into her deepest communion – until, UNTIL I got back on the lee side of the hedge where the calm brought me back my gaol of clay.'

That we should not resort to the earth's scenes for comfort, if not a cure, when our own clay begins to crack or warp is foolish, for as Wallace Stevens says, 'Our nature is her nature,' a concept he must have got from Pope, who was acknowledging holism as long ago as the 1730s when, in his *Essay on Man*, he states, 'All are but parts of one stupendous whole,/Whose body Nature is'. But it is easier to be poetic than scientific about what exactly takes place. The actual exercise of a long walk will be beneficial and yet, frequently we know for certain that it is more than just this which has revived us, killed a pain, healed us without a fuss. The land itself seems to have laid its hand on us. Dr Johnson, that very sick man, to whom Hawkstone had offered 'a kind of turbulent pleasure, between fright and admiration', was so put to rights by his long trek through the Highlands that no sooner had he got home to London than he had to set straight for Wales, saying, 'The longer I walk, the less I feel its inconvenience – as I grow warm, my breath mends, and I think my limbs grow pliable.' Goldsmith told young Boswell (aged 33) that the Doctor (aged 64) would be a dead weight for him to carry all the way to the Hebrides, and when Voltaire heard of the plan, Boswell said, 'He looked at me as if I talked of going to the North Pole,' but go they did and that great travel book is nothing less than a learned testimonial to the curative properties of a superb landscape. Johnson was indifferent to weather. He refused to believe that it was the sun which made one of Boswell's friends reluctant to return from Spain to England and insisted that it must be a woman.

For centuries healing was most sought after in water, spasmodically recognised as emanating from the sun, and vaguely discovered in a change of air. But those in search of health rarely attempted to find it by some kind of deliberate intake of scenery alone. When the latter did improve the spirits, and subsequently the flesh, as the sick travelled to distant wells and better climates, few seemed to realise it. Yet the beneficial effect of a variety of landscapes on pilgrim and patient alike must have been enormous, and often those who thankfully attributed their cures to certain springs and wells would have been on the road to recovery long before they drank from or bathed in them. Exercise and that most exquisite (and taken for granted) of pleasures, of having a rich sequence of near and distant hills, fields, woods, skies, buildings and landscape features of every hue and form fed through one's heart and mind, as it were, day after day as the journey progressed, had performed the miracle.

But holy water is not to be dismissed. To our ancestors, local water had something of the same reputation and distinction as local wines have for us. Among the countless sources of domestic water all over Britain there were found to be a great many springs and wells containing waters which did wonders for aches and pains and skin diseases: chalybeate (iron), sulphurous, lime, thermal, soda- and other mineral-filled special waters, most of which had long been placed under the protection of saints. Seeking cures from sun and air was altogether more problematical, and their recent elevation, really from the late eighteenth century onwards, as health-givers owes as much to romanticism as to science. When the Shah of Persia was visiting Edinburgh during the mid-eighteenth century, a Presbyterian lady accused him of worshipping the sun. 'So would you, Madam,' he said, 'if you had ever seen it.'

What we appear to demand of landscape in health-giving terms is something to soothe us at home and to stimulate us abroad. Take the remarks of two explorers, Fridtjof Nansen and Quentin Crewe, one on his way to an ice barrenness, the other on his return from a sand barrenness. Nansen, leaving his beloved Norway for the polar regions, wrote in his journal, 'You may shrug your shoulders as much as you like at the beauties of nature, but it is a fine thing for a people to have a fair land.' And Crewe, returning to England after crossing the Sahara, and asked what the huge desert had done to him, replied, 'It refreshed me.'

The word once most used medicinally about landscape was 'salubrious', or favourable to health, and it was generally affixed to some resort. Doctors need no longer pack us off to these watering-places but it wouldn't at all be a bad idea if they recommended more of us to sit on Pendle, walk along the Suffolk coast for a week, or give ourselves up to the Dee Valley for a fortnight, etc. Not for a holiday, but for a cure.

SIRKKA-LIISA KONTTINEN top, *Harry, St Peter's Allotment*; above, *Kids with Collected Junk near Byker Bridge*

Knowing a Place

BY PETER LEVI

No one can walk into the same stream twice, because the water has run on. No one can read the same book twice, because the reader is not the same. The taste of an apple will alter, not just with the ageing of the senses, and of the season and of the tree, but because life changes us subtly and deeply. And even if the landscape stayed the same, as a few landscapes seem to do by mothy magic, swallowing and transforming change into themselves, we ourselves alter so much with the increase of knowledge and experience of the world, that as we age we see things in a new way.

Without this constant refreshing of the senses, and this continual rethinking as we look, the world would go dead on its old observers. There are three obvious ways in which the world constantly revives in our eyes: by a deliberate searching look, 'Where were my eyes yester-day?', that every alteration of light and the seasons provokes: by the influence of painting and photography, filtered through the memory, so that one recognises someone's way of looking, or the tones of an English water-colourist, or something Japanese or Chinese, in the real landscape: and finally by the growth of knowledge.

As a young man, straight after Oxford, I was sent rather against my will to teach at a public school in Lancashire where the masters' windows gazed blankly across country towards Pendle hill. I recollect that I arrived in Lancashire with my brother, and at first he hated the untamed landscape but rather liked the school architecture, which was more grand than charming, but I loved the landscape and hated only the architecture. We were both, as some old men gently remarked at the time, difficult to please. In winter light there was something precise and terrifying about Pendle. It lay crouching in the middle distance like a sphinx of nature, untroubled by mankind. It had a disturbing perfec-tion, particularly when one considered the possibility, or in my case what seemed the likelihood, of living out a lifetime watching Pendle always framed in the same Victorian window. It symbolised my frigid circumstances, because it was a beautiful hill, almost a piece of mountain, but it was perpetually out of reach. To get there and back you needed a long summer day's walk.

But Pendle altered when someone explained the geology. Pendle represented the last push of the last glacier of an ice age. I stared at the map and began to plot the underlying stone. Not being a scientist, I have never really mastered more than fragments of the geological map of Britain. Greensand means to some people an exact area and almost a chapter in the prehistory of the earth. To me it only says something about what gardening the soil will bear. I have never been able to imagine the entire structure of even one district. I find the walls of freshly cut graves more fascinating than those of archaelogical excavations, and fresher and more intimate than railway cuttings. As a boy I read in an old book that the way to understand geological structure was to study newly made cuttings. That must have been true in the great age of railways, which ended only around 1900, but those cuttings were overgrown long ago. The only new one that recently offered the same imaginative pleasure to my scarcely scientific curiosity was the cutting through the western edge of the Chilterns where the M40 motorway climbs out of Oxfordshire.

This tiny scientific upheaval over Pendle took place in my head when I was nearly thirty. It was not just an idea; one could see that stubborn pushing and the slow timescale in the shape of the hill. Pendle became to me thrilling in a new way, like a mechanical model. I began not only to think about structure but to see it. I liked the tilted underwater landscape of the river Hodder where the brown water tumbles over ledges of very ancient rock like a collapsed staircase, and the tilted underwater rockface that now lies high up on dry land under the Glyder range.

English landscape is not intelligible without the sea. As a suburban London boy, I suppose I thought once that the only rocks were sea rocks and cliffs. They seemed intensely romantic, enlivened by the destructive sea, an extreme opposite of home. I never thought trees were for climbing, but I thought cliffs were. Climbing is an expression of love I suppose. The most enjoyable thing about it to my mind is the handling of the rock. But they say that the danger and the physical racing of the blood that comes from exertion combine with mountain air to create a unique sharpening of the pleasures of sight and smell. What the biscuit was to Proust by way of the fermentation of memory, the smell of bog-myrtle and of wet rock is to me. (Its opposite in my repertory, the most homelike and secure of smells, is the smell of mint under a James Grieve apple tree, paradise lost.) But the most exciting smell in England,

and the most exciting sight, is the sea. The action of the sea on the sand, on pebbles and on cliffs, is the first long process of nature that children appreciate, as if Britain made sense only where its edges are broken. How many British islands are there really?

The other day I saw by chance the watercolour drawings of a schoolmaster called Powell, who died in an Alpine mountaineering accident in 1933. He had a style that was delicate and even strong, and his work still had the freshness of drawings that have not been much exposed to sunlight. The immediacy of watercolours has nothing to do with the soul. It comes from technical originality, a continual impromptu of devices, an art that you make up as you go along. Once it has rules it deadens. Some of Powell's drawings had rules, though they were able, spirited performances. One of the best was of cliffs in Kent or Sussex or the Isle of Wight, with the sea fawning at their feet. His cliffs are a cascade of whiteness. No doubt schoolmasters in 1933 knew as much about chalk as mountaineers knew about rock, but he caught these cliffs in intense light, and somehow by contrast with other colours he showed their chalk surface, with every fold and crevice and shadow, as I have never seen them represented.

I think it was knowledge of chalk cliffs and slippery cliff paths that confused my ideas about the Downs for many years. A quarry or a pit in the Downs does reveal something about their structure, like a wound in a whale, but in childhood I mostly saw the Downs from a distance, from a train or on a bicycle, and they meant the sea. They had for me a merely mystical or harmonious beauty. I had read too much poetry about them by Belloc and Kipling, and if I had known that Gilbert White still called them mountains, I would have thought he was mad. They were just a beautiful, rolling barrage of sweet-smelling, sheep-cropped grass. (I supposed it was only the sheep that kept the grass short; I had never noticed the miniature size of the flowers.) They ended in cliffs and coves. They were the last obstacle before you got to the sea.

It was a stray remark of Geoffrey Grigson, that master of knowledge and particularity, that made me first see them as they are. I must stress here that I mean see, more than 'understand' and that the idea doesn't now have much geological respectability. Anyway, Grigson suggests that the Downs were once the floor of a warm and shallow sea. They are shaped by the sea, they were deposited and compacted. They are like vast sand dunes, like the sand dunes of the Landes, the final product of the Atlantic and its weather, but the Downs have a submarine quality, and shapes determined by the pressures of water and wind. The waves in spite of their foaming crests are only swellings and wind-driven heavings of the sea, and the Downs are like them but more solid.

Why do I find it comforting that there are fish-bones in the chalk, and fish must once have been gliding through the currents of salt water around Mount Tabor and Firle Beacon, and yet terrifying that human beings once roamed after reindeer and wild horses across what is now the North Sea? And it is disturbing to know the sea is not level. Its curve is not exactly that of the earth's surface. If the North Sea froze, you would be skating downhill from Aberdeen to Amsterdam, and uphill in the other direction. Even the island of Britain is heaving very slowly in three different ways, like three scales on the side of a breathing dragon. It is easy enough to consider why mountains are the shape they are; indeed that is the first question one asks about them. They seem to preserve the process of eruption and creation which is imagined in children's books about the origins of the earth. But what one likes about them is their slowness. The surface of this planet has settled itself into shape terribly slowly.

I have often been puzzled to know why we should think its proportions so beautiful. Not because of any objective mathematics, but because one likes best what one is used to, and certain places by association, other ones by extension, others again because they are so surprising. Yet people are shocked to think the Greek islands are like the Scottish islands. No one imagines that Cairo is as foggy as Bournemouth. The Alps at dawn standing up above the plain of Lombardy are always astonishing, and so is the sudden sight of the Himalayas. I once lived for a year at Tremeirchion in North Wales, where very rarely, just a few days in the whole year, you would suddenly see the Snowdon range standing high up in the sky above the Denbigh Moors. The effect is the same really. The glitter of snow is always new, even if you see it winter after winter, as you do on the White Mountains in Crete, or in the Cotswolds. Almost every landscape can make you suddenly stop and stare, at least on a few days a year, even if you were born there.

You learn the age and history of a forest only if you live with it. They say you can roughly estimate the age of an undisturbed hedge by a calculation based on the number of species of trees in it. You can often tell the beech trees introduced all over England by Scottish landscape gardeners from the late eighteenth century onwards, by their strangely divided trunks like Gothic pillars. They were brought down from nursery gardens too far north of the beech's natural range. Woods more than anything else in the English landscape become more loved the more familiar one is with them. They are a strong case of liking what one is used to, and of hating any change. I have seldom felt any change whatsoever in a wood was an improvement if I knew the wood well, even the most necessary clearing, even when I did the clearing myself.

Knowing the nest of every bird, and the noises of a wood at all hours and seasons, is almost a lifework. I was once in charge of a wood for a few years, and it took me half that time to see the meaning of its drainage system, let alone to disentangle it and clear the ditches. But learning the history of parks and artificial landscapes more swiftly alters the way you see them. I spent the afternoon of Mr Kennedy's missile crisis knee-deep in the muddy silted end of a lake, cutting down three water-rooted trees to restore an eighteenth-century vista. Seeing that the vista was meant to be there in the first place was a matter more of knowledge than of intuition. Taste is a very uncertain criterion, and geometry is even less help. Nowadays, garden historians use aerial photography to show the skeleton of a lost garden, which the turf can reveal just as crops can reveal an ancient settlement. One carries the plans and habits of long-lost gardens and landscapes in one's head I think, and one sees automatically the mutations of a landscape from century to century. One can read places like an antiquarian book. It is a matter of habit, not a difficult or very learned skill.

The problems thicken with the influence of human beings of course. It is well known that a landscape can be read in terms of social and economic history, and once one has read a little about the rural poor, about child labour in the fields for example, one can no longer see a nobleman's park or anything else in the country as pure idyll. Even 'The woods are in their autumn beauty' takes on another meaning, when one remembers the history of the game laws. Pendle was where George Fox, looking down on one of the earliest industrial landscapes in the world (though the Sussex iron industry, of which we have little visual record, was earlier) had his apocalyptic vision. The great American railways crossed the west on sleepers made of the ruined chestnut forests of New England. These are thoughts one cannot think away. But the tragic nature of our history does not make ruins or even graveyards less beautiful. Nor does it disguise a choice we have refused or are refusing to make.

It is part of the way we look at the landscape. We know more than any previous generation, there are more of us, and our anxiety is more acute, though our history is less obviously harsh. The effect is that certain ways of seeing are now excluded, or ought to be, because of their falsity. We say fondly, What a Christmas card scene, meaning in some way unreal though highly enjoyable. One says Chocolate box less fondly, and mostly about bad art, rather than banal, romantic nature. These are mere aesthetic matters. What is so false as to be ruled out is the Victorian sense of Merrie England, or the Georgian sense of Britain as an agricultural, perfect paradise, or the romantic sense that one can wander off into the countryside like the scholar gipsy, as if the late Victorian or the pre-war countryside awaited us. The sense of a crisis is universal. The landscape everywhere in Britain feels like a survival, but no one is sure of the future.

No one can look at a perfect ducal paradise like Blenheim Park any more without at least a shadow of several thoughts. How beautiful it was once, before it was full of people. How strange and in some ways how sinister a world built it. How lucky we are we still have it. Then some people will experience a kind of baroque triumph or a pastoral exaltation, which those who created this landscape intended them to feel. Some will think about Winston Churchill. Many more will feel envy. We are a society with a chip on its shoulder. We feel puritanic disapproval of the past, furious resentment of the old, complacent upper classes, and the odd illusion that all these landscapes and lakes and palaces are 'our inheritance', that they belong to us and they represent our creative powers. It is an astonishing claim when you come to think of their true origins and perhaps it comes from frustration, like identification with royalty or a football team. I have even read that the lyric poetry of William Blake is best understood as an expression of the emerging lower middle class.

All these illusions nourish a lost truth. Blenheim Park was meant to amaze and please, and so it does. Knowledge of its landscape history cannot take that away; this is a case where science is little more than a game. If you know enough, you reconstruct the old look of the little river before the lakes were dug, and you thank heaven the upper part of the bridge was left unfinished. It would have looked like a railway viaduct. But Blenheim is an extreme case of an artificial landscape. The sight of any oldish farm standing in its own fields raises thoughts almost as complicated. You can develop, as I have done, an eye for old field patterns and rural history. The map is what tells you most, and a study of the map certainly alters your eyesight. Almost every landscape in Britain is man-made; it is a reading of history. That universal fact itself, once you have swallowed it, alters the way in which you look more than the particular age of any one settlement or piece of cultivation.

You see the countryside differently by knowing or suspecting what lies underground: rocks or ruins or coal or a system of limestone caverns. Equally if you travel a lot in search of the bones and the variations of local landscape, you begin to notice whole river systems and the drainage and the variations of soil; you begin to love places for their specific quality: a lake island where you stand on shale and look at limestone, or in my own region, the differences of the three river valleys of the Cherwell, snaking in and out of the Oxford canal among water-meadows, the Evenlode, which makes constant love with the Oxford to Hereford railway, and the best and purest, the Windrush valley. You recognise with pleasure the same landscape effect in utterly separate circumstances. The house where William Morris lived near the upper Thames is in a thrillingly desolate, flat and medieval-looking river plain, threaded by the intricate brooks and ditches that make it habitable. You could as easily hate that landscape as love it. The playing fields of Eton lie in similar water-meadows, threaded by dark brooks and willow-sour ditches. Beyond the Thames at Oxford, in an area now abandoned to industry and sub-industrial desolation, I used to walk in the same rough fields. It is all Thames gravel I suppose. The gravel ponds at Staines must have been like that before they were dug. I bitterly regret knowing so little of the Thames below London.

One feels a loyalty to one landscape, the pleasure of a traveller in another. Even those who work the earth, who curse it as well as love it, are usually found to nourish a stubborn topographic affection. National patriotism is a mere parody of this feeling. The body and surface of a landscape can attract something like personal love. There is something deeply erotic in the relationship of man and place; it includes endless exploration and happy repetition and silent familiarity; smell, sight, taste, touch and hearing call it to life. I think it is literally too deep to be expressed in words, except sideways or casually, in the course of saying something else. Music about places has a false joviality or an assumed melancholy, an untrue melodrama. Cézanne and Constable are great topographic artists because of their patience, their endless dissatisfaction. No single picture of theirs taken by itself could quite tell you that. In Chinese topographic art every brush-stroke is like the fall of a leaf, and the drawing commemorates the soul, or the dying breath of the place. But I do not think it expresses stubborn local love.

Love is a constant discovery, and the exploration of a place never ceases. Many of us settle down in retirement to the thorough exploration of a single landscape. The most detailed, annotated map builds itself up year by year in the memory. One slowly recognises the shape of things and their inter-relation. I have always envied Peter Lanyon, the Cornish painter who explored his familiar landscape from a glider. I recollect the rush of air and sharpness of sensation that makes the motorcycle such an exciting engine of exploration, and earlier than that, the unique thrill of cutting across country on horseback. The truth is that one wants to come at the landscape from every direction, in every different way.

I live now on the edge of a few miles of flat land, dented with small valleys. This was once the shore of a subtropical sea, and one can recognise the seashore in its fossils. In the river valley below the village some horses, apparently escaped from a Stubbs painting, graze in water-meadows. Calling voices echo between hillside and wood. The railway lies beyond the river, but because of the woods and the echoes, the Hereford train when it passes fills the whole landscape with noises for a minute or two. Now that the elms have gone from the fields, the characteristic trees are willows, but the wood towards the river is a beech wood. It seems to have been planted by the Dukes of Marlborough to preserve pheasants or to shelter foxes, or to mask abandoned quarries and stonepits. The shape of the hillside above the wood comes alive with the geometric marks of ploughing. I love this landscape with an insecurity of passion. I do not own it, nor was I born in it. Most of us who live in a place will soon be forgotten. Our only immortal link with the landscape will be if we are permitted to be buried in it.

MEDICINE WHEEL

365 DAYS

12 MONTHS

1 YEAR

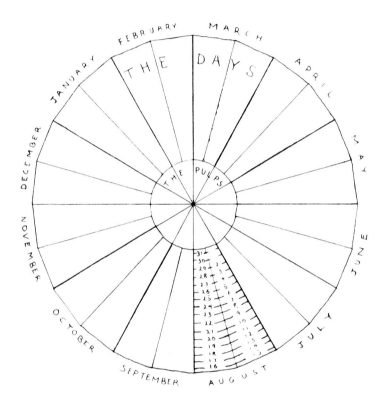

One natural object for each day of the year.

Twelve segments of paper, one for each month,
made during that month from the pulp of
particular plants.

A mushroom print

AUGUST 16 1982 – AUGUST 15 1983

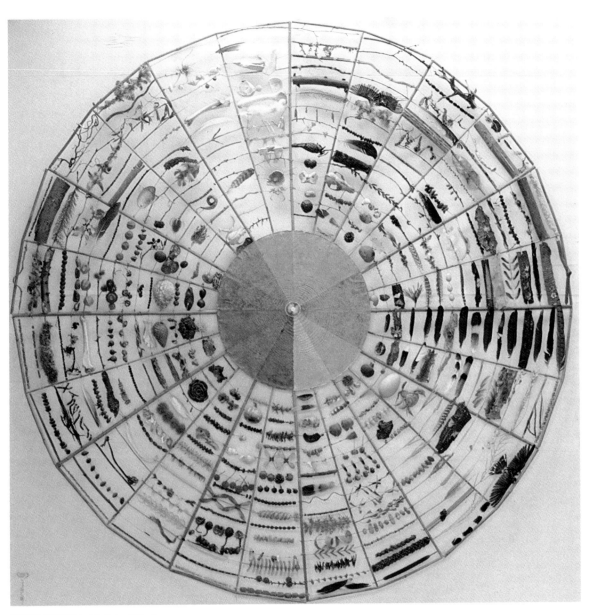

CHRIS DRURY *Medicine Wheel*

MOUNTAIN SHEEP

MOORLAND SHEEP

VALLEY SHEEP

WOODLAND SHEEP

COASTAL SHEEP

ESTUARY SHEEP

Sheep Spaces, North Wales. David Nash 1983

DAVID NASH *Sheep Spaces*

SOD SWAP

August – September – October –
1983.

CAE'N – Y – COED, N. WALES

A RING OF SODS, 35' DIAMETRE

N. Wales Ring

Common Mouse-ear Chickweed
Thin-runner Willow Herb
Thyme-leaved Speedwell
Common St John's Wort
Procumbent Cinquefoil
Common Hemp-nettle
Scented Vernal Grass
Creeping Soft Grass
Common Catsear
Lesser Stitchwort
Ribwort Plantain
Common Sorrel
Birdsfoot-trefoil
Common Bent
Sheep's Sorrel
Red Campion
Yorkshire Fog
White Clover
Hardheads
Cocksfoot
Hogweed
Soft Rush
Ragwort
Bramble
Bracken
Bluebell
Moss

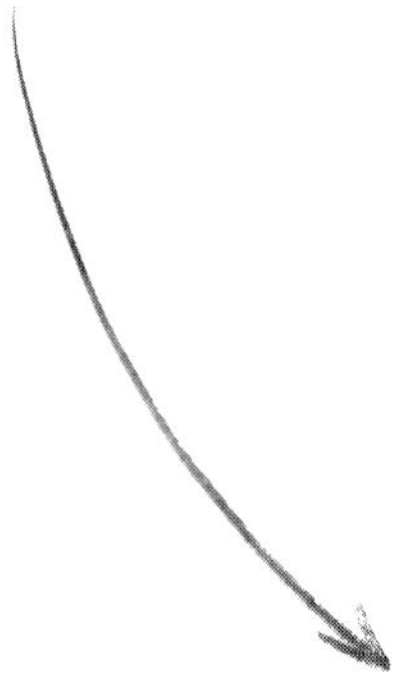

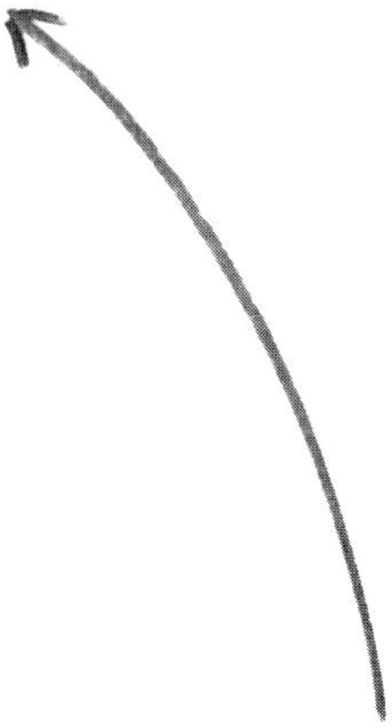

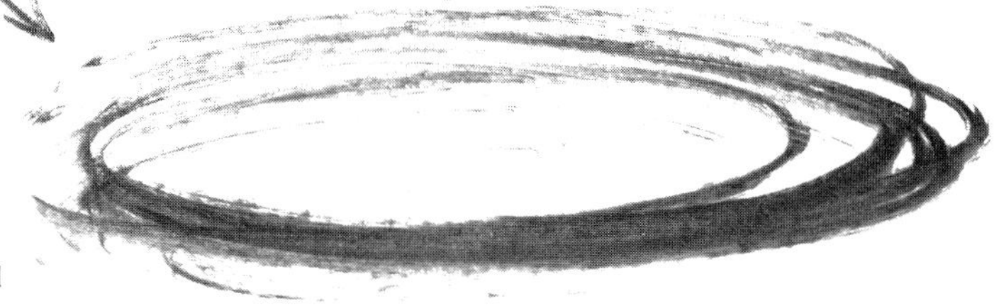

Kensington Gardens Ring

Daisy
Rye Grass
Common Mouse-ear Chickweed

KENSINGTON GARDENS, LONDON

A RING OF TURF   35' DIAMETRE

For the duration of an exhibition of sculpture at the Serpentine Gallery, London, a ring of sods from a field in North Wales was exchanged with a ring of turfs from Kensington Gardens, London –

A piece of rural environment in London, – A piece of urban environment in North Wales.

David Nash. 1983

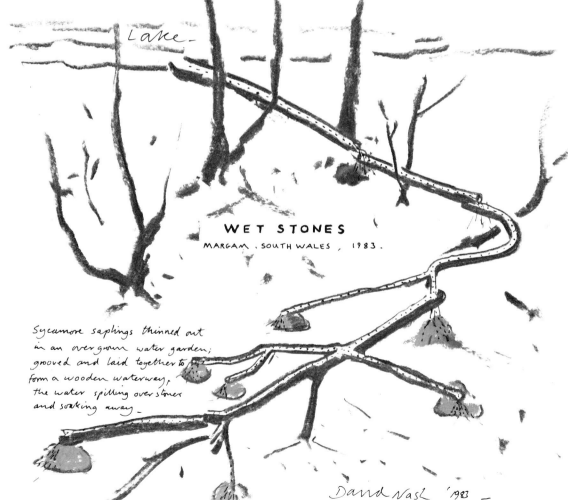

Lake.

WET STONES

MARGAM, SOUTH WALES, 1983.

Sycamore saplings thinned out
in an overgrown water garden;
grooved and laid together to
form a wooden waterway,
the water spilling over stones
and soaking away.

David Nash '1983

DAVID NASH *Wet Stones*

The Demanding Landscape

BY BEL MOONEY

> Man has lost the capacity to foresee and
> forestall. He will end by destroying the earth.
>
> *Albert Schweitzer*

I live in the country now, or more precisely, in a small village just outside Bath. Yet I am not of the country; it is as an outsider that I regard the landscape all around – an exile from the city. Exiles look with a clear eye at the unfamiliar terrain they newly inhabit; they may view it more vividly and with more awe than do those who truly belong. Trees outside I cannot name, fields I rarely walk on, hedgerows I never study, farm animals of which I feel nervous . . . yet still the view from the window (hills, sky, distant sheep) hauls my attention, and its lessons are still being learnt.

It was no romantic move from London: the back-to-nature fraud fashionable enough to inspire advertising copy for a shelf full of hair and beauty products. I wanted to grow no vegetables, nor walk around in Wellington boots, nor change my habits to echo the sincere convictions (wholefood, lentils, free-range eggs, and ecology) so cleverly parodied in Posy Simmonds's *Guardian* cartoons about the muddled Weber family.

Idealising nature is not new, but in the late twentieth century we are seeing novel versions of the pastoral way of life, principally amongst the young and middle-class. The concentrated involvement of women within the peace movement (represented most strikingly at Greenham Common) has evoked a symbol at once modern and most ancient: the earth mother herself, exalting a primitive feminine wisdom that owes much to instinct.

Interestingly, a political grouping based upon the peace activists, 'Woman For Life on Earth', suggests a concern very much connected with what I learn from living outside the city. The connecting idea is that of responsibility. Those who sit outside air bases which shelter American missiles, and those who stand for Parliament with the apparent temerity to speak for 'life on earth', and those like myself in broad sympathy with such actions – all have at the root of their ideas a passionate sense that there are permanent moral values which are symbolised by the planet itself; that we are but custodians whose grave duty is to ensure that the earth passes on to generations after us, in such a condition that they also have a choice about how they treat it. There can be no such choice unless we take a few hundred steps backwards from our original sin, unfolded with particular complexity in the twentieth century. The sin is arrogance. The lesson to be learnt is humility, and it is humility which the landscape outside my window demands.

The word 'nature' has many meanings, but central to them all is the idea that the 'natural' has its own life, unmodified by man. Nature untamed, nature red in tooth and claw, nature with its cycles of destruction and rebirth, nature as distinct from 'nurture', nature as evolution: all of these images flesh out the *persona* invoked by the demented King Lear, 'Hear, nature, hear; dear Goddess hear ... ' Implacable, obeying her own laws, nature *is*. It was that blind but awe-inspiring power which made primitive man shiver, and led the Greeks and Romans to see gods in every tree, as well as in the fruitful fields and treacherous oceans.

Two things stand in opposition to this vision of omnipotent nature: God and Man. By God I mean the giver of life, the Maker of heaven and earth, for if life is 'given' how can it then evolve according to its own dictates? This was the question that shook the edifice of Victorian belief to its foundations. It is certainly possible to look on nature as the perfect manifestation of God's grace, but if nature is Creation it is not creativity itself: it is made by God, a work of art, and (for the believer) an expression of divine will which must necessarily be subject to that will.

As for Man (and the masculine singular includes the feminine; women are not guiltless), his history is that of a suppression of nature, for his own survival or convenience. At its best this shows in the cultivation of field, park and garden, the domestication of animals and the development of medicine; at its worst, in the assumption that Man stands at the centre of the universe and must bend it to his will, by (for example) imposing artificial restraints such as chemical pesticides, so that in the end nature is perverted, its chains of dependence broken – with destructive consequences. There is an insufferable certitude behind the phrase 'the control of nature': the conviction that the natural world exists solely for Man's use.

If God and Man are, in different ways, controllers of Lear's rampant Goddess, they command separate but equally powerful armies with which to subjugate her. One attacks through complacency, the other through commerce. Those who believe in a God-created world have always shown a tendency towards fatalism: war, famine, pestilence and flood may bring horror, but are, after all, a just punishment for man's sins, and God's will be done. This is not so archaic as it sounds: it is fascinating to witness the attempts of some churchmen to justify the possession of nuclear weapons in spite of the wholesale destruction of man and nature they imply. At the root of all the circumlocutions seems to be an alarming fatalism: a willingness to accept that God, who created the earth, may allow Man to destroy it. The life to come, of course, is not temporal but eternal. Similarly, those who place all their trust in man and his works are likely to put commercial interests before conservation. The same people are also generally prepared to sanction the potential destruction of all living things to 'defend' one arid political philosophy or another, which matters, in the teeming history of the planet, less than a single plankton matters in the mass of ocean life. The end of the world is predicted by scientists and by the Bible and, brainwashed by both systems, most of us believe we can do nothing.

'L'homme propose, dieu dispose' will not do. We have no right to accept that either some unseen will or our intrinsic rapacity and ignorance prevent us from assuming responsibility for the future of the earth. We have no choice but to accommodate ourselves to the needs of the planet, for how can we expect it to accommodate itself to us, polluted and despoiled and threatened as it is? If we were to see ourselves as emancipated animals, we could not conceive of allowing the environment which is our home to be destroyed by our own actions. As a part (a small part but the one dignified by a moral sense) of the living world in its entirety we have a duty to understand the conditions of existence for all parts of that world, and not violate them.

The starting point is a sense of history, which in itself should foster humility. The chief problem in all questions of conservation is the apparent difficulty of reconciling the needs of past, present and future. The past needs to be preserved (whether represented by a patch of green belt land or an old church) though many would deny that in the name of progress – the present. We need, they say, to think of *now*: to streamline our agriculture, to get rid of certain insect strains, to harness nuclear power, to exploit animal products – we need it for our own good. If a certain butterfly becomes extinct, or a beach is polluted by chemicals, or fish die through nuclear waste . . . hush, protests like that are romantic or (worse) subversive.

As for the future . . . we have such a paucity of imagination that we cannot look beyond the next ten years. We devote our resources to immediate or partial interests, without stopping to consider the potential needs of those who will come after us. On a small scale this happens when a parish council decides to level an ancient sloping meadow to build a new football field, village hall or whatever. The notion that future visitors or inhabitants might well have preferred the chance to see the unique contours and features of the landscape unchanged is dismissed as fanciful or interfering. Of course communities must change and develop, but not at any price, only as a result of careful thought. On a large scale it happens when a nationalised industry is allowed, with the collusion of government and the protection of the whole establishment, to pollute the environment and endanger health until the public wakes up to the enormity of its actions. Too late, of course. On the largest scale of all, it happens when nations deem it acceptable to have the potential to use nuclear or chemical weapons, and so create a moral pollution far worse than anything we have yet done to the earth. And thus polluted, how *can* we have the foresight to forestall as Albert Schweitzer warned?

The growth of ecological awareness is often dismissed as unrealistic: a new manifestation of Luddite reaction. In fact, it shows extraordinary realism, and is in the vanguard of what I predict will emerge (if we survive) as received wisdom, although it is burdensome in its challenge. That is the point about this gentle English countryside; it is not an escape, but forces you to a toughly realistic reappraisal of your own values. That is what happened to me, and I am still rather dazed by the conversion to ideas I had never thought about, before the fields and munching sheep brought them to my attention. There is no escape; you are left no room to hide – just as the young Wordsworth found when he attempted to steal a rowing boat and imagined, in his guilty horror, that the mountain itself reared up to rebuke him. For Wordsworth, nature was a moral force which served not only as an object of poetic contemplation in itself, but also as the means to direct thought back to 'the still, sad music of humanity'.

Such thoughts can be bleak; certainly they are demanding, reminding you constantly of your own insignificant size, and the shortness of your time of choices. When I see the seasons change, and watch the bad weather roll itself into a ball and hurtle down our valley, or listen to the wind screaming through the cedars in the village churchyard, or think for a moment of the abundance of microscopic life within each clod of soil – I know what this landscape means to me and why I am so afraid for its future.

It is because we cannot live without some contact with the natural world: it is essential to our spiritual well-being – more simply, to our happiness. If we are indifferent to the fate of the world of which we are a part we have allowed our spiritual sense to wither and die. At that stage there is no point in survival anyway. The joy that medieval people felt in the spring ('Sumer is icumen in . . . ') at the end of the long, hard winter was no different in its essence from the rush of pleasure city dwellers experience today, at the sight of the first February crocuses in a municipal garden, and the warmth of first sun on the face. Such sensations connect us through the centuries; they alone transcend any technological 'fixes'. They give back to dreams, visions, instincts, emotions, and all the multifarious powers of the thirsty imagination, the proud centre of the stage; they push into the wings the paltry misapprehension that only through science can we now gain any knowledge of our world. And all of this implies no escape from logic, or reason. On the contrary, it is an expression of reason: an inescapable conclusion from the evidence all around, as well as the wisdom in the blood.

We have to regain a proper respect for natural processes, and a true reverence for the living world, ridding ourselves of all other allegiances − if we value, not *your* life or *mine*, but life itself.

FAY GODWIN *Peak District, Derbyshire*

FAY GODWIN *near Haystacks, Cumbria*

From Flint
to Shale

BY MICHAEL BERKELEY

In winter, the only visible inhabitants of the bleak salt marshes of the
North Norfolk coast are sea birds, scuttling gillies (small, evil-looking
crabs) and, when the tide is out, the occasional fisherman stooped over
a fork and bucket. He works his way across the mud flats leaving little
heaps of mud like the droppings of a large animal. He is digging for
lugworms which he will need on the next tide when he puts to sea in
search of the elusive shoals of mackerel. Frequently he will fish for
several hours and return with only a handful of dabs and black gillies.
The good days are becoming increasingly rare, though when he does hit
a shoal there is still the old excitement. For a few moments the world
seems to go mad with a dozen flashing streaks of silver to every line.
Then, as swiftly as it began, the turmoil will cease apart of course from
the thrashing haul on the rough deck.

Now the sea returns to its usual leaden black, an eerie mirror for the
chilled, magnificent light so essential to this landscape and its sounds –
the lonely cries of gulls, peewits, curlew and, inevitably, the wailing
wind. And what a wind it can be as it swipes across the punished flats;
for the land is all too vulnerable to a merciless sea which fingers its way
across the mud in a series of creeks. Occasionally the wind, moon and
sea join forces and then the menace of a flood is born. Not content with
the sodden marsh the sea gallops up the lane and rushes through the
already salt-encrusted gardens.

One year it came at night, dismissed the dyke as though it were some
childish seaside dam and plucked whole families from their beds. Even
houses quite far inland had water up to the mantelpiece and to this day
the salt has played havoc with the mortar, bricks and plaster.

The fishermen view the prospect of drowning at sea with a 'fair play'
philosophy; hardly any of them know how to swim and they treat any
suggestion of learning with derision. Maybe the centuries of hardship
have washed away the notion of the sea as a source of pleasure, or

perhaps they feel that to fight against death by drowning only makes that death more terrible. However, they do not extend this stoicism to their families and on that terrible night the sea violated the rules and in drowning their wives and children seemed to tear the heart out of the land. But life here has always been fairly hard and led from hand to mouth. It produces a people not given to great generosity but of fierce spirit and courage. These are the inhabitants of Crabbe's 'The Borough' and it is not uncommon to see a tortured, shunned character, 'A lost, lone man, so harass'd and undone'. If productions of Britten's *Peter Grimes* sometimes disguise the mad violence it is nevertheless there in the score. Indeed the turbulence of the storm-tossed sea is the mirror image of the tormented Grimes, and Britten recognised in his schizophrenic character the duplicity of the ocean. Could the full force of a North Sea gale have been so tellingly portrayed by someone who had not stood in the face of it and felt the exhilaration and terror, the almost magnetic force that draws you to the water and compels you to touch? It's the vertiginous sensation that Debussy captures so overwhelmingly and yet so subtly in *La Mer* and it's the feeling of powerlessness that catches your breath when you see sailors desperately hauling a line in a Turner storm.

That Crabbe and Britten were *there* in the teeth of a gale you know as surely as you know that Monet lived with his water lilies or Degas with his dancers and that the blackness of a squally sky was as menacing to Turner as were the black crows to Van Gogh. While wonderful things have been created from the pure and abstract imagination, there does remain a special quality of communication which comes only from direct experience. It is the becoming a part of your landscape as opposed to merely witnessing it. This is also true of abstract art in as much as the power of a Jackson Pollock canvas does not rely on a recognition of its starting point. But there remains in its abstraction something private where in realism we can all share.

An absorption of a particular atmosphere is often equated to the degree of familiarity. Britten, for instance, heard and was transfixed by the Gamelan music of Bali and its exotic sounds are evident in his later works, but it is not in his blood – or the music's blood – and does not strike you with the same impact as does the presence of the North Sea and the east coast of England, though had he encountered Gamelan at an earlier age it might also have become an intrinsic part of his make-up.

Timing is everything. In 1956 when I was eight years old my parents bought one of those salt-encrusted cottages on the North Norfolk coast. It was, appropriately called Cold Blow and lay just outside a village called Morston. You could rule an uninterrupted line between it and the North Pole. Even at that tender age it was an awe-inspiring place to spend your childhood. Those are the years when places steal a particular affection in the memory and are consulted and compared for the rest of life. On our first visit to the marsh we stood for a moment in wonder before getting down to the serious business of mud, sand, boats and sea.

After three years exploring the marsh I got my first and happiest job. Having learnt to navigate the complex channels and currents I became a boatman ferrying bird-watchers and holidaymakers down the twisting creek and across the temperamental channel to Blakeney Point – a sandy, dune-covered bird sanctuary which juts out from the coast and is an island except at very low tide when you can walk across the shoulder joint where it meets the coast some two miles below Morston.

When the tide was out the would-be traveller who wished to travel from Morston rather than Blakeney had to walk the slimy marsh since the creek would be completely empty. Quite how severely the sea dictated our fortunes became all too clear while sitting for several hours on a cold seashore longing for a hot drink and, occasionally, a bit of cover. Not to mention the two occasions on which I nearly drowned.

Cold Blow was sold when I was eighteen but because of the initial excitement and freedom from school and the prospect of foreign travel I did not at first notice the gap it was to make in my life.

Now was the time for the intoxication of new smells, colours and animals: the unforgettable sensation, as you land in Africa, of a wall of heat hitting you like a bomb blast. I was so fascinated by this that I found the one hotel in Dar-es-Salaam that had air conditioning, then walked in and out of the reception area to savour the experience. In the hall of this impossibly grand hotel there were little morsels of paw-paw liberally doused with fresh lime juice. It was the one luxury I allowed myself – to go into the cool air of the hotel and the unbelievably refreshing paw-paw and, when thoroughly cool, plunge once again into the exhilaratingly dry heat.

It was from a whole series of contrasting tableaux around the world that I gathered the musical stimulation I have always needed from a landscape. Back in London I would draw on these images and as a writer keeps a diary, or an artist a sketchbook, so I kept a notebook into which went hundreds of fragments; the sounds of new continents and the ideas that those sounds suggested to me. Sometimes sitting in some ravishing setting – under a Baobab tree near a Masai village in Kenya or on the coral beaches of the Comoro Islands in the Indian Ocean – I would simply scribble whatever notes came into my head and now when I look at these portraits, the sound jogs the visual memory and I can transport myself back to small pockets of exoticism. When you rely on your ears, silence and tranquillity are essential and it was invariably in sparsely populated and rather desolate areas that ideas came to me.

Back at home the synthesis began: from a walking expedition in Greece, snatches of ancient folk tunes became *Variations on Greek Folk Songs* for unaccompanied viola. The bleached dusty plains between Cordoba and Granada set the tone for *Iberian Notebook* for cello. The click of cicadas, the darting geckoes and the stunted trees of a Provençal olive grove dominate *Three Moods for Oboe*, while the clarity of light and sound of the Mediterranean night pervade *Nocturne for Flute, Harp and String Trio*.

As my music began to be performed, travel became somewhat dictated by the location of concert halls. Once the performance was over I would find myself anxious to escape, to cleanse my ears of the city and would eagerly set forth to discover the local countryside.

There are such endless surprises in a landscape. After the hurly burly and excitement of a first visit to New York and Boston, I headed north up the coast to discover in Massachusetts, New England, a sister to the Morston Marshes. Here once again were the same birds, creeks and even samphire and gorse. Yet there was also a very different quality to the land and the fishermen. Neither have been punished in quite the same way; the land feels less ancient, the people less craggy and more giving. The contours of history are less deeply etched and you sense the optimism that you find in much American art – in the music of Copeland or Ives – and where here there is warmth, in comparable parts of Britain there is an eternal sadness. In Scotland, for instance, the rub of sea and weather has produced the granite-like expressions that you find in the stony beauty of Peter Maxwell Davies's music, which reflects not only the harshness but also, in *Mirror of Whitening Light*, the fusion of land, sea and sky of Hoy in the Shetlands to conjure a miraculous and radiant light. In this music of the Northern Lights I find something of Sibelius's relationship to his native Finland, which shows that with time an acquired affinity with a landscape can be as telling as a native affinity, since Maxwell Davies was no more born in Hoy than Gauguin was born in Tahiti.

Even with artists who write less specifically about the land there seems to me to be an aura of geography. The lyricism of Michael Tippett's music, so full of references to the elements in general, conjures up the sweeping plains of Wiltshire where he lives and works. Would the rounded figures of Henry Moore be sharper if he had set up shop on Max's Hoy? And by the same token I am hardly surprised by a violence in the art of the city; it's not the abrasiveness of a savage coast but all too often the language of despair raised to a higher level. I see it in the faces of Francis Bacon, in Brecht and Weill's portrait of Berlin and in the tragedies of *Wozzek* and *Lulu*.

I saw it too when I left the Royal Academy of Music and played in a rock group which rejoiced in the salubrious name Seeds of Discord. (Sadly neither in name nor talent did the 'Seeds' have quite the same impact as the 'Stones'! Perhaps a decade later, as punk seeds, we would have come into our own.) Seediness does seem the product of the urban environment and is not a word one would find easy to use in open country. Playing rock music gives one a tremendous feeling of sheer power and it is exciting to experience the gut reaction of hundreds of people, but the need to escape always struck me as more desperate when we were playing in large towns.

I soon began to yearn for a more peaceful existence and returned to the scene of my childhood in an attempt to recapture its more tranquil happiness. Not far from Cold Blow and just beyond Blakeney lies the silted up port of Cley with its stunning church. And then comes the village that bore the worst fury of the flood, Salthouse. Here there is another bird sanctuary, this time on the marsh itself. A small cottage was for sale and I determined to have it. Walking had by now become a passion and was undoubtedly safer than boating so with my dog Trout, I set out to cover the four or five miles from Morston to Salthouse to attend the sale. During that walk along the coast I began to realise that the memories of early days are best left enshrined by time and that you cannot hope to recreate them. What I needed was a new landscape, a new adventure, and so though I began to bid at the auction, and thought the final price was within my grasp, my hand was not raised as the hammer descended.

Instead fate took me in a straight line west from the flint of Norfolk to the shale of the Welsh Marches and a countryside ostensibly different though not without similarities. For although the pastoral lyricism of the west of England stretches into the foothills of Radnorshire there is already a strong flavour of the wildness to which they lead. This is one of the least populated areas of the British Isles as you soon discover if you try to travel without a car. But what wonderful compensations are to be found in the empty green valleys and the rolling acres of sheep country.

In the distance you can see the Black Mountains and to one side of them the Brecon Beacons. Here there is a touching respect for the soil, or 'him' as it is called. In fact everything is 'him' or 'her'. While building a new barn I was momentarily baffled by the following instructions; 'Fetch him over here and winch her by the truss then we can sheet her purloins while we have our bait.' I feel a great joy as I work with these friends who are so direct. We have a farm which has grown from nothing to a respectable smallholding and when I am helping to make hay, feed the calves or dip the sheep I feel the sense of peace and camaraderie that has been absent since my boyhood on the boats.

As I arrive from a hectic tour of duty in London, a weight seems to be lifted from the shoulders and I drink in the wonderful quiet. Music has priority in the morning (except in lambing time); then there is a long walk to mull over the day's ideas – if there have been any. It's an opportunity to get away from the notes themselves and consider the overall perspective of a piece in progress. I feel I belong in the rolling hills which allow the mind to float freely, and now that walking is such an important part of my life here I cannot imagine how I ever did without it. It has been fascinating to see how Trout, a Cockney mongrel, has adapted to the countryside. At first, when he encountered a gate he would whine like a baby. Now he's learnt from a local sheepdog to look for a hole or a loose rung.

There's great satisfaction in learning about an entirely new way of life: to know how to help a sheep in distress, how to shear and how to lamb. Gradually I have become able to identify trees and birds and tell from the sound of the brook how high the rainfall has been. In this border country you walk through a series of wonderfully contrasting land-scapes, from low rich pasture to high moorland, and these suggest great sweeps of sound.

Without the cleansing cold, pneumonia soon sets about the young calves and the racking coughs of sheep echo across the valley. I cannot immunise myself against the distress of a suffering animal whose plight can colour an atmosphere for days. So sometimes I have to fight off the external sounds which can appear as actual notes or as an abstract feeling only to be realised later through the labours of pencil and rubber.

As the addiction to walking in the country takes over so your psychological well-being cannot do without the daily ration.

It seems to me that we must be grateful to the land on so many levels that its gradual destruction has to be viewed as a form of spiritual suicide. When a hedge is ripped out to make two nine-acre fields into an eighteen-acre expanse worthy of modern machinery it's not just the loss of the hedge and its aesthetic value that we should mourn but the deeper implications. The loss of wildlife and the ruin of a natural scheme. When, centuries ago, farmers laid hedgerows they did so for very good reasons. The soil on one side of the divide is frequently different from the soil on the other, where conditions will now change because there is no shelter or break from sun, wind and rain.

Just as we erode the land so too do we erode the communities who best know how to husband it. Whole villages have been dismantled and not just because of modern technology, which certainly has its place. Rather, I am thinking of the ludicrous laws which help no one and have caused the number of farm tenancies to dwindle to such an extent that it is virtually impossible to start farming unless you have the vast amounts of capital needed to buy land. In the hill farming country that I know and love, the big farms get bigger and the characteristic smallholdings gradually disappear. It is also a tragedy for the architecture of the English landscape which has for centuries been sculpted by farms of varying size and as its boundaries and natural barriers are removed so the lie of the land falls a little more off balance.

Sadly, those of us who draw our inspiration and sustenance from the land can only grieve for the future and wonder what would have happened to the great pastoral canvases of the past had there been no sweeping fields in Elgar's Worcestershire, no lowing cattle in Constable's Essex, no twisting lanes in Hardy's Wessex and no marching hills for the lines of Langland, Kilvert and Housman.

As one remembers how much of what's worth remembering is married in some way to the land it is hard not to feel anxiety. What inspiration will be left as new centuries unfold, both for the artist and for the soul of the common man, unless we cherish the soil and the sea today and tomorrow? This was part of the overall concern for our time and our children's time that led Ian McEwan and myself to write our oratorio, *Or Shall We Die?* We simply felt the need to voice our fears and those of our friends. 'Shall there be womanly times', we ask, 'Or Shall We Die?' Sometimes the land seems to be posing just that question as it heaves under an all too masculine hand. Can we bind feeling to the intellect, have strength without aggression? Blake's apocalyptic lines ring horribly true:

> *Did He smile His work to see?*
> *Did He who made the Lamb make thee?*

JOHN HILLIARD *Revelation*

JOHN HILLIARD *Isle of Arran*

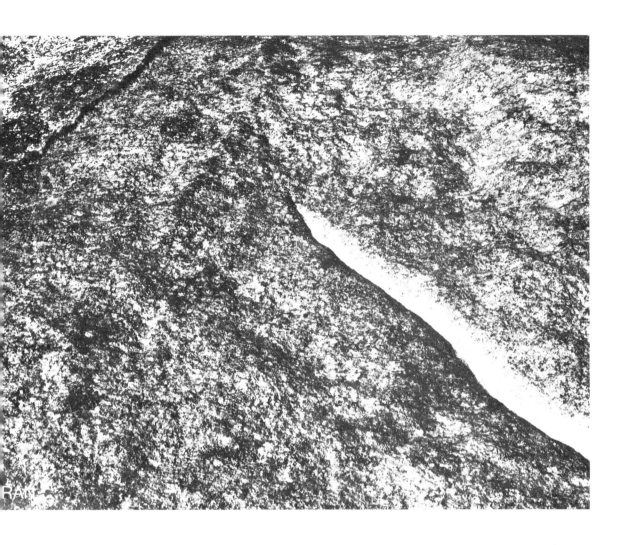

VISION

JOHN HILLIARD *Vision*

Letter to Laura

BY FAY WELDON

My dear Laura,

You write to me from Sydney and say that you and Ray are coming home to England, and are thinking of living in the country, and do I think that's a good idea?

My dear Laura! It all depends, as you must know I'll remark, on what you mean by living, on what you mean by country and mostly, on what you mean by 'good idea'. The last two words, I fear, are simply not equal to the awfulness (in the old sense of the word) of what you have in mind. You might, I suppose, describe it as a 'good idea' when proposing to build a cathedral or write the New Testament but I think even you'd try to find a loftier way of describing so profound an aspiration. Living in the English countryside is a very, very serious matter. How can you be so blithe?

Living in Australia – where they don't, come to think of it, have countryside, merely outback; the interior being altogether too large, too hot, too unregarded, too unobserved and in general too alarming to be described as anywhere but somewhere else: namely *out the back* – is dangerous but hardly serious. Snakes, spiders, sharks, bush fires, rip tides – all out to kill and if they don't get you, skin cancer will. But these concern survival in the outer world, not, as does the English countryside, survival of the soul itself. Australia, in this as in all, is O levels, England is A levels.

Nature in Australia is something external – humans live perched on the surface of an unfriendly, uncomfortable, wildly beautiful land: its flora is stark and ravishing, its fauna raucous and bizarre: south of the Wallacean line, in the hard bright sun, nature experiments; who can take an emu seriously? Or the koala bear, who lives his life altogether zonked out by the drug-filled leaves of the eucalyptus tree he favours. So much so, he's for ever simply falling off, spaced out as he is.

Here in the shadowy North nature long ago settled into sedate ways, incorporated human beings into its scheme of things. We are, here in England, part of the landscape. We have to be. Every acre of this tiny, densely populated land of ours has been observed, considered, valued, reckoned, pondered over, owned, bought, sold, hedged – and there's a dead man buried under every hedge, you know. He died of starvation, and his children too, because the common land was enclosed, hedged, taken from him. We owe the neat, patched, hedgerowed beauty of our countryside to unwilling human sacrifice: that, I suspect, is its power over us. We owe it to the past to appreciate its beauty. It's the least we can do. It's *serious*.

Now you will find it strange to hear me talking like this. I, the Londoner, who used to hate the country. But I was younger then – by all of three years – and had fallen prey, along with everyone else, to the Notion of Polarity – the feeling that if there is an evil there is a balancing good, and vice versa. That if the Russians are bad, the Americans are good, that if workers are exploited, management are exploiters, that if Palestinians are to be pitied, Israelis are to be blamed, that if the Conservatives are wrong, the Labour Party's right – and that if you love the town, you must hate the country. One proceeded by corollary, falsely.

What happened was that I investigated my love of London, and discovered it was not crowds I loved, nor power, nor conversation, nor the literary world, nor parties, nor L.B.C. – it was landscape. What I loved was the familiar as it changed suddenly to the unfamiliar with the shift of season and sun. The city skyline seen from the top of Primrose Hill as a rainstorm swept the Thames; Regent's Park astonished by a sudden snow-fall; the icy silence of the Serpentine on a January morning, the Hilton misty and irrelevant behind; the wide wild sky as you drove down Westway into the sunset – it was, after all, only landscape.

Landscape wins. I told you that in my last letter. I told you that Australia was only an extension of Indonesia and becoming more Indonesian every day, and Ray, Wasp and furious, answered my letter instead of you, so incensed was he by the very notion. But isn't that why you can never get an Australian typist to work over the weekend? They're down on the beach, *having a good time*. I ask you, is that European?

Landscape wins. Europe can't survive in Israel for that reason, or only for another couple of generations. That's obvious when you look at the faces of the young. They're desert faces, growing back into landscape, part of the landscape, olive faces, dark eyes, beautiful, unworried, as the yellow sand sweeps back over everything, making all things equal, empires rising and falling, yellow stones crumbling: all passion passes, and a vengeful God prevails over the ochre land. What price Nietzsche now?

Landscape wins. Look at the flat faces of Norfolk and the craggy faces of Yorkshire.

Incidentally, I recently had a letter from a lady in Freiburg who is doing a Ph.D. in Women's Studies with particular regard to literature. She objects to a statement of mine that writers are born to be writers, on the grounds that to claim anything is in the genes is politically and socially dangerous – especially in Germany. Writers are made merely by their circumstances, she claims. It is, in fact, a talent anyone can acquire if they only put their minds to it. What do you make of that?

She certainly wouldn't like me saying that people in Norfolk have flatter faces than people in Yorkshire, so I withdraw the remark. Nevertheless, I continue to maintain, landscape wins. It triumphs over political parties, social ideologies, individual will. Catholicism in cold wet Ireland, where the grapes won't grow, is a different, sourer religion from, say, Catholicism in vinous Mediterranean Italy.

You add a brief postscript to your letter: the momentous news that Ray has given up his job as assistant controller of A.B.C., and taken redundancy money early, in order to 'develop his talents as a writer'. I take it that's what all this English countryside is about. Your husband sees himself as a latter-day Hardy, I daresay. Well, why not?

But, Laura, *what* talents? I hope he's sure. I know all too many men in their middle years who have mistaken the general malaise of boredom and vague life-disappointment (if that's not a phrase in common use, it ought to be) for a soaring creative talent gone to waste, never given the opportunity to flower. They give up their jobs, and often their wives too, and retreat into garrets to write. (Or, more often, to rather nice villas, somewhere warm, with swimming pools.) And they find eventually, too late, that it wasn't time they needed, or peace, it was ability. But I daresay for one in ten it's true; there *is* a talent, it can be developed, it is not too late – and who is to say that Ray isn't the one in ten? Let me not wet-blanket – it's too late anyway! You're on your way.

A friend of mine in her middle age, a traditional wife and mother, happily ironing her husband's Tuesday shirt on Monday evening, was disturbed by an estate agent, showing clients round her rather lovely home. Her husband had put the house on the market, without telling her. He was afraid to. He had given up everything, job included, to write. He went to Spain on the proceeds of the house, which was in his name. She got a job as a laundress. (She was skilled and experienced, and did all right, and he never got further than Chapter 3 before suffering from Writer's Block. Presently, when drunk, he fell off a mule and broke his back and had to come home and live off a disability

pension. Some people will go to any lengths to avoid finishing a novel!)
Never mind, but it was a nasty shock for her, at the time. So consider
yourself lucky, Laura, that Ray, in this Life-Change-Situation, includes
you in his plans. It is nice for a writer to have a wife, especially if she can
type.

As for writing in the country – well. The country in this respect isn't
really any different from the town – only further. What you see out of
the window is obviously different – in the country I write at a first-floor
window, creeper-frilled, and see fields, stream, cows, sheep, moorhens. The cows are of the anonymous modern kind, without apparent
personality. The sheep are commonly mistaken for goats, being brown,
lithe and hairy. Their social organisation is enthralling. But mostly I see
what is in my head, not what is out of the window. In the town, you
raise your head from work and see houses and people. It depends on
your nature whether you find this interesting or distracting. I rather like
it.

But the problem is not really what you do or don't see out of the
window – it's having something to say and the means to say it. I was
reared in schools and offices, and don't mind distraction and am
oppressed by silence. Ray may well need total solitude and you creeping round the house in soft shoes. Everyone's different.

I know a poet who so needed silence he sound-proofed his room
thoroughly – so thoroughly he collapsed and had to be taken off to
hospital suffering from oxygen starvation. That was in the town. The
country is draughtier: I don't think it would have happened there. Make
of it what you will.

I will say, for myself, that when I'm in the country I tend to write *long*,
considered things, things like novels and plays, and when I'm in the
town I write for television. This latter may be because of the nature of
T.V. drama, which I like to see as a city thing, a gathering up and
focusing of group energies: a holding up of the mirror to urban society,
thus enabling it to understand itself, and so make changes, however
minor. Or it may be that T.V. Companies, reluctant to pay too many
train fares, simply prefer not to commission out-of-town writers – make
of that what you will.

I can't make up your mind for you. I will warn you of the sheer
practical difficulties of living in the country: how to keep warm, how to
keep fed with the take-away five miles distant, how to get the children
to school: I will encourage you with talk of the natural harmonies: of
how the writer in the country feels less professional, and more simply
human, and as if writing was a natural overflow of animation, rather
than a matter of contracts and residuals and royalties. It takes the writer
back, in all humility, into himself, and his original vision of the world,

and his desire to communicate it, rather than to gain a writing credit on some screen or other, and if I may venture the suggestion, this is more important for the male writer than the female. He is more easily divorced from the realities of the world than she can ever be: she goes on dusting and sweeping and being pre-menstrual like anyone else – he retires into his Ivory Tower and his wife brings him coffee and admires him, and he thinks that is the world and grows smug and boring, and has nothing left to say. Could I suggest that that is why we now have a dearth of young male novelists?

It is exciting to think that you're coming back! Laura, the *greenness* of England. You think you remember it, but it will shock you when you see it again. Try to come in April, when you get that extraordinary new acid hedgerow green which can reflect back from a grey sky and all but blind you. Mind you, as the season advances, the fields of England can be seen to be altogether too brilliant, these days, in the texture and depth of their poster paint green. Too rich, too perfect; sweetened with nitrogen, phosphates, fungicides, insecticides, pesticides: waving altogether too thickly and slowly in the wind: the cows eating the chemical grass, their diet liberally salted with antibiotics and hormones – well, you know all that. I deplore along with everyone else even as I munch my own mega-multi-mineral tablets, and remember what a scientist friend once remarked in irritation as I stared into the window of a health food shop and he strode by – 'What do they think we're all made of, if not chemicals?' I take comfort from that – otherwise I'd never eat steak again, and as for water-injected pigs, and as for battery hens . . .

Listen, Laura, forget landscape, forget carcinogenics. If you're going to live in the country and enjoy its flavourful, natural goodness, Be Rich. We costed out our free-range home-grown organic eggs at 50p the piece, and that was leaving out the cost of the hen house and the mortality loss from foxes. Ray will want to own a dog, of course, with which to have himself photographed, pipe and all, in front of the new country property. So be prepared for mud not just in the hall and kitchen but up the stairs. You'll never keep the animal out of the bedrooms, your heart will melt at its howls, and it will roll in strange stuff known as Fox Trot and the stench is phenomenal, and no amount of Chanel No. 5 will drown it. You'll want to own a car, of course, and be able to afford petrol for it, or you'll find yourself living 2⅞ miles from the school and so not eligible for school transport and yourself walking twelve miles a day, there and back, there and back, winter and summer, as an alternative to letting your five-year-old walk by herself along a narrow arterial road with no footpath – which is what the Education Department will expect her to do. That's the English countryside, for women and children. Have a car, also, because there are no buses to take you about any more, not even to the Job Centre. Not that there are any jobs, anyway. That is how you define the country. It's a place without jobs. That is why there are so few people in it: that is why it is so nice. So have a source of income, and a good one, before you contemplate living in the country. But I'm sure Ray will see to that.

You see how I am torn? My love of landscape, and my feeling that the countryside is a dreadful, fearful place: a place that the rural young have for centuries done everything they can to leave, and with reason (in the cities there is freedom, independence, company, excitement, a cheerful sexuality. There's sex in the country, Laura, in plenty, but mostly of a rather doomy, suicidal, incestuous kind); the place which a new breed of self-deluded, middle-class rural sentimentalists, ecological obsessives, who believe that everyone in the world is *bad* except them, and they would live for ever if only the capitalists weren't poisoning them, now infest, ignoring – nay, blocking – the needs of the genuine rural inhabitants who want *more* industrial development, factory farms, council estates, not less, and a cheap jam butty made of white sliced bread, vitamin enriched, for tea, and why not? And who are cheered, not appalled, by the sight of a row of electricity pylons marching forcefully across the land.

Laura, this letter is turning into a confessional, not a reply to yours. Forgive me. When required recently to pin a photograph on the Greenham wire, it was one of the English landscape I put there, and not, as I would have expected of myself, a family group. I can, it seems, tolerate the death of people more easily than the death of landscape. So much of our past, of human aspiration, and struggle, and joy is invested in these hills and fields of ours, that the present pales beside it. People, after all, are replaceable, renewable. And then I think – but that statement puts me in the ranks of militarists, who prefer the neutron bomb to 'ordinary' nuclear missiles because the former destroys life but preserves *things* – and wonder down what alarming paths this passion for landscape is leading me. Mao said, two decades ago, in the days of our simplicity, dragging us enthralled into our dangerous new world of polarities, of death sentence by corollary, love what your enemy hates, hate what your enemy loves. Define yourself by the company you keep. What am I to do, Laura? What are any of us to do?

All I know is that on a winter's evening the road from Shepton Mallet to Wells can be almost intolerably beautiful – when the road stops curling between treacherous stone walls and opens up over the hills, and there is a view to the west, and the low sun breaks through the rain clouds that cluster over the sudden hummock of Glastonbury Tor, and the plain between is patterned by shadows of grey and gold.

Come and live in the country, Laura. It's a good idea, if you can forget the remnants of the socialist principles you once had and don't mind the mud from your car splashing the rural unemployed. You might even bring some money into the area – builders, plumbers, grocers, domestics – all will benefit. You could even come and live near me, if you can bear the sight of me growing roots, so that lifting my feet out of the water-logged clay beneath the drizzling, drifting sky, is every day more of an effort. It's very windy where we live: and high: and sometimes the wind keeps up for three weeks non-stop and I think I will die from the horror of its wailing around the house: and if it's from the north, and especially cold, why then the fires smoke; and just when I think I will go mad from frustration and irritation, and sit at my desk at the upstairs window and the rain blows so hard against the pane there is no view of anything at all – I might be on a high speed train going through a hurricane – why it is then that *something happens*. The rain will stop: and there below, where normally the stream goes under the lane that leads from our house to the road, thus discommoding the moorhens, who can never work out which side of the divide they live, and have to keep getting out of the water and marching from side to side to find out, the water level has risen to flood the drive and the moorhens have at last solved their problem, and there they are, swimming in the drive itself, triumphant. Or I go down to the kitchen and find sitting in a circle, on the floor, a very small child, a cat, a dog, and a hen, each studying the other, trying to find a likeness, other than life itself, and failing . . . So I stay another day, and perhaps the snow falls, and adds excitement and the edge of danger; and then I find myself looking at the overflow graveyard – a few simple stones on a bleak hillside – and I think, yes, well, that will do. You have to end somewhere. Why not here? Better than Golders Green Crematorium, any day.

So come along, Laura. Hold your nose and jump. When terrified, it is the only honourable thing to do.
With love,

Cousin Fay.

JOHN HUBBARD *Abbotsbury Gardens*

Nature and Culture

The Blinded Eye

John Fowles

BY JOHN FOWLES

A sparrow's life's as sweet as ours.
Hardy clowns! grudge not the wheat
Which hunger forces birds to eat;
Your blinded eyes, worst foes to you,
Can't see the good which sparrows do.
  John Clare – 'Summer Evening'

One September day I was standing with an American friend beside a small stream in the Massachusetts countryside. We were talking literary shop when suddenly, without warning either to him or to myself, I began running away like – I am afraid as much like an excited ten-year-old as a bearded and not conspicuously slim man four times that age can. I did not run very far because the thing I was chasing disappeared, like Hemingway's colonel, across the river and into the trees; and also because, as I could see by my friend's face when I turned, serious writers just don't break off conversations like that if they want to go on deserving the adjective.

He was not to know that I had just had my first living sight of the sublimest fancy, the summit of exquisite hope, of every British lepidopterist. During the last hundred years 157 brave expatriate specimens of the milkweed (or monarch) butterfly, *Danaus plexippus*, have managed to get themselves netted over here; and where other small boys dreamed trains and aeroplanes, I used to dream black-veined whites, mazarine blues, and milkweeds. But though my first reaction was instinctive I was not simply running, as my shocked friend supposed, after a large – and in the United States, quite common – tawny-brown butterfly. I was really running after a whole buried continent of memories . . . and also, I must confess, after a whole series of blind attitudes to nature.

I began very young as a butterfly collector, surrounded by setting-boards, killing-bottles, caterpillar cages. Then I went in for birds and compiled painstaking lists of the species I identified: an activity closer to writing down the makes of cars than to ornithology, though I suspect many misguided amateur birdwatchers still think the spotting of rarities is what their hobby is about. From birds I moved on, in my teens, to botany; but I was still a victim of rarity snobbery and for years hardly spared a second glance for any plant I had already ticked off as identified.

Then I went through a shooting and fishing phase, a black period in my relations to nature, and one which now, taught by Clare and Thoreau, I look back on with an angry shame. That phase ended dramatically one dusk when I was wildfowling in the Essex marshes. I winged a curlew. It fell in the mud beside the Thames, and I ran to pick it up. Curlew scream like children when they are wounded, and in too much haste I reversed my gun in order to snap the bird's head against the stock. The curlew flapped, the gun slipped, I grabbed for it. There was a violent explosion. And I was left staring down at a hole blasted in the mud not six inches from my left foot.

The next day I sold my gun. I have not intentionally killed a bird or an animal since.

Now, when I observe myself, a specimen of that vicious parasitical predator *Homo sapiens*, I see that I fell into all the great heresies of man's attitude to nature.

First of all, I was a collector. One of the reasons I wrote – and named – my novel *The Collector* was to express my hatred of this lethal perversion. All natural history collectors in the end collect the same thing: the death of the living. And in this age of 'environmental control' (so often a barefaced euphemism for the annihilation of any species of life that threatens profit margins) collecting animate objects such as birds' eggs or insects for pleasure *must* be evil. No moral choice of our time is clearer.

Then secondly I succumbed to the heresy of destroying other life not to keep myself alive but for the pleasure of hunting and killing.

Finally I was trapped by the subtlest temptation of them all: rarity chasing – still a form of destroying, though what is destroyed may be less the rarities themselves than the vain and narrowminded fool who devotes all his time to their pursuit; who, in Clare's image, blinds his own eyes.

Now I suspect this last abuse of nature is closely connected with the notion of nature as a 'hobby'. To my mind 'hobby' is a deforming word: that is, it deforms anyone who uses it to describe his own relationship

JOHN HUBBARD *The Sunken Lane*

ANDY GOLDSWORTHY top, *Bracken Leaves*; above, *Sycamore Leaves*

ANDY GOLDSWORTHY top, *Ice Stacks*; above, *Ice Arch*

ANDY GOLDSWORTHY *Snowball in Trees*

with natural life. Perhaps especially in Britain it has crippling connotations of the spare-time and the peripheral, of petty expertise, a clever
little amateur skill at making or identifying. Only too often this hobby-
mindedness engenders the vain (in both senses) attempt to ape a
professional exponent in the field – especially the established masters
and ideals of yesterday . . . in other words, the very models and theories
that any genuine contemporary professional (be he a biologist or a
painter) is trying to escape, or at least to question. We can see this in the
work turned out by people who go to amateur art classes. They are all
trying to paint like Cézanne and Van Gogh; and a great many natural
history hobbyists pick on equivalent gods, such as the great classifying
naturalists of the Victorian period. Indeed, a kind of Linnaean nostalgia
seems to hang over them. It is as if the whole ecological and ethological
bias of the new field biology never took place – just as if, for the
evening-class painter, Picasso (let alone Mondrian and Jackson Pollock)
never existed.

I saw recently an exhibition of an elderly woman painter's work: a
genuine Essex primitive in the Grandma Moses line. The gallery owner
told me that the great problem was keeping this gifted old lady away
from art classes. She had no notion that her talent was remarkable
precisely because it was so innocent. She thought she ought to be taught
to paint better, not realising that teaching is always teaching to imitate
someone else. As she is, she is nature; and any 'guidance' must be a
form of pollution. This illustrates perfectly the deformation, the blind-
ing, brought about by the hobby attitude to nature. It turns nature into a
sort of golf-course where you go to amuse yourself at weekends; into
the mirror in which you flaunt your skill at naming. It drains nature of
its complexity, of its richness, of its poetries, of its symbolisms and
correspondences, of its power to arouse emotion – of all its potential
centrality in human existence. And far worse than the damage it does to
the misguided natural historian is the damage it does to the vast
majority who are neutral or indifferent towards nature. If this is the one
avenue of approach, then it is no wonder they shrug and turn away.

Some fifteen years ago I became interested in Zen Buddhism; and among
other debts I owe that very un-European philosophy is the way it
brought me to examine the Western attitude to nature. I came to the
conclusion that we ordinary nature-lovers have had a miserably one-
sided vision of the proper relationship between the human and the
natural worlds foisted on us by our science – though rather less by our
genuine scientists than by their amateur fellow-travellers.

Our illusion is that nature *must* be dryly classified and its behaviourisms analysed like so much clockwork – or rather, since of course I am

not denying the necessity and utility of this approach in its proper context, our illusion is that this is the only *serious* relationship we can have; the implication being that any other relationship must be fundamentally superficial and dilettantish. I find this view ominously like that of our science-besotted Victorian ancestors, who thought that if you know that *Luscinia megarhyncha* lays eggs averaging twenty-one millimetres in longest diameter you are far more highly evolved in your understanding of nature than poor Keats, who knew no better than to write an ode to *Luscinia* – vulgarly called the nightingale.

I believe myself that Keats's attitude to the nightingale has very arguably more *scientific* validity than that of the worthy gentlemen who pursued the bird with their brass dividers and rulers. All the hard taxonomic facts in the world don't begin to add up to the reality of the nightingale; and if a visitor from outer space wanted to know that reality he would do much better with the ode than with *The Handbook of British Birds*. The greatness of the ode as a piece of science is precisely that it decompartmentalises the phenomenon; it discusses manbird, not just man and not just bird. Today, with all our talk of the global village and the world environment, we ought to see its relevance; we ought to see that the lack of a right ordinary *human* attitude to nature has become of far greater moment for effective conservation than accurate scientific knowledge about this or that species. We know quite enough facts now; where we are still miserably retarded is in our emotional and aesthetic relationship to wildlife.

Nature is a sort of art sans art; and the right human attitude to it ought to be, unashamedly, poetic rather than scientific.

Such a bald statement may sound dangerously like the Romantic Movement's theory of nature – Nature with a capital as an evoker of beautiful and noble sentiments ... a theory memorable when transmitted by genius but only too repulsive when couched in the purple prose of debased 'Nature Corner' journalism. We are not the age for beautiful, noble sentiments about anything, let alone nature. For all that, I think we, in our present vilely polluted world, had better think twice before we sneer the Romantic theory into oblivion.

It came, we might remember, as a reaction against an age very much like our own: a highly cerebral and artificial period and one that would have raped nature quite as abominably as ourselves if it had had the technology and population at hand. And the theory did two other things: it re-asserted the identity of man and nature and the dangers of splitting that identity. Most important of all, it suggested, both explicitly and implicitly, that the celebration and health of that state of identity is much more a matter for art than for science. The very nature of science is to split, to break down, to reduce to a special context; and the only human science of comprehensive reality is art. Let me give an illustration, from that famous ode by Keats I mentioned just now. These lines:

> *The voice I hear this passing night was heard*
> *In ancient days by emperor and clown:*
> *Perhaps the selfsame song that found a path*
> *Through the sad heart of Ruth, when, sick for home,*
> *She stood in tears amid the alien corn . . .*

Lines we all know (though we may have forgotten that here 'clown' – as in my opening quotation – means peasant and not buffoon) and lines that may seem to you to have no scientific validity at all. But what I see in them, besides great verse, is a classic statement about the situation of man in evolution. Both science and our everyday lives make us exist in the now – so to speak horizontally, not vertically back 'down' through time. And then we are evolving much more rapidly than any other species on our planet: our thrust is ever onward and forward. Both these factors tend to detach us from the stable flow of evolution; we lose contact with our earth, in every sense of the word. The urban world is everywhere too much with us, so that the experience of nature becomes almost a historical, 'antique' sensation, like standing inside a Norman castle or an Elizabethan house. A wry-minded New York friend put it very succinctly to me the other day in my garden, when he heard the blackbirds and thrushes singing. He saw one and turned to me. 'Good God, you mean they're *not* recordings?'

Keats's point, of course, is that they are indeed in a sense recordings. My friend and I could have been taken back through two, through ten hundred years of May evening; and very probably we should have heard exactly the same sounds. More and more it is this stable evolutionary continuum that I see in nature, this plunging back like a knife through recorded time, to Ruth amid the alien corn. Nature was not born for death, but to remind us of the continuity of life. It is a kind of brake, a sanctuary, a system of landmarks in time; a check on our craze for meaningless 'progress'.

The practical point I am trying to make, behind all this rather abstract literary stuff, is that our education about nature remains much too orientated towards scientific views and ends. Of course intending professional scientists must be trained; but I don't see why the rest of our children (those well-known fathers of men) have to suffer on their behalf. They need much more an education in human relationships to nature, in man's responsibility to other forms of life; and the clues and roads to that lie far more in the work of the countless great artists, both literary and visual, who have tried to define and expand this key relationship than in the recognition of species and the explanation of behaviourisms.

Science may understand nature; but it can never understand what nature requires of man. Of that, poets like Wordsworth and Keats knew more in the tips of their little fingers than all the biologists in creation.

It is, alas, unrealistic to hope to persuade born name-droppers like Europeans and Americans that knowing the name of a thing has extraordinarily little to do with its intrinsic beauty and value; and I will not attempt to plead the extreme Zen Buddhist position, which quite simply states that the name of an object is like a pane of dirty glass between it and you. We of the West are conditioned to need some background knowledge of the objects of our appreciation. But our contemporary addiction to such information is unhealthy – as if a nameless flower cannot be worth looking at, as if this salt-cellar by Cellini can't be enjoyed until we have checked in the guide that it really is a masterpiece.

I think the first thing to gain, in the appreciation of nature as well as of art, is confidence in one's ability to see beauty for oneself. This has certainly never been more difficult. Like all successful species, man attracts parasites, and in this category I number many functions of the mass communications media. They are the lice that infect our minds – all eager to tell us what to admire, all eager to see and think for us. Just as the car and the plane have made us physically lazy and cholesterol-prone, so does all this appreciation-moulding induce a fatal hardening of the observational arteries. To that must be added the high pro-gramme priority (especially in nature films) put upon the exotic and the rare. I look forward to the day when the B.B.C. will spare us a trip to the Galapagos or the Great Barrier Reef and give us a series on common British garden birds; look forward to it, and don't expect it, I'm afraid. We have very little national genius for seeing the familiar with fresh eyes – another ability, let me add, more commonly found in poets than in scientists.

But here nature has at least one thing on its side. Unlike art, it is uncomposed and ever-changing, and therefore not nearly so amenable to appreciation-moulding. Anyone who has kept up with his or her culture will find it difficult to see famous paintings with a fresh eye; but nature inherently forces the new appreciation on us. It obliges us to make poetic judgments.

Above all we need to learn to distinguish our total human awareness of a natural phenomenon from our specifically scientific knowledge about it. In the field, so to speak, I find this scientific knowledge usually presents itself first. If I see a bird, its name (or my uncertainty about it) is the first reaction; then the typicality and likely explanation of its behaviour, assessed against my previous knowledge of the species. But unless it or its behaviour is very unusual, this scientific processing is very rapid – a second or two at most. From then on I let the poetry take over. Now this poetry is very complex. It has to do with pure movement, sound, shape, colour; it has to do with the framework, blue sky for this buzzard, bramble thicket for this warbler, in which the bird is. It has to do with what other birds are about, what flowers, what awareness of the place I have, what season it is – the migrant arriving or departing; what mood I am in. It has also very much to do with previous history, since just as nature can take me back through time and turn history on its side, so can many species of bird, butterfly, and flower lead me back through the maze of my own life.

I will try now to describe what it is like and I shall probably make it sound too conscious a process, a calculated system of free association. But the only really conscious part of it is my rejection of the narrowly ornithological or botanical approach. I believe in fact that this is the natural and normal way of seeing wildlife; its effect on us, and probably in strict inverse proportion to our scientific knowledge, is largely emotive and aesthetic.

A North London garden. Winter. A spot of cerise, grey, and black, in an old pear tree. I am standing at a window, there is snow on the ground. A cock bullfinch. A sporadic winter visitor to outlying city gardens: not unusual. Looking for clematis or forsythia buds; or honeysuckle berries. A week before, in Dorset, I counted twenty-seven cock bullfinches in a grove of bullace. The bullace in blossom. Bullace jam. 'Whistling' bullfinch – I could do it as a boy. A Devonshire combe and our cottage there. Waking up and hearing the whistles very close and looking out and seeing six cock bullfinches sitting in the first sunlight on an apple tree. That apple tree, with its yellow-green smoky-tasting apples no one ever knew the name of. That same bullace grove in summer. I lie in the shade there and a bullfinch sings overhead: its strange monotonous little five-note fluting chant. Like Webern. Like a last cardinal, in the freezing wind on the dying pear tree. The future, a jet heading for Heathrow, whines over. I feel depressed. I have a busy day I don't want ahead. I hate cities and summer will never come again. The bullfinch drops down into the garden. A flash of white rump. Then nothing, I can't see it any more. A squirt of green memories, like a brief taste on the tongue. But enough to keep me going, the bitter and dull day through.

Or this, something rarer. Late May, on the fringe of an Oxfordshire beechwood, sunshine, growing half-shaded under a whitebeam. A fly orchid. I have seen this species only twice before in my life. Once during training, during the war. Flinging myself and the Bren I was carrying to the ground and there, a foot from my face, was my first fly orchid and I had twenty seconds to enjoy it before a Royal Marines sergeant (when he was drunk he used to chew razor blades, his mouth dribbling blood) shouted us up and on. The second time I saw it I was with a girl, and botany was the last thing on my mind. And now it is here again, mysteriously survived and resurrected; and when I find my fourth *Ophrys muscifera* I shall remember this, my wife kneeling beside me, the Chiltern sunshine, the good day; and the second time again, and the first.

This highly associative and personal relationship with natural phenomena may seem, to many scientists, narcissistic and introverted. But the one thing it does not breed is selfishness; what it creates is an intense need and affection for the *direct* experience of nature. And that, in my opinion, is the only kind of soil in which a really effective general social demand for conservation can grow. It is no good the scientists alone wanting to defend wildlife from industry and over-population; the human in the street has to want it as well.

Always we try to put the wild in a cage: if not literal cages of iron, then cages of banality, of false parallels, of anthropomorphic sentimentality, of lazy thinking and lazy observation.

For this reason I am far from convinced that pet-keeping has the good educational value some teachers maintain. Personally I hate the pet mania, as I mistrust zoos and all other compromises between man and nature in the wild. Once, in Crete, I was climbing a mountain alone. Heavy snowdrifts made me give up the attempt to reach the top, but before I began the descent I lay down on my back between two boulders in order to rest out of the icy wind. A minute passed. Then, with an abruptness that stopped my breath, I was not alone. A huge winged shape was hanging in the air some twenty feet above my head. It looked like an enormous falcon, its great wings feathering and flexed to the wind current, a savage hooked beak tilted down at me. I lay as still as stone, like Sinbad under the roc. For some ten seconds the great bird and I were transfixed, in a kind of silent dialogue. I knew it was a lammergeier, one of Europe's largest birds of prey – a species few ornithologists have seen in the wild at all, let alone from a few feet away. Ten seconds, and then it decided I was alive and swung a mile away in one great sweep on rigid wings.

Now I could go easily to a zoo and see the lammergeiers they have there. But I have never done so. Although I accept that the bored eagles and vultures of our zoos cannot, lacking an imagination, be bored in fact, *I* suffer when I see them. I used the word 'dialogue' just now. What passed between me and that splendid bird in the azure Cretan sky was simply this: Cage me, cage yourself.

I know encaging is not the worst of our crimes against nature in this century; and that with some danger-list species it has now become their only hope of survival. Indeed I have only to go back to the woodlands I knew as a boy in the 1930s to see the greater crime: how once common birds are now rarities, how glades once full of butterflies are now empty of them, sunlight without wings. Here, as in every other heavily farmed area in the world, the silences and motionlessnesses of a dead planet begin to steal up on us.

This guilt, which we all must share, makes it impossible now to write of nature except in terms of lamentation and sermon. I have very little hope for any form of real progress that is not broadly based on the pleasure principle. The archetypal human demand, when faced with change, has always been 'What's in it for me?' – what new pleasure shall I get? And this is the strongest argument for trying to change ordinary attitudes to nature from the pseudo-scientific to the poetic, from the general to the personal.

Poetry, then, not science; or rather, just as much science, as much knowledge of names and natural machinery, as the poetry requires. For we must learn to accept that nature is always finally mysterious – a place where the killers and collectors and name tickers will finally see nothing, hear nothing, and understand nothing.

The deepest thing we can learn about nature is not how it works, but that it is *the poetry of survival*. The greatest reality is that the watcher has survived and the watched survives. It is the timelessness woven through time, the cross-weft of all being that passes. Nobody who has comprehended this can feel alone in nature, can ever feel the absolute hostility of time. However strange the land or the city or the personal situation, some tree, some bird, some flower will still knit us into this universe all we brief-lived things co-habit; will mesh us into the great machine. That is why I love nature: because it reconciles me with the imperfections of my own condition, of our whole human condition, of the all that is. My freedom depends totally on its freedom. Without my freedom, I should not want to live.

CHILDHOOD GROUND   ABIDING PLACES

The cliff ledge den
The look-out tree
The bicycle racing track in the wood
The dumps
The long grass place for stalking
The cave in the cliff
The slide
The footpath where we dug a trap
The smoking-cane place
The place of the secret grave on the scree
The tobogganing zig-zag
The place where we dug quartz with hammers
The place of some soot behind a wall
The swampy place

City of Bristol   The Downs and the Avon Gorge

AVON GORGE WATER DRAWING

RICHARD LONG

A Line in England
Richard Long Yorkshire 1977

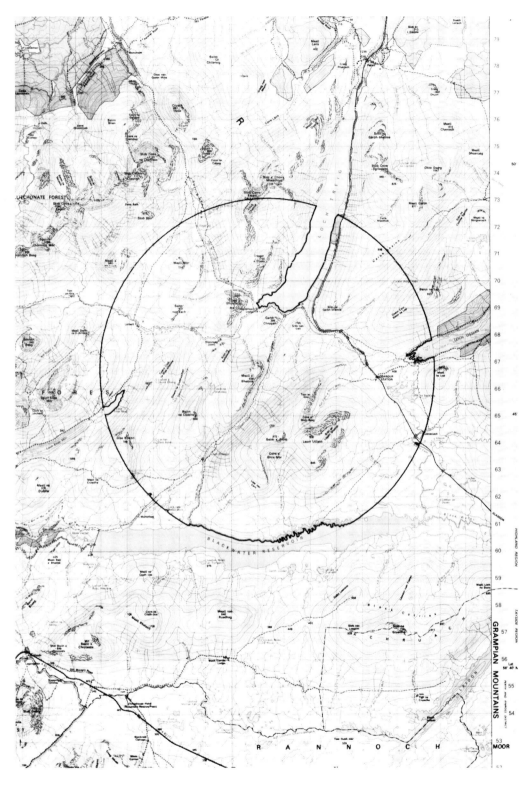

Low Water Circle Walk
A two day walk around and inside a circle in the Highlands
Richard Long   Scotland   Summer 1980

JOHN BLAKEMORE *Wind Series, Ambergate, Derbyshire*

JOHN BLAKEMORE *Wind Series, Ambergate, Derbyshire*

Animal World

BY JOHN BERGER

> I am Ashurbanipal, king of hosts, king of Assyria. In my abound-
> ing, princely strength I seized a lion of the desert by his tail and, at
> the command of Enurta and Nergal, the gods who are my helpers, I
> smashed his skull with the axe in my hands.

This boast was made in about 650 B.C. Two thousand five hundred years
or more later, in a manuscript smuggled out of a Greek prison, Professor
George Mangakis wrote as follows:

> I would like to write about a friendship I formed the autumn before
> last. I think it has some significance. It shows the solidarity that can
> be forged between unhappy creatures. I had been kept in solitary
> confinement for four months. I hadn't seen a soul throughout that
> period. Only uniforms – inquisitors and jail-keepers. One day, I
> noticed three mosquitoes in my cell. They were struggling hard to
> resist the cold that was just beginning. In the daytime they slept on
> the wall. At night they would come buzzing over me.
>
> In the beginning, they exasperated me. But fortunately I soon
> understood. I too was struggling hard to live through the cold spell.
> What were they asking from me? Something unimportant. A drop
> of blood – it would save them. I couldn't refuse. At nightfall, I
> would bare my arm and wait for them. After some days they had
> got used to me and they were no longer afraid. They would come to
> me quite naturally, openly. This trust is something I owe them.
> Thanks to them, the world was no longer merely an inquisition
> chamber.
>
> Then one day I was transferred to another prison. I never saw my
> mosquitoes again. This is how you are deprived of the presence of
> your friends in the arbitrary world of prisons. But you go on
> thinking of them, often.

These two quotations, which are in every respect antithetical, remind us of the range of the human attitude to the animal world. Furthermore, they show how much a particular attitude may reveal of personal and historical circumstance. Animals have always been central to the process by which men form an image of themselves.

Animals were the first subject in art. The blood of animals was perhaps the first paint. The depicted was the quarry. Not only by way of magic but, at first, factually. Before they were ever painted, animals were probably represented in ritual by the hides of animals already successfully hunted. Realism was borrowed from reality. To depict an animal's appearance was to capture what lay behind it. Yet the notion 'capture' is wrong. By taking the animal's appearance it was possible to become the animal. Becoming was the only way of possessing.

Up until the Renaissance when animals ceased to be an ever-recurring subject, there is an unexpected continuity in the way they are depicted. I have on my table Francis Klingender's *Animals in Art and Thought to the End of the Middle Ages*, which is open at a Spanish rock shelter painting of a man being attacked by bees. Not far away on the table there is a pot of local honey and on it a label showing a mountain landscape with bees in the foreground. The way the bees are envisaged in the two images, separated by at least 10,000 years, is similar. There are fish engraved on Egyptian reliefs which resemble eighteenth-century engravings and are as accurate.

The realistic depiction of animals, with which art itself began, seems to have changed very little from civilisation to civilisation; and, at any given time, it appears to be in advance of the depiction of anything else (the human figure, landscape, utensils) in terms of accuracy and subtlety of observation. There were of course periods, beginning with the neolithic, when animals were incorporated in highly formalised, ornamental, unrealistic styles. But even here one is struck by an unusual continuity. Many of the animals of medieval heraldry, for example, were first 'composed' in Mesopotamia in the second millennium B.C.

Animal appearances, as depicted, seem highly resistant to cultural or ideological change; whilst, at all times, men have seen animals more clearly than anything else. Or is this true? Is it only apparently so because we, as we look at these images, simplify them so as to accommodate them within an atavistic response?

Either way, the answer points to our special relation with animals. Until recently this specialness would have been taken for granted because everybody was familiar with their own familarity with animals. Now animals have become rare, marginal creatures of childhood, nightmare and dream. They are what meat was before it was meat. And a dead animal in the cities is first thought of as an object of disgust. (The fact that the same may be thought of an *unknown* dead man is not unconnected.) Today we have to remind ourselves of our special relation to animals.

Written descriptions, because they are mostly concerned with significance rather than appearance, do not reveal the same continuity as images. But they often demonstrate the ambiguity of the human relation to animals. The English Franciscan friar Bartholomew wrote in the thirteenth century a book which remained, until Shakespeare's time, the standard work on natural history. Here he is describing the cat:

> He is a full lecherous beast in youth, swift pliant and merry . . . and is led by a straw and playeth therewith: and is a right heavy beast in age and full sleepy, and lyeth slyly in wait for mice . . . in time of love is hard fighting for wives, and one rendeth the other grievously with biting and with claws.

Five hundred years later Buffon, the French naturalist, describes the mole:

> The mole, although not blind, has eyes that are so small, so covered, that it cannot make much use of its sense of sight; to make amends, nature has munificently provided it with the use of the sixth sense, a remarkable apparatus of vessels and reservoirs, a prodigious quantity of seminal fluid, enormous testicles, a genital member of inordinate length; all this well-hidden within, and therefore warmer and more active. The mole in this respect is the most favourably endowed of all the animals, the best supplied with organs and, in consequence, with the sensations which relate thereto: it has very acute hearing, and little five-fingered hands very different from the lower extremities of other animals, almost resembling the human hand; a great deal of strength for the size of its body, a firm hide, a constant weight, a lively and reciprocal attachment between the male and the female, fear of all other company or disgust therefor, and gentle habits of repose and solitude.

In both passages, the writer's pleasure in identifying himself with the animal while he is describing it is evident. Becoming was no longer in those ages of property the only way of possessing. But it was the only way of describing an animal affectionately.

By identifying with the animal, man anthropomorphises it. At the same time he measures himself, as he is, against the animal. Occasionally with undiluted pride. Often with surreptitious envy.

With and against the animal. The duality begins with the magical belief in man's kinship and descent from the animal. Here it may be worth noticing that it is the male who inherits the animal's positive qualities abstractly; woman – the mother of all living things – is the mysterious physical intermediary. The first great epic poem – from Mesopotamia – describes how a woman is sent out to tame a creature who is half-human and half-animal by sleeping with him. After seven days with her he is fully humanised and thus ready to be useful to the King of Uruk. Similar themes recur many times, such as the legend of the unicorn who can only be captured by a virgin, and the various versions of beauty and the beast.

Man's mastery over the animal could never be complete because of his own biological inheritance. He often experienced this incompleteness as fear. He was bound to fear the eye of the animal *as the carrier of a view of himself over which he had no control.*

Gradually animals ceased to represent spirits which had to be propitiated, ceased to coexist with the gods but became a gift or message from the gods to man; and, in sacrifices, vice versa. So the animal world, from being mysterious in itself, became a reference for religion, a metaphor. Men domesticate animals, use them, but they also explain by them. Animals supply examples for the mind as well as food for the body. They carry not only loads, but also principles.

Until the discovery of Newtonian physics and modern chemistry, animal life occupied a central place in natural science. From Aristotle onwards all scientific and moral systems paid special attention to animals. They were there to demonstrate laws to men because there was nothing else in the world through which men could so subtly define themselves. But all the systems (in Europe) were more or less mathematical, positing always a single centre of reason or a single godhead. 'Every law deals with the passive – and that is why a law, every law, is restricted, incomplete, approximate' (a note by Lenin in Hegel's *Logic*). The movements, pauses, glances of animals are incompatible with such passivity; whereas in humans passivity can nevertheless be a determining state of mind. This is why the strain of subordinating life to the laws of the closed symmetrical systems was often betrayed by a response to animals.

For example, on many twelfth-century churches there are, besides monsters, animals who, precisely because they are soulless and destined for neither heaven nor hell, look freer than any human carved there.

For example, men have recurrently looked at human society and been reduced to asking: does not the bee do better? The answers may have varied, but the question has persisted.

Uneasy inversions of moralising have taken place. Take the pig. It is true that the wild boar from which the pig has been bred will eat − if necessary − almost anything except what is poisonous to it. But this does not make it greedy. It is an intelligent, fast, active animal. The pig is the only animal bred by man entirely for the sake of its meat. It is fed inordinately on garbage in order to make it fat. It becomes dirty because it is kept in a sty. It is made lazy only because it is confined. Yet the pig − not the breeder − is designated piggish. A similar inversion has taken place with the donkey, who, because he is made to work for man, is designated *stubborn*.

The character of man's favourite animals indicates the same strain. For example, the cunning of the fox, as soon as it makes its appearance in legend or art, is perfunctorily condemned and actually admired. The fox is treated as the most human of all animals because it is thought that to survive it, too, has to be double-faced: what the fox promises is one thing, what it does is another. The laws of symmetrical systems are not adequate. The imagination knows it and the fox knows it.

With the advent of modern science and capitalism, all laws became mechanised and purely quantitative. Descartes defined animals as machines. Every law then became a 'natural law', inexorable and impersonal. At the same time 'nature' acquired a compensatory meaning: 'the natural' in man came to represent all that his laws failed to embrace. 'They are what we once were,' wrote Schiller of the forms of nature, 'they are what we should once more become.' Most animals in romantic art were painted in the spirit of Schiller's intuition.

Today animals are studied in laboratories, and the findings are used to excuse, in so far as they are philosophical and popular, our present social nature (Lorenz, Ardrey and others). Most people scarcely ever meet the gaze of an animal. The eye of the pet acts only as a coloured mirror. Theoretically a world without want is possible; in such a world men would see animals as they have never before been seen, because every view concerning animals is a comment on human history to date. If today we regulary confronted animals we would have less reason than primitive man to fear their look; yet it might still give us pause. As it is, we are alone.

THEY ARE THE LAST

Behind her tongue
with its language of grass
and passion for salt,
behind the heavy tongue
deft nevertheless
as a blind man's hand,
a cow in good health chews
approximately fifty times
before reswallowing the cud.

It appears the animals
Beverly
are emigrating: their America
the constellations in the sky
Lizard, Lion, Great Bear,
Ram, Bull, Crow,
Hare . . .
Perhaps the more prudent
like the agouti
have chosen the milky way.

Put your ear to her flank
and you will hear
the tide of her four stomachs.
Her second, like a net,
has the name of a constellation:
Reticulum. Her third,
the Psalterium, is like
the pages of a book.

When she falls sick
and lacks the will to chew
her four stomachs fall
silent as a hive in winter.

Each year more animals depart.

Only pets and carcasses remain,
and the carcasses living or dead

are from birth
ineluctably and invisibly
turned into meat.
'I believe it's completely feasible',
said Bob Rust
of Iowa State University,
'to specifically design
an animal for hamburger.'

Elsewhere
the animals of the poor
die with the poor
from protein insufficiency.

When fetched from the pastures
they bring into the cool stable
the heat of the orchard
and the hot breath of wild garlic.

To clean out the cowshed
scatter a little of
the mare's dung
it absorbs their shit
liquid as springtime
and green with grass.

And fasten them well tonight
bed them with beech leaves
Beverly
they are the last.

Now that they have gone
it is their endurance we miss.
Unlike the tree
the river or the cloud
the animals had eyes
and in their glance
was permanence.

It was the same fox for ever and ever.
To kill him
was to drag him
momentarily
from the earth
of his eternity.

Once flies and crows
when devouring the dead sheep
began with the eyes.
Yet the ewe
had already lambed
her permanence.

The buzzard circled
biding his everlasting time
as repeatedly
as the mountain.

Out of the single night
came the day's look,
the wary animal glance
on every side.

Once the animals flowed like their milk.

Now that they have gone
it is their endurance we miss.

'The breeding sow', it is said,
'should be thought of and treated
as a valuable piece of machinery
whose function
is to pump out baby pigs.'

Sometimes still
when you are pouring
from the blue jug,
the milk
reminds me of the geese
who like dogs
guarded the house.

ELISABETH FRINK *Dog, 1980*

ELISABETH FRINK *Barn Owl, 1974*

Closely-observed Creatures

BY DAVID G. MEASURES

26 November: 5.30 p.m. A sudden sharp yelp nearby and your blood quickens. In this encircling darkness the unknown alarms. You turn to the west, to the direction of that single sound . . . and make out a glow in the sky over the dark woods and the deep darkness between, that holds the pond, its trees, and somewhere within it the fox . . . to you, once an animate creature of the land yourself, yet living today a world apart, that unknown yelp at night is more eerie than any daytime and familiar sound. No other sound comes as a confirming clue. Just that one yelp . . . so you sit, wait and muse.

To be idle in landscape, to be still, silent, alone − it is impossible to feel lonely when watching the day-to-day activity of other life forms. It was because I had stopped idly to paint butterflies, captivated by their

iridescent colours and patterns, that I developed a curiosity about what they were doing. I began the habit of jotting notes between drawings in order to find out what happens to a butterfly at a particular time of the day. Thus, gradually I became acquainted with the everyday lives of the butterflies of my locality.

The best place in the area was a curving stretch of old railway track sheltered by a plantation on either side where about twenty different species could be seen each year, including one of the county's rarest butterflies, the grizzled skipper ... alas, that half mile of trackway burgeoning with wildlife has now been bulldozed away. Its embankment, formed of pure sand, above the low-lying land, offered a commodity which the owners decided to sell. One half has gone to increase the area of the town tip, the other, now levelled, has been brought back into arable cultivation, so marginally increasing the total acreage of the fields on either side.

Consequently, I had to go somewhere else. I found a long thin strip of woodland, in places reduced to avenues of elms and hedgerow, sandwiched between farmland.

Divided in ownership, it owes it existence partly to the right of way that runs along its length. To a degree its wildlike potential is affected by the seasons and by the changes the farmers make; ploughing, drilling, and harvesting – destroying some field habitats and creating others. Here I was not so much aware of butterflies – fields and woods cannot generate the heat of the clinker of the railway track, and there are fewer species associated with trees and mixed farming land. However, by using the habit of keeping still formed in watching butterflies, I began jotting notes of what I saw and making drawings of anything that aroused my interest. An early jotting reminds me how I began:

12 March. My first sight of a fox, on a newly seeded field between two coverts. In the soft evening glow it sits on the fine tilth dried by the day's sun. It rises to its feet, showing a chocolate-dark tail, then sits back on its haunches again. Tom, our golden labrador, sits obedient beside me, oblivious. It is too far off for me to see any detail, just a shifting of its shape and colour.

It was this chance sighting of a fox that prompted me to return, hoping to draw it. I have always found that drawing increases my interest in a living wild creature. With a Biro and a miniature box of watercolours, I attempted to note my experience of animals' habits in pocket sketch-books. Spittle and my finger provided the water and brush. More recently I have bought pocket field-glasses of minimum weight. With patience and luck I can get close enough to make some sort of sketch and write a description of what I have seen before I move on.

6 March. I get up to the dividing hedge and crouch under the hazels while a pair of English partridge sits sentinel in open grass. I make myself comfortable on an earthy bank and watch through a con-venient break. Two hares are keeping together – the rabbits in the background tear about.

All the variety of farmland creatures seem to be assembled and peaceably feeding in their separate groups and different ways. This is a gentle English version of the films we see of African savannah with its mixture of grazing animals and birdlife.

When you move away from the cover of hedge and ditch to get closer to your subject then domestic animals can be helpful; their clustering presence disguises the human one!

25 August. Whilst I've been peering through the glasses, drawing a pair of partridge, heifers have grouped behind me. I hear them approach, blowing as they draw closer. A nudge on my jacket shows they are right up to me. I'm pinned in by the curious gentle black and white beasts but they serve my purpose and the two partridge show more erect, and gaze back in my direction puzzled and intent. The midges are frightful and send me wild with their biting beneath my hat and all about my head. As I rub and scratch for relief only the snorting and blowing walrus-like cows keep the partridge from instant flight.

To get drawings of rabbits, lapwings and hares and all the other less wary creatures is relatively easy, but sightings of fox, sparrowhawk or woodcock are rarely repeated. A fox is usually some distance from you and to get even the merest scribble seems impossible. You are left with a vision more like a dream than a reality.

Well though you may know a place by day, darkness brings that borderland between reality and imagination. You are no longer sure. There lingers that inexplicable vague feeling . . .

> 5 October. The moonlight sits on the land like a mist and floats on the top of the grasses. It pierces the dark shadow of the wood and is caught suspended in pools on the grass heads. It disorientates you as you stumble along the rutted track. The desire to cross the stubble and enter the familiar yet transformed landscape draws you on.
>
> You walk through cattle that lie about the wood's edge. If you stop you hear their breathing. The sheep too are lying down and make pale patches in the meadow. Not a leaf rustles. Peewits cry from afar, night-flying waders call in single musical notes. Even the roads are quiet. From far off comes an overall hum . . . is it the sounds of the city on this the second night of Goose Fair?
>
> The sky is so light it merges with the fields except where it is marked with a hedge line. I return with a fallen branch for the fire and leave before the night air turns chill. The exceptional day passes through its dusk and merges with night so gently there is no jarring change. In contrast, behind me the brilliant moon dazzles the eye and turns every feature of the land to silhouette.

I often paint landscape as the light fades. If there is no moon there is usually sufficient illumination for me at least to be able to assess tonally the painted marks, and a painter is familiar with the arrangement of colours in his box.

Driving rain, unless there is shelter in the vicinity, makes painting almost impossible. But during the winter if you dress warmly you can withstand the coldest days and still do a certain amount of drawing and writing, wearing gloves.

> 6 December: dusk. As I paint the temperature drops below zero and from that moment, every brush mark I flood across the paper freezes like a snail's silvery trace.
>
> 29 January. Thank goodness the hedge cuttings have been fired during the afternoon so that at the glowing heap I can bring life back to my finger ends.

In zero temperatures you can no longer use fingers for painting. A clip-on water pot and a brush are needed. At dusk, when the frost tightens its grip, each dip of the brush into the pot reglazes it and each application on to the paper sheds less and less of its colour load. You need to work fast to get your effect before the brush is clogged like a mop and the water pot choked with ice. Once home the frozen painting must be left in the coldest place in the house to dry slowly, for if you take it into a warm room, the layers of coloured ice melt and merge in a flood.

Watching when linked with drawing and note-taking brings in its own time a knowledge of a creature and its identity; and whether you intend it or not, you gradually learn something of the plant world that is linked with it.

> 23 July. There seems to be something marvellously satisfying for the human in using the ability to distinguish and separate the mass of plants into groups and colonies of like kind. Here, I journey through a patch of the softest downy grass, then brush against the misty heads of another species, then walk through swaying foxtails and in dark conifers come upon a ride of rosebay, another of creeping thistle, whilst the wood's edges bloom with creamy roses. Sensing such distinctions gives a satisfaction to a journey. Awareness of the commonplace forms the familiar fabric against which you notice something different.

Before long and without knowing it I had begun to build an acquaintance with a place, its flora and its fauna. The birds and mammals of this arable farming country may be ordinary, but are no less interesting  because they are common species – hare, squirrel, stoat, skylark, lapwing and partridge – 'Common' creatures of the country that we daily pass in our cars and rarely get to know better as they are wild, shy and easily disturbed. But the intimacy gained by care and effort ensures an interest in them which exceeds the momentary excitement that you feel at the sight of a visiting rarity.

Again and again, whatever your starting point, you find that it is people's use of land, in particular by farming, which determines the variety of wildlife within it. The farmers here, mostly family farmers, are proud of their piece of land and good naturalists.

> 21 November. D.T. rang to say he'd seen a short-eared owl while spraying the chickweed before the winter plough. As he took me up to see it he told me how tame the owl had seemed, flying up and resettling close by, ignoring the spraying booms his tractor carried – 'so tame I stopped and climbed down to see if it showed any injury. A marvellous sight, so I read it up over lunch in *Birds of the County*'.

The strip of woodland has a substantial elm content. The farmers cope with the formidable task of replanting, as the elms gradually succumb to Dutch elm disease. Each year they clear a small area of bleached dead wood and its broken litter and replant with mixed stocks of trees, usually supplied by the county council. In 1977 there was new planting in the coppice, including alders.

> 1984: 3 January. Sleet in the air; down in the coppice hanging from the cone clusters of the alders a small group of redpolls feeding from their seeds. To think seven years ago I saw these trees planted, now twenty feet high and offering a winter seed supply.

Being out of doors a long while can make you 'weather drunk', and if you do meet someone it is difficult to be sociable.

> 22 October. A family, mother, father and children, smartly dressed, avoiding puddles, with their County Leisure Services Map guide. 'Where are you walking?' I asked. 'A circular tour' the man replied . . . and nothing else was said. They looked and smiled, but my head was swimming.
> 'There you are', I heard the man say as he briskly opened the gate for his family. I just drifted through with them, and let him close it behind me, as in a dream.
> All the world seems streaked; the passage of falling leaves streaming and the dappling from the sun, the wind's noise in the trees, make my path bewilderingly slanted.

There are occasions when it occurs to me as I sit enjoying the rolling farmland that it is the experience of a particular moment, which is the quality most difficult to convey; that of tranquillity, the open space and stillness in which the sounds of a finch and a skylark are enriching sensations.

Notes from any one year usually record a stretch of weather that has affected the district's inhabitants – domestic and wild creatures, so that you are able to remember a year for its abundance or absence of one species or another. Seasons, therefore, can be remembered as entities, each distinct, some exceptional. The year's batch of drawings and photographs confirms this.

Summer 1976. I shall always associate this year of drought with elm sap and a flush of Red Admirals. From the fresh holes left by the elm beetles' sap was welling and attracting all sorts of insects – ladybirds, wasps, bees and butterflies – perhaps the more so because wild flower nectar was so scarce.

Such extreme conditions provide examples of how common species survive. December 1981 brought an early spell of three weeks' unbroken snow and ice. Wildfowlers were asked not to shoot the starving birds: our local Boxing Day shoot was cancelled.

19 December: 4.30 p.m. Already too dark to make out the markings of its face, next moment the owl is down on the snow crust beneath the hedge, a round dark blob. It is crouching, working at some prey; after ten minutes whilst I draw it from the car, it is suddenly gone. So I get out, cross the field and find a hen reed bunting – its body stiff but minus the head. The owl has flown further down the roadside field and is working away at the head paying no heed to my presence forty yards off. It is feeding on the frozen brain which, being granular and crumbly, is the only part it can manage – for the frozen muscles of the carcass would be solid.

I shall remember Summer 1983, for the prolonged period of sun which allowed Clouded Yellows (not seen in such numbers since 1947) to invade our country on southerly air streams from Europe thus giving me that season's particular flavour.

A naturalist progresses towards an increased awareness of the life of an animal, bird or insect in relation to its environment. In endeavouring to judge and render the shape, tone or colour of a subject in relation to its background a painter also develops a way of seeing things very much as a whole. Gradually my attention has expanded to include other relationships that seem to fit into the shifting pattern of life within a site.

I try to visit my area of interest at least once a week and so over the years build up an acquaintance with the ways of its inhabitants. By arranging the written notes and drawings of the different species in chronological order, hints of their seasonal existence can be discovered. You quickly become aware of the overall pattern of their daytime existence. Take hares for instance. Hares like to lie up singly and remain mostly inactive, crouching in their 'forms'. Not until the end of the day or approach of dusk do they begin to roam, congregate, chase and graze. The hare 'form' is the seat to which they return. Depending on the season and condition of the land they will select a tuft of grass or stubble, a depression in the soil or lump of clay into or against which to press themselves; any means of camouflage, any feature in the open land that will mask the outline of their body.

At the appearance of a human, a hare has the curious ability of physically changing its shape by the use of its long ears. These they can curl and manipulate, as though throwing over themselves a transforming cloak, so as to assume a nondescript appearance which you can mistake for a clod of earth or a horse-dropping. If you remain motionless long enough the inanimate 'thing' will relax, cock an eye, lift an ear and become a hare again. On occasions when you find one whose activity is not conforming to this overall pattern, an extra interest is stimulated: the following selection covers only their response to weather and their whereabouts.

18 September: 2.30 p.m. A hare is lying against a verge at the edge of a rape crop, getting the full benefit of the afternoon sunshine. Whilst I've been drawing it, only once has it shifted position to sit up, stretch, arch its back, then resume its former position exactly. Two hours later that afternoon it was still there sunbathing!

As many other animals appear to benefit from and enjoy lying in the sun, I wonder if all hares sunbathe? From several other records, it seems as though they might. Do they sunbathe at any time of the year – or is the need for sunshine greater, prior to winter extremes? My other sightings of them, stretched out, basking on the hot earth, or 'sitting warming like a cat' are in May and October. Unlike rabbits, hares live without burrows; theirs is an open air, open field existence:

6 June: 6.30 p.m. (daylight). A hare, making its way up the farm track, is stopping to feed at the verge grasses. I remain behind the wheel of my car and wait. Huge rain drops begin, preceded by violent wind movements. The hare is forced by the cloudburst to squat in the long grass of the verge and sit out the downpour, alternately closing, then squinting through its eyelids. By 7.30 p.m. the thunderstorm is over and the hare begins grooming, licking its matted, sodden fur back into condition again. The sun shows, the hare nibbles a grass, becomes active and continues up the lane.

In response to another weather extreme:

20 January: mid afternoon. A hare prominent on the icy surface of packed snow. The curious thing is that it allows me to crunch my way across the snow field and get close to it. Caught out of its form it is a conspicuous silhouette. The little dark shape sits on the snow crust, shuffles, turns a little and watches. Sleet irritates the exposed portion of my face and collects on my field glasses. I have to get to the fence to prop the glasses before I can settle to draw it. Finally I cross and walk to within ten yards of it before it bounds away.

During these conditions its food supply is the bark of hedgerow shrubs. Somewhere will be its form:

> 28 January. Only fourteen feet away from the tracks of a fox, a hare form within the deep snow. Its sides show two obvious levels – sedimentary layering – revealing that this hare sat throughout the two major snow falls – and that it has used this form throughout the last ten days since the first heavy fall. Most likely it was sitting in the same field seat long before the snow fell and covered it.

Such findings in any one species prompt future visits.

The lure for the painter is the chance of an encounter with a wild creature that allows time enough to make a drawing. Contained in that scribble, in that response of marks and dashes, is something perhaps of the creature's vitality and elusiveness. I find the need to depict, peculiar to man, fascinating, for what a strange desire it is to recreate the intangible quality of things seen.

> 9 December: 3.00 p.m. In the marshy pasture there is a sunny scene of melting warmth at the edges of the wood. Where it remains in shadow the frost's hold is unquenched. A rabbit lies at the edge of a briar, two moorhens and a snipe feed close by him, a robin flies down and beyond it a moving 'log', an impossibly difficult brown shape to distinguish – a woodcock. The slightest call from an agitated blackbird near me was enough to send it running back into the wood. The moorhens took cover but they were quicker to reappear. When the woodcock shows only its movements reveal it and with what care it slips through cover. Eighty yards away I remain stock-still behind two screens of thorn hedge and yet the system of the wild is so tuned that the slightest indication of my presence is sensed. At sunset the frost reclaims the marshy meadow which drifts back to a pale and ghostly world. As I move to go, the woodcock flies up and disappears around the edge of the wood.

DAVID G. MEASURES top, *Hare, 1982*; above, *Lapwings on Stubble*

STEPHEN DALTON *Carder Bee*

STEPHEN DALTON *Swallow Drinking*

DAVID G. MEASURES *Night of Total Eclipse*

Possession

BY KIM TAPLIN

Richard Jefferies was a man whom the reality of the countryside possessed and who responded with a quiet, intense and abiding passion. In an essay called *Meadow Thoughts* he leads the reader step by step through a landscape along a footpath, until we encounter a spring where it 'rises in a hollow under the rock imperceptibly', and its hidden beauty is revealed as the goal of a quest, the quenching of a growing thirst. Beneath it 'the basin is always full and always running over. As it slips from the brim a gleam of sunshine falls through the boughs and meets it . . . The water', he goes on:

> was more to me than water, and the sun than sun. The gleaming rays on the water in my palm held me for a moment, the touch of the water gave me something from itself. A moment, and the gleam was gone, the water flowing away, but I had had them. Beside the physical water and physical light I had received from them their beauty; they had communicated to me this silent mystery. The pure and beautiful water, the pure, clear, and beautiful light, each had given me something of their truth.

Any natural thing truly seen and told conveys essence – and that is one reason why we need art as well as committees in defence of nature; but Jefferies is so great a master of seeing that his spring and basin, a real but unnamed, unhistoric place, becomes a metaphor for life itself. Jefferies has been known and loved by many general readers, and writers as different as Edward Thomas and Henry Miller have praised him, but he does not get taught in schools and colleges. This may be a fortunate thing because when gospels become respectable it is harder to hear them, and the need for us to hear his is urgent now as never before.

From Jefferies you can learn how to love ditches with nothing but a little dry grass in them, ditches far poorer than that which forms the western boundary of our garden. The water of our ditch flows after one more field, in which are the green mounds of a deserted village, into the River Cherwell. It has alders growing along it and in it, willows and hairy willowherb, hawthorns, forget-me-nots and meadowsweet. So many creatures live there – crayfish and dragonflies and a host of insects that I don't know how to name, snipe, owls, kingfishers, moorhens, ducks and small birds of twenty kinds. One humid afternoon after blundering about and getting hot and stung looking for nests, and not finding a single one, I sat down to rest in the shade. Obliged to give up trying to possess the secrets of the place and sit quietly, they had a chance to take possession of me. The warm and powerful smell of water-mint at once began its two-fold trick of refreshing body and spirit. And then a warbler began to sing. It was very close: I saw down its throat as it sang.

Its song was of this earth. It was full of delight but it did not have me rapt, nor was it wistful or cheerful or any of the anthropomorphic adjectives we use in trying to 'capture' birds' songs in words. And I have no view on whether it sang 'I love you' or 'Keep off' to some invisible mate or rival. I only know that it seemed to sing itself, as it was itself, without self-consciousness, and that I felt beyond measure lucky to be there.

I think it may have been a marsh warbler: they are not *very* rare, but they are local. Oxfordshire has been one of their counties, and our ditch is the right kind of habitat. This bird sang from an exposed branch, which one book said was characteristic, and there was something else – the colour of the legs I think – that seemed to fit. Perhaps after all it was a reed warbler. But whatever kind of warbler it was, and despite its being a summer visitor, it seemed to live there by a much more certain right than mine.

That I'm only a middling ornithologist only adds force to what I have to say: most people don't know a sparrow from a chaffinch, much less can tell the warblers apart, yet in our crazed, fearful and ignorant possessiveness we are prepared to put at risk the lives of creatures that we do not even take the trouble to know. For Upper Heyford will grasp that warbler's territory within its hideous hug, if that particular nuclear base should get its nuclear mate.

The bird lived there for a while, and its voice lived in my mind, there under the roar of the F-111 bombers and all the other bogus thunder we pollute the world with. It spread out rings like a leaping fish in the Cherwell, coming to speak for all the other creatures living there, for the creatures living in the shadowed circle of the other British targets, for the creatures living near the targets overseas, for all the creatures in this world our species threatens to lay waste. Can you look the bird at your own back door in the eye? A black mood can make a clean sweep of our species seem as sensible as the eradication of a plague virus, but of course that kind of despair is part of the disease and has to be fought. Clean it couldn't be; and in any case it couldn't be done without taking the rest of creation with us. But looking at nature as it is, existentially, renews a sense of responsibility. What hurts the marsh warbler hurts me.

Creation falls with man. To me the story in Genesis seems to describe not a punishment but a consequence: knowledge thus wrested from nature is bad for us, and leads to our being pitted against nature instead of living in harmony with it. A mark of maturing in the individual is that she learns what is harmful and avoids it of her own free will, but collectively we remain childish. And yet myth − collective wisdom − and the individual mind alert us to the source of evil. Like Faust we go on extorting from the earth a knowledge that afflicts us. The prohibition in the Garden was not on knowledge but on havingness, having to have no matter what the cost. In the glittering range of ways that man has outraged nature for the supposed benefit of the species, nuclear weapons are the splendid masterpiece; and in the face of the guilt that now possesses us there is a choice. We can recognise the guilt as a warning symptom. We can begin to atone by identifying the disease and setting to work to heal the common weal. Or we can refuse to recognise it; either by turning deaf ears and blind eyes to the unfaceable facts, or by justifying such evils as necessary. The aggressive are the ones who actually do the damage; the passive do not become politicians and military men. But the passive by their weakness empower aggression and they therefore share responsibility. As Shakespeare's Cassius said:

> I know that Caesar would not be a wolf,
> But that he sees the Romans are but sheep.

Tolstoy in *War and Peace* put it another way, pointing out the weakness of an emperor were it not for the combined strengths of the men he swayed:

> . . . in order that the will of Napoleon and Alexander [the people on whom the whole decision appeared to rest] should be effected . . . it was necessary that millions of men in whose hands the real power lay . . . should consent to carry out the will of those weak individuals . . .

In the huge tracts of land that are controlled by the Ministry of Defence

we can once more see the sheep – Caesar's sheep – 'eat up the men'.
For these are the new enclosures. Like the old ones they have a lot to do
with profit. Like the old ones they break hearts, spoiling and shutting us
out from loved and local landscapes. Many are occupied by Americans
who not surprisingly know nothing of the places they're living in and
try to feel at home by turning them into little Americas. John Clare's
poetry of mourning for the murder and theft of his landscape by
enclosure can help us to recognise what is happening today and make
us more determined to resist. And other mute inglorious Clares must
find a voice, avoid the elegiac tone that tells of defeat, and speak
effectively for life.

There are those who believe that 'Defence' protects the countryside
they love. Wild flowers, embosomed spires and cricket on the green are
under serious threat, yet all these seem, to them, to need those places
with their bunds and bunkers, monoculture grass, their concrete and
their steel, their barracks and their hangars and their wire. Perhaps they
feel it is a pity that those paths are shut, those trees are down, those
views are out of bounds; but they believe that nature, like religion, can
be kept in reserves, and that it is the price of the freedom of our country.
Perhaps they have not reflected enough upon the wire. There is the
wire, and there are the paths. Public rights of way across 'private' land
are at least channels of life, veins through which freedom's blood can
flow: yet they are under constant attack from those who claim to 'own'
or 'defend' the land. Paths and wires are actual; but they are also
metaphors. Confronted by stockades on every side, we need to hear
again the gentle questioning of Robert Frost:

> *Before I built a wall I'd want to know*
> *What I was walling in or walling out . . .*

We have to question the new imperial assumptions, just as we questioned the old. We have to question a socio-economic system that
denies people jobs on the land, just as we questioned the way of life that
tied people to it. 'Jobs', like 'Defence', we are not supposed to question.
When the word 'jobs' is dangled as an excuse for another military
installation, or some other wasteful, polluting, ugly and unnecessary
industrial 'plant' in the already groaning and travailing land, those who
have jobs are shamed into silence. Most of those who have not can see
and hear nothing but that word, and feel savagely towards those whose
protests seem to mean to deny it to them. It is a torturer's technique to
squeeze until the victim will agree to anything: of course people need
work, but we must dare to think about what that is.

Real work cannot be created, any more than the raw materials that provide it can, whether those are the land itself, its plants and animals, or the human beings who need teaching, healing ... Caesar cannot create. But there is plenty of work for hands and minds to do, cultivation in the widest sense, turning the planet we have plundered and fouled into something like a garden again, and if our society is truly free we ought to be able to choose and reward real work, work that is properly human.

I was once at a meal with a 'member of the personnel' from the military base at Upper Heyford, and when he was told that the vegetables he had eaten had come from the garden he began to feel ill. He was an intelligent man, a teacher and not one of the military; but his predicament was horrifyingly symbolic. His body proclaimed the outrage he was doing to his mind; he was suffering from the really dangerous escapism of our time, the refusal to recognise the basic reality that our food comes from the earth, that we are dependent on it.

Forgetfulness of our dependence is relatively new, but the other pretence, that we shall never die and can therefore 'own' property, has an older pedigree. Two thousand years ago Horace saw its absurdity and wrote:

> nam propriae telluris erum natura neque illum
> nec me nec quemquam statuit
> (for nature has ordered it that neither he nor I nor anyone is master
>   of the land he holds).

Whether we acknowledge Caesar and his claims on anything at all, it is plain that land cannot belong to him: money and machines and weapons are man-made things, but not the land.

The knowledge that comes from possessing things, knowledge that is taken forcibly, is in the end harmful and not nourishing; but if we can love something without wanting to possess it it becomes part of us by increasing our understanding. 'Knowledge puffeth up; but charity edifieth.' Sheep get puffed up if they eat unsuitable food, and die if they go untreated. To prevent this ludicrous, horrible death by wind the surgery must be swift and skilled: those who can speak or write must bring sharp piercing words.

T. F. Powys throughout his parable-fictions makes the connection between possession and cruelty. Powys – if you can find him, for most of his books are out of print – is strong stuff, and should be taken sparingly. A good way is in alternate doses with his brother: John Cowper Powys's shifts for saving 'the whole round earth ... bleeding and victimised, like a smooth-bellied, vivisected frog' are sometimes strange, but at least he imparts optimism, a feeling that it is possible.

Looking out on the ancient tree-lined ditch and a field with a path across it, and a blue sky full of autumn cumulus that Ruskin would have delighted in, the distant planes homing in on Heyford do not look very threatening. Even here it is easy, and cosier, not to acknowledge what is going on. We have to make that effort. We have to see that we can't afford to keep ourselves fastidiously apart and our opinions veiled. Solomon saw that the child rightly belonged to her who cared for its life and not to her who would have it at any price. It is time to pull the armour off the false St George, who swashbuckles so dangerously, and show the scaly hide. But polemic is a prickly thing, and figs don't grow on thistles. Means matter.

Muniments

The following poems are about four of the hundred and more places in Britain alone where nuclear targets have been created.

Muniments are defences. But muniments are also documents preserved as evidence of privileges or rights. In these four places, as elsewhere, people have lived, adding their lives to the humus of history; and I realised as I read that their chronicles, the books and essays and articles by and about their inhabitants and them, were muniments in that sense. The writing of the local history of unhistoric places tacitly asserts the privilege of being human and the rights of man. There are records too of the local plants and animals: they too have their muniments.

Much of what is here is written by other people: what I have done is to make gatherings of their observations, often in their own words. I want to bring home that all places are home. Greenham Common, Lakenheath, High Wycombe and Faslane, like other places in Britain and all over the globe, are places where people have lived and died alongside their fellow creatures and among the plants in mutual dependence on the earth. They speak in its defence.

GREENHAM COMMON, BERKSHIRE

When the earth was unsettled
I was exalted; my gravel floor held
while the rocks that made my sides
were washed away.
The valley of the shadow is as old as man
but I am older.

Then I was settled.
Bury's Bank crosses me
by which there are or were
five round dips in the grass,
the British hutments or their cattle-pens,
with a ditch and mound enclosing them
to fence outsiders out and cattle in.

My name means 'green river-valley',
referring to the land beside the Kennet.
But later I was called Red Heath
although, ironically, that name was lost.

I am there in Domesday
twenty years after the Conquest,
with land for ten ploughs
and more than a hundred acres of meadow.

People brought beehives to me in the summer
so that the bees could browse on purple heather.

I see strange sunsets.
A man named Hockin prophesied ' . . . the downs
and this high weird common go livid
and the valleys seem like cracks in the moon,
and yourself much less than the dust . . . '

The earth is unsettled
and they have built a fence of fear
nine miles round on me.
Kennet and Enborne
clasp my three hundred feet.
The sunsets may grow stranger.
The radiant dust may be the last to settle.
I am green pastures and now
I am valley of the shadow.

Women watch with me continually
certain that peace is conceivable.

Know me for what I am.

LAKENHEATH, SUFFOLK*

Flint axe, copper dagger, Roman brooch:
always people there between fen and breck
alongside the rabbits and plovers and curlews
scratching the sand.

Ground they broke with plough or spade
the Celts called breck; but breck goes back
and to Saxons the word meant waste,
where water is brackish and bracken grows.
Now it is land that is tilled from time to time.

Over the North Sea and up the Ouse
and up the Little Ouse to a hythe on the fen's edge,
unpromising land, Danes came and settled.
'Landing-place of Laca's people': Lakenheath.

Others make tunnels besides the rabbits.
There are tales of a passage under the fens:
they say it was there that Hereward hid.

Alan of Walsingham, Prior of Ely,
owned land there under Edward III;
and inquisitors sent to assess one ninth
of corn, lambs, wool, for fighting the French,
wrote: 'nihil solvit, nec solvere vult'.
Alan, in English, refused to pay.

This was the muster of Lakynghyve,
its civil defence in Tudor times:
princypall archers xii
able archers ii
fifteen princypall bylmen
and thirteen able.
And the store of arms was seven halberds
seven swords and seven daggers
and seven harness for three horse.

Small slidings of sand are incessant;
it moves and settles like the people.

---

* First published in *Peace News*.

Once the wind whipped up
a giant sandstorm like a revolution,
but they shovelled and patched and life went on.

'Nothing can be more desolate and forlorn
than the situation of Lakenheath . . . '
David Davy hurried away
after noting a galilee in the church.
Some find God in wilderness;
but if some have found it godforsaken

do we still give Caesar more than his due?
Here, now, is his camp that can lay waste
the earth and all that therein is.
O the sweet cry of the ringed plover
over the breck . . .

HIGH WYCOMBE, BUCKINGHAMSHIRE

What does it mean to talk about our country?
In Bucks it used to mean this bit of Bucks.
Batter *was common for a sloping bank*
and blizzy *was a blazing fire.*
The grey herb southernwood that has so many names,
lad's love, that Edward Thomas wrote about,
they knew as kiss-i-my-corner, *wren was* tickety,
and creeping saxifrage was thread-of-life.

He would have been a bodger,
turning the local beechwoods into chairs.
She would have got her living at the pillow:
bone-lace and chairs our country's noted for.

The Chiltern hills have mainly dry valleys
so Wycombe grew and took its name from water:
'valley-in-which-there-is-a-stream'.
And the hills surrounding it seemed good defences.
But neither Keep nor Castle Hill availed:
a Roman pavement in a nearby field

has 'a Beast at the centre in a circle
like a dog standing sideways by a tree'.
Deliver my darling from the power of the dog
that still stands at the centre of the circle
pissing on the Tree of Life.

The mayor and corporation in the eighteenth century
received a distribution for defence
of muskets swords and bandoliers.
Now they get pamphlets with tall stories in.

A local poet wrote in 1848:
  'And here the young, oh! guard and bless!
  And may they, as their days increase,
  Find wisdom's ways are pleasantness,
  And all her paths are paths of peace.'
God guard them still in 1984
crouched in the mud beside the peacecamp fire
disheartened after having flu in tents.

In 1936 'on a starry night . . . Bomber command was born':
glad tidings from a history of the Air Force . . .
What does it mean to talk about our country?
Beneath this batter *is a life-proof bunker.*
Tickety *go computerised controls.*
(Outside the wren is burning in the blizzy.*)*
O quickly kiss-i-my-corner *while there's time!*
Parodied by the wires beneath its roots
can thread-of-life *survive at Walter's Ash?*

FASLANE, IN THE PARISH OF ROW, DUMBARTONSHIRE

This is how Faslane was fashioned,
the small and beautiful bay where the burn
ran murmuring into the loch:
all these lands and lochs were the slow work of ice
and species by species after the thaw
the kingdoms began to colonise until
all along Garelochside whins and wild roses
ramped, and sloes, and there was sweeting of birds

and sweet scents from copsewood and shrubs,
and there was man.

Climb from Faslane
up the glen, over heather,
past ancient boulders left by the ice
through the peat hagg where white
pebbles glitter in the sun
and up the grassy face of Maol am Fheidh:
there's a fine peep of the loch.

Or look, doubled beauty:
moonlight on Gareloch,
stars in the water.
Still reflections . . .
such abundance:
why is peace so hard to grasp?

If not beauty, fear might teach it:
each croft kept its crosscuts of iron;
flesh cooled to hear the wolf's howl
beyond the circle of firelight.
Or grief? Fire and sword, Haco the Dane,
always 'thift, reff, and uther ennormities',
Colquhouns and Macgregors,
blood in the rowanhung waters of Fruin,
blood on the blue-grey rocks of the Glen of Sorrow,
and still a mound to mark the mass grave . . .
How much is enough?

John McLeod Campbell believed that love was
and he preached that love in his parish of Row
saying that Christ had saved every one.
And his people loved him and might have loved God through him.
But the Gospel of Peace is too lawless for churches and synods.
The General Assembly made him leave his kirk
though his father said he was proud of such a son
'and although his brethren cast him out
the Master whom he serves will not forsake him'.
He settled in Rosneath, across the loch,
and called his home Achnashie: Field of Peace.

SOME SOURCES

English Place-name Society county volumes
Ordnance Survey Maps 1:50000
The Oxford English Dictionary
The Victoria History of the Counties of England

J. R. A. Hockin: *On Foot in Berkshire*, 1934
Philip Morgan (ed.): *Domesday Book 5 Berkshire*, 1979
Transactions of the Newbury District Field Club Vol. 5, 1911

W. G. Clarke: *In Breckland Wilds*, 1975
Proceedings of the Suffolk Institute of Archaeology and History

B. E. Escott: *A History of the Royal Air Force in High Wycombe*
H. Harman: *Buckinghamshire Dialect*, 1929 repr. 1970
Henry Kingston: *The History of Wycombe with Recollections of my native
    town including anecdotes, biography, oral reminiscences, poems, etc. etc.*
    1848
Thomas Langley: *The History and Antiquities of the Hundred of Desborough,
    and Deanery of Wycombe, in Buckinghamshire; including the Borough towns
    of Wycome and Marlow*, 1797
L. J. Mayes: *History of the Borough of High Wycombe from 1880*
Parker: *Early History and Antiquities of Wycombe*

W. C. Maughan: *Annals of Garelochside*, 1896

A HOLLOW LANE ON THE NORTH DOWNS

THE PILGRIMS WAY 1971
ANCIENT PATHS FORMING A ROUTE BETWEEN WINCHESTER AND CANTERBURY
10 DAYS IN APRIL   A 165-MILE WALK

HAMISH FULTON

NO HORIZONS

A ONE DAY 50-MILE WALK   SOUTHERN ENGLAND   1976

HAMISH FULTON

BARKIN

A NON-STOP 82-MILE WALK LASTING A DAY, A NIGHT AND THREE-QUARTERS OF A DA

OGS

DADS AND PATHS   FIELDS AND WOODS   KENT   AUGUST MOON 1978

The Time
Things Take

BY DAVID POWNALL

In the first week of the great July heat wave of 1983 I rowed the Thames from Maidenhead to Oxford and back with a friend. The 122-mile journey took us eight days. Within that period everything belonged to the river. It imposed its own authority over time and distance. From the boat we would see a signpost on the road showing three miles to the next town but we knew that for us it was seven miles still to travel, winding a separate way through the land. Even with the holiday launches streaming up and down rocking us in their wakes; the High Speed 125 trains flashing across bridges towards Bristol; Concorde bellowing its way over Oxfordshire; the heavy traffic on the Thames valley roads audible; we had the satisfaction of being in a different dimension that employed separate laws. We were not encountering Nature as something passive and hidden. Its authority made itself felt in the way we felt connected to what we were doing. For so much hard work we could get so far – no motor, no compromise. There was no need to do it this way. From start to finish would have taken us an hour and a bit in a car. When we completed the journey, returned the boat and got ready to drive back to London we immediately ran into a fifteen-mile traffic jam on the M4. Inside the mind all the river's longer, deeper relationships shrivelled like lengths of string in a fire and we were left with the city and frustration. The benefit of the trip seemed to die in the sense of wasted time, polluted distance and our participation in something dull, desperate and mad.

In September of the previous year I walked the 220-mile final leg of the medieval pilgrim road to Santiago de Compostela in north-western Spain with another friend. We started at the ancient city of León and spent the first day following the trunk road as we had not been able to find any map that had the old pilgrim road marked on it. Leaving the still centre of León in the early morning we walked through industrial estates, massive roadworks, excavations until, ten miles later, the four-lane highway got free of the city and we were able to feel and see the plain of León. We were never alone, having the lorries always with us. For a journey that we had been talking about for several months and which meant a lot to both of us, it was a nightmare beginning. The modern cladding of the city just went on and on many layers thick. Fences kept us penned in, forcing us to keep on the tarmac with the traffic. We began taking ridiculous detours through fields and orchards, casting about like hounds to find the scent of the old road. It took us three days to find it. By that time we were nearly across Marageteria, a region of desolated villages and bald hills that had all the resonance of a non-mechanised era but which had steadfastly refused to reveal the ancient route. It was not until we met a man from Madrid who had started up a café in the middle of the ruins of Acebo that we discovered that the Camino de Santiago – the thousand-year-old road to the shrine of Saint James – was marked out with small yellow arrows all the way from the Pyrenees. When we started to follow these markers – they had been daubed on trees, wayside stones and walls – we found what we had been looking for. It crossed the trunk roads, ran into the industrial zones, burrowed through the towns and tourist traps, but it always re-emerged and wavered on towards Galicia, always feeling its way through the landscape with a walker's canniness, conscious of contours.

We were then in a different country with different rules. The effect of the journey was no longer involved with resistance to the earth we were covering, or resentment at what we had to look at or listen to: the journey had a natural meaning that had nothing to do with speed or anxiety. We were walking out of one half of ourselves and into another.

I have never been so aware that I have to endure an alien environment as part of myself, living with that tension, that hostility to the landscape that surrounds me and is me: the great smooth highway, the industrial estate, the pipeline, the whole ugly, shabby, loveless mass of the habitat we have created for ourselves is grafted on to our sense of Nature. We struggle for our personal harmony of mind within that dichotomy, knowing that the future will not resolve the argument. From now on we have to survive within the structure we have imposed on the world as well as the world's ancient natural functioning.

Will the value that we place on the river and the old road always match the worth we put on this alien civilisation we are creating? It must have worth because we persist in working for it. It may be that there is an evolutionary mechanism that is fitting us for the unnatural life required by a high-technology existence. There may be a greater degree of comfort and equilibrium to be found by rejecting the old natural order. It does not refresh, it sets up antagonisms between the man-made world and our known, animal needs. We are perfectly conscious that the river and the old road are part of ourselves, that they have strengthened and sustained us for all the history of the species – but is the tension they create still beneficial, or necessary?

When I was working as a personnel manager on the Zambian Copperbelt during the 1960s the problem of recruiting British expatriates was seriously worsened by the mining company's policy of flying new employees out to Africa rather than bringing them out by sea and train. A family from Swansea or Leicester would move from their house in Britain to their house in the African bush in the course of one day. It does not need a psychiatrist to analyse the tensions and difficulties that this created. I remember one Welsh rigger demanding to be repatriated within the week – a not uncommon occurrence – and the man had to struggle to explain why. His mind was in such a confusion that he finally settled on the grievance that no one had told him that there were so many black people in Zambia! I did not have to believe this idiocy, neither did he. What we were both aware of was that the pace of change over physical and cultural distance had been too fast and he, with his wife and children, had been victims of cruel, commercial stupidity. But the mining company steadfastly clung to its short-term, cheap policy of catapulting employees from Britain to Central Africa, refusing to spend the extra money on a sane, tempered introduction to the new continent via boat and a week on a slow-moving train through the deserts and savannas that prepared the recruits for their new lives; as a result they suffered alienation, unhappiness and disorientation, and a wonderful adventure for them was often ruined. Big money is not conscious of Richard Murphy's definition of natural pace – the animal chronology within which a balanced development can take place: 'Time that they calendar in seasons, not in clocks.'

Self-knowledge and Nature are two slowly-turning wheels of revelation that should work together. It is not in innocence that we are most sensitive to the land but, if we have the strength and purpose, it is when the selfish centre is being broken down by experience and wisdom. Nature is that which exists or would have existed without human endeavour or interference. Today we accept that the photon and the Z-nought particle are as much a part of that power as the obvious Wordsworthian landscapes. But their speeds within matter are not comprehensible in terms of the seasonal toll that is taken of our lifespan. As we get older it is the winter to summer calibration of time that becomes most important – that is the dimension that we feel and suffer. Meanwhile our society rushes forward at a pace that is hysterical, artificial and harmful to the people that it is supposed to serve.

The estrangement between the artificial and natural parts of the human self is not as acute in those countries where the population retains its relationship with the land. That does not prevent the allure of the city from working its lurid, deceitful magic on even the canniest country minds. The young still flee from rural dullness. The potential for the crisis is there. With a less romantic view of Nature than the city-dweller, the peasant attributes life-giving qualities to urban culture – variety, stimulation, entertainment and liberties. As far as the peasant is concerned life is *too* natural and lived at the mercy of a harsh, arbitrary power that is as hostile to him or her as the city is to me. Profound dissatisfaction would result if we suddenly switched places. Both of us would be confused.

Within this split between the developed and underdeveloped societies and their views of Nature is the beginning of a far more fearful division. We are politically conscious of it in as much as we recognise the problem of first, second and third worlds and how they must be brought together. But the actual worlds we are concerned about are not kept apart by boundaries established by governments but by the separating attitudes we have to what form of life is most desirable and how this should be achieved. The developed world needs happiness but can only imagine economic advancement. Nature and its powers appear to be the province of other, poorer peoples. What we are able to deal with is the pastiche of the land – we walk on it but it has no meaning except as an imitation or reproduction of what we used to understand. So, the third world will remain the old world and we will create the new – which we know contains the seeds of an unnatural unhappy, anxious prosperity that the third world will crave in its innocence. Should war arise from this separation of environments it will not be between the superpowers but by the superpowers against the alien but natural world that they have lost.

All these prophecies are false if it is the intention of an intelligent natural authority to have the human animal evolve into a self-subsisting creature that has shed its need to integrate with its environment in the immediate sense. It is possible that the mental direction of the species has always been towards the artificial and in the security of a man-made environment is its only salvation. All the major religions of the world are supernatural. They do not attempt to bring the intelligent soul closer to the natural world but press for understandings beyond the immediate environment. It is the end of Nature – death – that has emerged as the desirable state in all our organised spiritual experiments. Nature is the enemy.

Man survived the great age of religion and has struggled into an era that belongs to the huge political machine and its vassal technologies –

war and media communication. We emerged lamed and sick from the journey from one destructive epoch into the next. If we had adapted ourselves completely to the demands of either religion or the state the present division of the civilised self would not have taken place. Nature would have its subservient place as either demon or resource and no further significance would need to be tormented from its endless coils of meaning.

All that saves Nature from this demotion is guilt – a spiritual emotion that could be defended as the most powerful force in the survival instinct. We feel guilt because we know that we are natural animals who are increasingly becoming unnatural because of our terrible appetite for witless ease and facile substitution. We feel guilt because we know that the easiest way is not the best way, that the line of least resistance leads us to the imperial authority of the television, drugs, desperation and the politics of hysteria. This guilt is not articulate in all of us but it exercises itself in our continual taste for mundane serfdom – giving away the time and effort of our lives to what we recognise as shabby, make-do and outside the discipline of our natural past. The guilt tells us that we are still animals that have a conscious appreciation of the parallels between our existence and the physical expression of the world's motion and energy. We do belong to a natural order. If there ever was an original sin it was not of pride but of lust for the easy way out – an easy way out that changes, cruelly, into an act of self-exclusion.

The alleviation of poverty, the increase of leisure, the improvement of living conditions, was never imagined by philosophers or revolution-aries as a means of creating more unhappiness. People did not sacrifice their lives in order to build a hell on earth for innocent people. We envisioned Utopias that were balanced, fruitful, peaceful and just. No thinker before the mid-nineteenth century was able to foresee the shrill, unbalanced, neurotic condition of the new society that would provide the setting for horrific wars and unhappiness on an unprecedented scale. If the history of the last hundred years has been governed by the unknowable laws of Nature and what it must do with the human animal then we must look at what we mean by Nature – re-examine the land, even the picture postcard, the bee in the flower. Whatever is being worked out in terms of our evolutionary destiny is already part of ourselves – we define Nature within our animal mind – and it may be that what has caused the division between the unnatural and natural state and its attendant misery is all bound within the framework of a perfectly natural overall programme of growth. If this is so, our trust in Nature – something we still retain in a somewhat corroded form – has been greatly misplaced. Our best course of action may be resistance to it;

its beauty, healing powers, richness, encompassing harmonies, are treacherous if they are leading to the evolution of an unhappy but efficient machine animal better equipped to grow out into the cosmos and become involved with the greater structure of a Nature that is – as far as our concept is concerned – supernatural itself.

In our search for the benevolent and regenerative power of Nature are we merely isolating one aspect of an alien mystery in order to pretend that we can cope with it? To glory in the land and the wealth of life that it bears may be an act of subservient respect and affection that is costing us too dear. We have always known that we die by Nature, sharing this sentence with all things, even our material universe that science has now condemned to ultimate extinction. We are finite and always in the grip of that hapless insecurity. Religion can square this with our sense of justice but if we labour to live by battling through the experience of life alone, intellectually exposed and isolated, we encounter the monolithic caprice of Nature. It does not care in terms that we can understand. It is inhumanly structured, savagely aloof. There is evidence that it reduces physical pain where it can – animal mechanisms contain natural opiates; we are equipped to shut off the main channels of consciousness when massive traumas afflict us. But the progressive deterioration in our sense of natural compliance with the environment is not reduced by any agency. We are kept sharply aware that it is wrong, harmful and our own fault, that this is not the direction nature wants us to take. That guilt is a piercing signal. The romantic search for landscape's curative goodness; the frenetic pursuit of a health that proves only superficial; the entrusting to societies, artists, politicians of the custodianship of our sense of harmony with Nature; are not enough. There must be a single, recognisable symbol that can be cherished and shared. It cannot be as abstract or miasmic as the philosophies and religions that superseded the early forms of worship. They worked on the principle that people surrendered that part of their minds to experts who would sort out some easy expression of ritual or observance – much as they handed over political authority to the warrior who would protect them best. That situation has not greatly altered. We are kept in touch with the natural world and governed by a similar structure of experts but, unlike the original citizens of the crudely centralised tribes, we are not bound to a Nature that we understand by force of a mean daily existence. Ease and convenience have thrust us out of that rough church where one could adore, resent, hate and be grateful to a powerful god who never promised that human life was sacred, or gave guarantees of a facile, easeful existence based on superfluities. It was a god that was grim but full of beauty, appallingly complex, insensately merciless, unjust but bountiful. The workings of the god were in tune with the blood, babies, the presence of moving stars and the mathematical reliability of seasons and death.

It was the kind of god that could be responsible for earthquakes but not for what has happened to modern, developed man. We know that what has been done to us we have managed ourselves. When we come across a landscape that suddenly fills us with wonder a part of our response at that moment is always a question – why did we think ourselves out of this land?

Any imaginative extension of the meaning of Nature by priests or poets is possible and permissible. Underlying the disciplines of science and philosophy is the belief that all concepts are already in existence and we create nothing new, only manufacture parallels and reflections of what has already been provided. We do not invent but discover our essentials. When we can claim to have created something it has the identity of a gadget: a means of getting away from, or circumventing, Nature. But the physical principles that govern it belong to the authority that it bypasses. It is for those escape mechanisms that we reserve our loudest applause. Aware that Nature is sufficiently profound to exhaust all our present genius we love the trick that gets round it, even though the apparatus – be it an inter-galactic rocket or yet another patent tin-opener – will not alter the laws that rule our individual fate through time and degeneration. The gadget is the most intoxicating evidence of progress and the cunning and awesome brilliance of mind that goes into creating it persuades us that here is a dancing, unconquerable area of our common genius that Nature cannot quell. In it we put much of the trust we once reserved for that primordial god, even the warped deities that came shimmering out of the Middle Eastern deserts to confuse us for a thousand years. It rested on a talent for getting round those huge, mind-numbing physical problems that faced the farmer and the builder. As they saw the power of intelligent human guile cheat matter and time, Nature was diminished. From the brute authority it was relegated to a status of an impossible prophet or something up the sleeve of the state's god. As we have surged forward in our ability to outmanoeuvre Nature by gadgetry on a colossal scale – both materially and intellectually – we have suddenly perceived that we have pushed Nature from being diminished though ever-present into a position whereby we cannot even maintain a relationship with it. It is slipping from our perception of reality, which means that we are becoming incapable of seeing ourselves as real. The appetite for robots is not a manifestation of the need to play or be entertained, or be industrially efficient. It is the urge to look at what will be our new selves in the world we have created. Now we have satisfied ourselves that our industrial future will be controlled by this technique of production and surrendered our leisure to the autocratic, centralised systems of television taste and media interpretation we have to ask whether this *feels* like our natural destiny – for it is only feeling that retains our respect as a truly natural function. But within that feeling is the division of selves and it is capable of taking two decisions at once.

A simple and crucial test of our attitude to Nature is the way we deal with the land when we have to. As a nation the British are strongly motivated towards home ownership which means land ownership. However, the feeling is for the house; even the garden is an extension of the interior decor and design. There is no emotional bond with the parcel of soil and stone that the building stands on – the eternal part of the mortgage. With present trends in house building in the private sector it is estimated that another quarter of a million acres of land will be required by the end of the century. All agree that this is a crowded island. We are not struggling with an escalating birth rate or in the middle of a population explosion. This acreage will not be commandeered because of land-lust by the house owner, or folk-movements, wars or imperial ambitions. It will be steadily ingested into a system of national economy whereby each mature, responsible citizen in the United Kingdom accedes to priorities – the first being that everyone has the right to own a house if he or she can afford it. The question of whether we, as a people, can afford it will be raised by the media perhaps, discussed, then it will fade. It will be assumed that it is either settled or no longer news.

The land will go. The woods will go. The rivers will go. The responsibility for keeping the earth revered and respected as our natural habitat will be allowed to slip away from government – wherein we have invested it, too confused to suffer it ourselves – and government will pass on that responsibility to the image-makers. Nature already lives half its twentieth-century life inside a television tube. It is the most photogenic face of all. We have a constant assurance that the land is still there, still unspoilt, still unpolluted, radiant as ever. Even the environmental debate is turned to good use. The battle for the land is carried on as surrogate theatre, a long-running series with the same characters and arguments repeating their appearances week in, week out. The critical sense of the individual is eroded by this familiarity. His assumption has to be that all this cherishing and concern must mean that the land is safe, somewhere. The artificial, political half of the mind will believe this: the natural, realistic half will know that it is a lie. But the false truth is easier to live with than the true lie. The ability to analyse and perceive that the destruction of the land is a destruction of the vital self has long decayed. It died with the media conquest of the 1950s and the extension of its empire to the present day. Like the land under the house, Nature is hidden in images of false ownership.

More ease, more opportunity to forget or delegate the mind's function, more high-speed materialism divorced from the known natural rhythms must produce a crisis unless either Nature is destroyed as a basis for a happy human life or the present tide of alienating technology is slowed or turned. There is an in-built defiance of the old truths that we have learnt about ourselves. Privately we might admit our awareness that Nature is finite in as much as it works within our lifespan. Whatever happens to us is governed by stern laws of time, growth and degeneration. Beyond our individual fate there is the vulnerable universe that must die. Nature itself is mortal and can therefore be cheated, warped or ignored. This has created a conspiracy of indifference. Most of the conventional melancholy, grief and complaint of the twentieth century is not to do with the failure of democratic politics or the several horrible proofs of the profanity of human life – it is to do with a bewildering grievance against Nature which is considered to have collapsed alongside God when faced with the challenge of the terrible twins, science and profit. Released from the worst excesses of natural power, sheltered by gadgetry, confused by space mathematics of phenomenal complexity we no longer ask Nature 'What are you made of?' but 'Why are you letting them do this to me?'

Such pessimism is, in itself, unnatural. It may have served its purpose in awakening people to the gravest condition of the human spirit that is known – the rolling despair of *too much* going down the hill of *too little* – and there are signs that the separation between Nature and our society is becoming detectable to the many rather than the few – a few who often appear to be inspired more by the pleasures of opposition than by any desire for the general good. By the time that the various European and North American ecology movements have collected enough support to alarm the establishments in their respective countries the gap may have widened to the point where people are left stranded on either side. All that will bring them together again will be a consensus of belief in what goes to make a livable life. By then I think the argument that life acquires significance only through accumulation of chattels and more material nonsense will have been rejected by all but the addicted and the insane.

There will be a new religion. Out of the destruction, waste and divisions of the twentieth century will come a resurgence of spiritual optimism. The alternative view is too harsh to be reconciled with life. The new religion will draw a minimum of inspiration from the existing creeds.

No mention will be made of sacrifice because it accepts that all the sacrifices have been made already and there is no need for more. It will be an heroic creed based on the career of one who learnt his lesson – Ulysses, who returned to claim a shattered inheritance after a prolonged, wasteful journey that provided amusement and horror but no growth, no onward motion towards human integrity.

The new religion will not be druidical or based on any known form of Nature worship. Those cults worshipped that which was in total authority over them. They had no need to see themselves as people who had defied and desecrated the power that they were subject to. In the twenty-first century we will be adoring a god that we wounded – apologising, trying to compensate for our mistakes but, most of all, for our greed – the oldest, most-wicked and comprehensive of our vices. This relationship to Nature has obvious parallels with the guilt the Christian feels over Christ but it is one that was never shared out to the plain, demonstrable god of Nature who was always seen as a minor function of Christ and Death. Out of the husks of the old religions and their obsessions with death, their hysterical guidance on how to poison the material world and elevate hypocrisy into majesty, will be pressed some good. At last they will be employed in a natural function of our universe – the universe that has life in it – they will adapt to bring about benefit, and become servants to a much greater cause.

JAMIE McCULLOUGH *Beginners' Way*

HENRY MOORE *Sheep Grazing in Long Grass (No. 1)*

HENRY MOORE *Henry Moore and Sheep Piece*

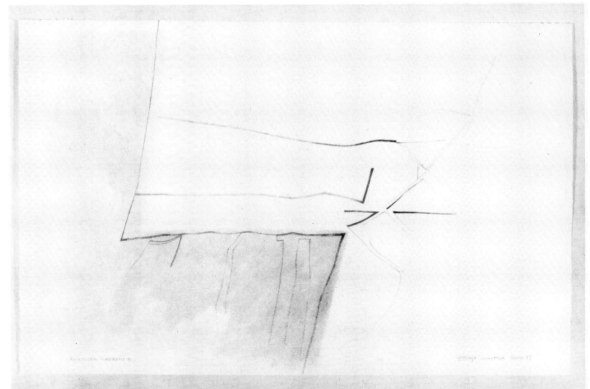

ALEXANDER MACKENZIE top, *Farndale*; above, *Grange, Cumbria*

ALEXANDER MACKENZIE *Lee Moor Variations*

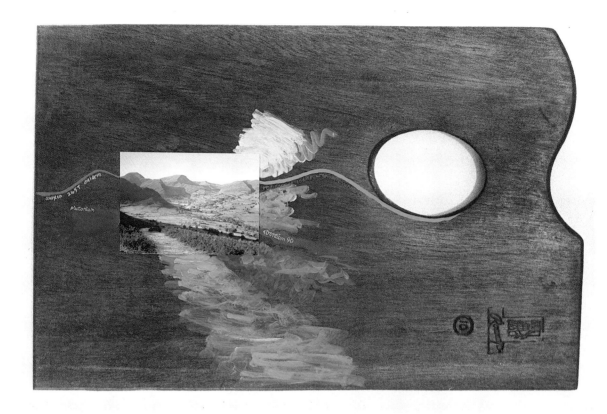

CONRAD ATKINSON *Plutonium Landscape*

PAUL HEMPTON *Stone Staff and Triangle (No. 13)*

Beyond the Golden Age

Home is Where the Heart is

BY LEONIE CALDECOTT

> I, the woman who circles the land,
> Tell me where is my house . . .
> The bird has its nesting place,
> But I – my young are dispersed,
> The fish lies in calm waters,
> But I – my resting place exists not,
> The dog kneels at the threshold,
> But I – I have no threshold . . .
>
> (Song of the Sumerian goddess Innana)

I am looking at a photograph of a cottage. It is the classic kind of English cottage, four small windows grouped about a wisteria-draped porch, chimney stack poking through a thatched roof pulled down low about the red-brick walls. In the foreground, a river runs along the bottom of the garden, and the wide stony lane which passes by the side of the cottage disappears straight into the calm waters, as though suddenly to send the traveller on a different journey, in a different element.

The season in the photograph matches the season outside my window now: it is winter. And yet my memories of this cottage and its surrounding Berkshire countryside, where I spent some of the happiest moments of my childhood, are mostly summer scenes. I recall the dahlias in the garden with their riot of shaggy colour, the sweet, maternal scent of lavender, the hovering hum of the bees, the rustling and calling of birds in the trees up the lane.

On the other side of the river was a large stretch of woodland known as the 'wilderness'. At least it seemed large to me, as a child. Once I got past a certain age, I could cross the narrow wooden bridge and venture into the area closest to home. There I would spend hours in some small clearing, running my fingers over moss and bark, mapping out a territory in which to enact some miniature, imaginary walkabout. At the edge of the woods, where the fields which skirted the winding river Kennet as it flowed on towards Newbury began, I found a hollow tree. Inside it was charred and blackened, with a dull charcoal shine in places. Lightning had struck this tree, I was told. Lightning, I thought, as I hid myself inside the trunk and stared up into the darkness. What is it like to be struck by lightning?

If I walked upstream along the river bank, the path would eventually leave the shining band of water and plunge into the heart of the woods. This was forbidden territory, unless I was accompanied by an adult, in which case my perception of the surroundings would be diminished by the necessity of making polite conversation. I would re-enter this place in my dreams, alone this time, and there I would come to the edge of the world. I would know this had happened because the path would come to an end, and a thick canopy of trees would surround me, containing all the species of plant and animal that had ever existed, assembled before my dreaming eyes. At the centre of this scene was a large owl with outstretched wings.

This then was the landscape of my childhood, one-third reality, and two-thirds dream. Idealised, exaggerated, remembered like a lover one is ashamed of having lost. A countenance of tenderness amidst a murmur of mystery, the murmur of the river sliding into the distance. Yet this wintry photograph, with its bare trees, flaking red paint on the door, the roof in need of re-thatching, brings me aptly to the present.

For although this cottage is the closest thing I have ever had to a true home, in the sense of a place where I felt rooted as well as sheltered, it is also the symbol of exile for me. It was from here that, at the age of three, I accompanied my mother out of her marriage. I returned many times to the cottage and the wilderness, but with my father not my mother. I wandered in the woods, peered carefully into the hedges to glimpse a bird's nest with its small blue eggs, saw the white flash of rabbits' tails in neighbouring fields, paddled in the cold water of the river with my minnow jar and watched my father patiently casting flies in graceful loops on the surface of the water, until a gleaming trout rose to the illusory offering.

My father re-married, and had several more children. My time was divided between this new family, and my mother, who lived alone in the city. Coming down to Berkshire with my father's family during the holidays, I could almost imagine that our holiday home was my true home, here amongst the familial comforts of the cottage and the gentle landscape that surrounded it. But the knowledge of exile had entered my soul, a knowledge associated with my mother and therefore with my own, growing female self. Like Persephone, I had eaten a seed I could not spit out, and thus winter had entered my world.

Then, when I was in my teens, the cottage was burned to the ground. A fire had started in the fuse-box in the kitchen, and soon engulfed the vulnerable thatch above. By the time some people at the top of the lane had seen the flames, it was too late to save the cottage. My family were all up in London, and we only heard about the destruction when it was a fait accompli. I sometimes wonder whether, if we had been there, we could have prevented the disaster. But the fact remains that because this home was a part-time, a seasonal affair, there was no one present either to preserve it or to witness its ending. To me it represented the final exile, the sweeping aside of childhood. Any lingering feeling of belonging somewhere went up in flames along with my father's maps and fishing books. The landlord never rebuilt the cottage: a modern construction could not have replaced it, in any case.

Although my father and stepmother did eventually move out of London altogether and settle in another part of Berkshire, my own attachment to this particular area of Britain had died with the fire. My relationship to nature in general, however, has remained – universalised out of this particular time and place, carried in memory and association, borne along in the very cells of my body. It has become the relationship of a traveller to chance encounters, rather than the settled intimacy of a long-standing connection with a familiar landscape.

As I write this, I am living in a flat in South London. It looks out on to a stretch of tree-lined common, and this is a blessing. But I know I shall not be living here for very long. Even now, I frequently travel away from it. So for the moment, my contact with nature is of necessity diffuse and haphazard, drawing on fleeting moments of wonder. The moon hanging out of the oak tree on the common. A crocus pushing up out of the earth in readiness for spring. The exhilaration of emerging out of fog into bright sunshine on a winding country road.

There is a part of me that longs to settle somewhere, to put down healthy roots away from the sprawling alienation of the city, to be done with itchy feet and the insatiable lure of the strange and the new. None the less, I have yet to find a place that feels rightfully mine. Like the Sumerian goddess Innana, I can only circle the land asking questions. Some of these questions are personal, some more general.

For example, I wonder if a feeling of being exiled in our own land isn't something that many modern women have in common. Everywhere we turn, we can find ourselves with the ground cut from under our feet. Harassed in the streets at night, told we are hysterical when we speak out about the dangers from nuclear technology or chemical waste, trapped by the conflicting demands of family and paid work, the need to be true to our feelings and the need to 'keep the peace', it is often hard to see *where*, in the deepest sense, *we can rest our heads*.

People are apt to say that a woman's place is in the home. But people have to be made to *feel* 'at home', which is different from simply finding yourself in an environment which somebody else calls home. Take patriotism for instance: the supposed conservative, home-loving nature of women has long been used to symbolise a whole sphere, domesticity conflated with territory, which is supposed to motivate men who go off to war. 'Women of Britain Say Go!' gushed the First World War poster, showing the dear feminine creatures keeping the home handkerchiefs fluttering as they drove their menfolk out to the slaughter. But what if, as Virginia Woolf argued shortly before the Second World War in *Three Guineas*, women are not in fact the protagonists, but rather the outsiders in this scenario?

> 'For,' the outsider will say, 'in fact, as a woman I have no country. As a woman I want no country. As a woman my country is the whole world.' And if, when reason has said its say, still some obstinate emotion remains, some love of England dropped into a child's ears by the cawing of rooks in an elm tree, by the splash of waves on a beach, or by English voices murmuring nursery rhymes, this drop of pure, if irrational, emotion she will make to serve her to give England first what she desires of peace and freedom for the whole world.

At this point in my life, the self that is available to me as a woman and as a writer is a self in motion, a seeking self. If home is where the heart is, then because my heart reaches out to the world outside my immediate sphere, I am obliged to make the world my home. And so I find myself travelling a great deal. Yet, as I set foot once more on British soil, I am often overwhelmed with unexpected emotions. 'Some love of England' was indeed dropped into my ears during the times I spent as a child in the Berkshire countryside.

Recently, I visited the place where the cottage in my photograph once stood. The elm trees in which the rooks had cawed were gone, casualties of Dutch elm disease. The sheltered landscape of field and hedgerow had been transformed into a bare expanse stretching from the river to the Bath road: a reminder of the shift from agri-culture to agri-business. The site on which the cottage had stood, now covered in asphalt, seemed too small ever to have contained the home I remembered.

Yet the river was still there, no greater and no smaller than in my dreams and memories, flowing inexorably under the same narrow bridge. I ran my hand along the rough wood of the rail and remembered a strange story that a friend of mine had unearthed in the British

Museum. During the seventeenth century, soldiers came across a woman who was seemingly walking on the surface of this river as it passed near Newbury. When they got closer, they could see she was standing on a raft; none the less, they decided she was a witch, and so shot at her. She reputedly caught the bullets in her mouth and chewed them up. This confirmed her as a witch in their eyes; thus they ran her through with a sword.

This river, I realised, runs on to Greenham Common, just as my life has run on from childhood security to adult uncertainty and questioning. And as I stood there, I became aware that this was the sound that had battered my heart over the years, battered it and kept it beating. The sound of water passing by. And for a moment I tasted a powerful paradox: the river remains, unchanging and constant, because its movement never ceases.

The highest good is like water.
Water gives life to the ten thousand things and does not strive.
It flows in places men reject and so is like the Tao.
(from the *Tao Te Ching*, Chapter Eight)

England, Home and Beauty

BY FRASER HARRISON

On a burning August morning in the summer of 1983 as I drove along the north Norfolk coast, I was suddenly overpowered by doubt. The scenery between King's Lynn and Burnham Market looked so beautiful it defied all thought of rural spoliation and its traumatic effects, though these were the themes I was then brooding on in preparation for a doom-laden contribution to this book. It may well be, I thought, that this stretch of countryside used to be prettier and richer in wildlife forty years ago, and even more so in the last century, but, for all that, nobody can dispute that it is exceedingly lovely today.

On my right, appearing to lift itself now and again above the sloping fields, was the summer sea, as blue as ink and enamelled by the sun. The fields themselves, which are still relatively small and bounded by hedges and copses, were smug with ripened crops, while the verges blazed with sulphurous ragwort flowers. The narrow road squeezed and wriggled between farms and villages, never forcing its way. To my Suffolk eye, accustomed to our cool blues, the pink and yellow flints of the cottages and churches looked hospitably warm, and with their earthy colours these Norfolk villages were agreeably married to their landscape. All this homely beauty and fertile contentment, as I said, made my proposed jeremiad not just alarmist, but churlish too.

My destination was in fact Lincoln and so, bypassing King's Lynn, I took the A17 for Sleaford. The county boundary is near the little river port of Sutton Bridge, where King John, while marching across the flats, was overtaken by the tide and lost all his baggage and treasure. His, however, is not the only treasure that turns out to have disappeared in the quicksands, for no sooner had I passed into Lincolnshire than all my blackest fears for the future of the countryside were abruptly revived.

The road straightened and broadened as the land flattened and emptied beneath an awesome, boundless sky. The tubby, rounded towers of Norfolk's churches were replaced by needle spires, for which the marshland is famous, stretching their ascetic necks to pierce the unapproachable Lincolnshire heavens. The clusters of honey-coloured flint cottages had vanished as well, their place taken by the odd isolated and featureless brick affair, whose few charms had as often as not been crusted over with pebble dash.

I exaggerate, of course, and for all I know the place may abound in attractions which simply happen not to be apparent from the road. But what I found so chilling about this unexpected contrast with north Norfolk's amiable qualities was that the alien Lincolnshire landscape seemed to represent everything to which monoculture threatens to reduce the countryside at large. All natural and human obstacles to agricultural efficiency had been razed and there was nothing to be seen that had not been adapted or sacrificed to the cause of expanding productivity. The level, immeasurable fields, if they could be called fields, with their treeless, hedgeless boundaries, gave the ruddy earth the look of a Martian landscape, but they were also perfectly designed for today's massive implements. Indeed, as I drove deeper into this prolific no-man's-land, I actually came across no less than five combine harvesters working abreast, a spectacle I had never seen before, though it must be commonplace enough in those parts.

I am not really suggesting that any other county stands in danger of being turned into a Lincolnshire. Obviously, the unique features and history of the marshlands around the Wash, not the exigencies of modern farming, are chiefly responsible for the making of this land-scape and its social geography. None the less, at the level of metaphor only, the marshlands impressed themselves on me as a horrific pre-figuration of the countryside that agriculture will bequeath our children if we do not halt the present mode of unbridled 'improvement' and production.

It was therefore with confused feelings that I approached Lincoln cathedral, the object of my journey. Surmounting its little nipple of a hill on the flat chest of the fens, the minster's huge towers and frontage can be seen from many miles away, floating above the city; no other English cathedral enjoys a more spectacular situation. To walk, as I did, from the Brayford Pool, in the modern part of the city, up High Street, up The Strait and Steep Hill, up the ever-narrowing streets and then up the steps of the medieval town, and finally to arrive, panting and dazzled, at the summit of Castle Hill, where the cathedral's astonishing west front suddenly looms like a mountain-side, is to experience with the legs and lungs what the eyes and imagination have apprehended long ago: that everything about this magnificent building has the effect of hurling the mind and spirit like a spear into the celestial blue above. And within the church itself this same sensation of being thrust irresistibly upwards is felt again, as your eyes compulsively race up the pillars and arches to play among the roof ribbing or swim in psychedelic stained glass. Up, up, ever upwards is the whole force of this glorious creation. Why then was it that I found myself grovelling about on the floor in the half darkness looking at the underneaths of seats for carvings which, being hewed out of blackened wood, were almost invisible?

Lincoln cathedral in fact is extremely rich in carvings of all sorts, both in wood and stone. For example, its impressive stone screen is alive with carvings, which seem to have grown out of every crevice and on every surface, like ornamental lichens. But I was particularly interested in the carved misericords or little shelves on the underside of the seats in the choir stalls. They were mostly carved in the fourteenth century and were designed to give relief to the clergy during long services by enabling them to sit, or rather perch, while appearing still to be standing.

It would be absurd to claim for these humble works that they were as moving as the more elevated and conspicuous masterpieces created by the same carvers throughout the cathedral; on the other hand, they do possess a decided fascination of their own. Turn up one misericord and you might find an Ascension scene or some other, predictable biblical topic. Turn up another and you might find a conventional motif of oak leaves, or a vine bearing grapes, or perhaps a traditional mythological beast, a griffin or a pelican 'in her piety'. But turn up a third and you will be confronted by a dead monkey carried on a bier by two others, or a naked child rising from a whelk shell to attack a dragon, or a wife holding her husband's beard in a fierce grip while she slaps him round the head.

The appeal of these lowly, laughably sited carvings is that they are accessible, in every sense. They provide the visitor with a sample, which he can literally grasp, of what lies elsewhere in the cathedral but is concealed or so high as to be out of sight. As well as being visible and tangible, they are accessible as iconography. In fact, their subject matter was largely drawn from bestiaries and other literary sources now known only to scholars, but the graphic manner in which they are carved and the earthy, commonplace incidents they depict make them intelligible to a modern audience. (I know of no earthier incident than one to be found on a misericord in a church near my home, which shows a mother smacking her child's bare bottom.) Regardless of their precise symbolic meaning, we feel an instinctive affinity with these vivid, essentially human works. Our sense of recognition, across history, of common experience is important to the atheist visitor, such as myself, who is unable to identify with the cathedral's religious significance, but feels the building to be more than simply beautiful.

While walking round the cathedral you are constantly reminded of the countryside, not least by the farming backgrounds to many of the biblical carvings and stained glass scenes, and it is this rich, harmonious blend of the natural and man-made that makes the place so exhilarating, and soothing, to the modern eye. Nowadays, the average visitor to the cathedral is of course not a pilgrim, but a tourist, on whom the theological significance of most of what he or she looks at is quite lost. For the tourist, the cathedral is primarily an aesthetic object. The religious inspiration which motivated its craftsmen is not felt as such, and only impinges in so far as it determines the unique atmosphere found in any cathedral. And yet, despite our secular point of view, cathedrals do continue to excite our deepest feelings, and in this respect there is a very close analogy with our response to the countryside. Cathedrals, as works of art, and certain types of landscape both tend to induce a sense of the numinous, of extreme spiritual sensitivity. In our faithless age, it is beauty which arouses intimations of a discarded God, and no longer God who bestows beauty, man-made and natural, as His gift.

A majestic Suffolk sunset, the Gulf Stream rolling its green breakers across the Atlantic to sap the embattled granite cliffs at Stackpole in Dyfed, where I was born, the river Wye snaking out of Wales across the valley floor below Hay; these are some of the natural phenomena that have the same emotional effect on me as Lincoln's soaring trio of towers. Despite their very different associations, each produces an almost inexpressible feeling of being engulfed and overwhelmed, while yet being lifted, melted and fused, body and soul, with the illimitable.

In the eighteenth century such feelings were classified under the Sublime, and later they were at the heart of Romanticism. In their calmer manifestations they are close to that state of mergence of self with non-self that some forms of Zen meditation aspire to maintain as a condition of existence. But whatever their culturally specific expressions, these 'oceanic' feelings would appear to be an irreducible potential within the spectrum of human emotion. When stimulated, they make up part of our response to the profoundest existential questions; they both enhance our sense of being and alleviate some of its burdens. In the days of commonly shared beliefs, they were assimilated into ordinary religious life, but as faith receded they were invested in those other fields of 'spiritual' experience, notably pastoralism, which came to fulfil some of the functions of religion.

But these delirious sensations by no means exhaust our feelings for either cathedral or countryside. Misericords, after all, hardly conjure up impressions of the infinite; on the contrary, it is their very earth-bound concreteness that makes them moving. In the same way, nature's own misericords, as it were, give us some of our greatest pleasures and satisfactions, and this in itself amounts to a very powerful argument for conservation at the parish level.

As I type these lines, my hands are still dirty from digging up a honeysuckle (*lonicera flexuosa*, its label informs me) which the dry summer killed off. To be frank, it was never much of a plant and its natural frailty was aggravated by my inept handling, for I moved it too often and watered it too little. Originally it had been planted in a tub with the hope that it would climb over our porch, but it never grew enough to gain a grasp on its trellis. Each spring it would throw out a cluster of shoots, which would grow a foot or more and then, in May or June, shrivel and blacken before any flowers appeared. I moved it to different sites, but it never improved. Ironically, it probably died in its most favourable position; this summer, for the first time, it managed to throw out a sprinkling of red blossoms, which had a gloriously sweet scent, but then it declined and dried up.

Looking at its twisted, withered skeleton, I could easily retrace its calamitous odyssey round the garden: each abortive spurt of growth was registered in a thick, stunted stem, with its own shock of desiccated shoots. Its death, though a good riddance in every practical respect, saddened me deeply, because I could also read in its crippled branches the sequence of our history here in the house: the years our children were born and the year my first book was published. This visible record of the accretion of their growth, which climbing species show especially clearly, is what makes the presence of particular plants in our lives so affecting – and so essential. Their parallel existence, intimately observed and nurtured, goes some way to ease the overshadowing knowledge of our own finite passage through time. Conservation is not only an ecological, but a psychological imperative too, and I do not think it is fanciful to talk of our having a need, in fact an indispensable need, of a direct, personal involvement with some aspect of nature. At the least, it can be said that we are saner, more contented people when we have the chance to enjoy a close familiarity with a small, parish-sized patch of countryside, in which we can plant our own experience, watching it grow and become over-grown.

Just as a village values its church and other historic buildings as symbols of the community's endurance, so each of us cherishes the private symbols of his or her own security in time and place. The charm of a parish church derives from the fact that the history of its village is to be seen uniquely represented, layer by layer, in the accumulation of its styles, additions and alterations, and in the cluttering-up of its tombs and treasures. These buildings are a testament to survival in the face of change, as well as survival by means of change. In the same way, it is nature's misericords, more than its marvels and vistas, that console and reassure us by marking in the singularity of their form the passage of our individual history and endurance.

The ordinary places and objects that make up our everyday land-scape, our personal countryside, stand as living monuments to our continuing survival and feeling response to the world. Without such monuments, and they are not necessarily a rural monopoly, our sense of identity begins to crumble and warp. We need little, low, unspec-tacular corners, which can carry special resonances for us alone. These local views and familiar landmarks, these commonplace flora and fauna, are the more valuable for being easily accessible. Like the Lincoln seats, they can be seen, touched and understood in the course of our daily round. The plants and creatures that populate our local landscape give significance to our lives simply by changing and enduring beside us, witnessing our experience, while always baring the intimacy of their own to our eyes and ears. They age with us and yet are constantly reborn; they are killed and rot at our feet, only to spring up again next year. The robin that nests in the niche of a bridge we cross every day is dead before a tenth of our life is spent, but our lifespan is hardly enough to grow the upper branch of an oak tree. All this complex intermingling of our emotions and their reflection in nature makes possible the birth of a powerful sense of rootedness and meaning in a world which other-wise yields little but confusion and futility. By conserving the mass of precious detail in our parishes, we conserve ourselves.

In the same way as the environment is suffering from a gross diminution in the variety of its life forms, our means of self-expression are being taken away, making it less and less possible for all but the most fortunate to fulfil their potentiality as creative, loving and social beings. Where they have not actually collapsed, ordinary family and social relations appear to be growing more brutal, while our inter-national relations are becoming uncontrollably murderous. An ever-encroaching uniformity is causing time and place to lose their distinctiveness, and work, when it is to be had, gives the majority no chance of using either imagination or initiative. Change at every level, but especially technological change, now happens at a speed and with a conclusiveness that leave us unable to absorb and digest our own history; we are helplessly whirled along like leaves in its slipstream.

Our loss of familiarity with nature is only one of these constrictions on our humanity, and it has to be admitted that a successful conservation programme, in itself, would not usher in a new, liberated phase of history. On the other hand, a renewal of our relationship with nature, which on a limited basis is within the reach of our present institutions, would be inseparable from a greatly sharpened awareness, if nothing else, of the other forces belittling our capacity for self-realisation.

As *homo sapiens* evolved, the formation of his unique mind was inextricably bound up with his anthropomorphic perception of the physical world, from which a newly dawned self-consciousness had only recently put him apart. The behaviour and appearance of animal prey and predators, the vicissitudes of the weather, the motion of the stars, the power and regularity of the sun, the mysterious variability of the moon – all these and every other observed feature of their environment provided primitive humans with material for the symbolic systems, and mythologies, which they invented in order to understand the world and their destiny. Religion and science – magic and the daily business of survival – were indivisible.

The objects of thought on which the human mind nourished itself as it matured were inevitably drawn from the natural world. In time, of course, with the sophistication of human technics and society, nature came to be invested with very different sorts of significance, though certain traditions of symbolism, deriving from our ancient agricultural past, have survived even into our own time. For instance, a clear line of heritage can be traced from the earliest religions of pastoral tribes through to Christianity's Good Shepherd and Lamb of God. However, this is by no means to infer than an immutable attachment to natural or agricultural symbols became rooted in the human psyche. The extreme longevity shown by some complex symbols only goes to illustrate the essentially conservative make-up of the mind, which prefers to use the same material over and again, reshaping it to meet different ends, rather than turn to something new. What I am suggesting, however, is that a predisposition for natural symbols has embedded itself at the deepest level in our *poetic* sensibility, and that this is partly the result of the pre-eminent suitability of these symbols and partly the result of their ancient familiarity.

Even over a period as brief as the last four hundred years our attitudes to the natural world have undergone a complete reversal, from the Elizabethan belief, sanctioned by Genesis, in the earth being created solely for Man's benefit and pleasure, to our modern ideas of conservation, 'speciesism' and so on. However, throughout these years, nature has nevertheless prevailed as the richest source of metaphor concerning the human condition. The cycle of life and death in nature has continued to offer the most accessible and the most emotive representation of our biological fate. This metaphysical view of nature helps us to reconcile ourselves to those aspects of our flesh-and-blood being which are least compatible with our self-knowing intelligence. By identifying our feelings and experience with animal behaviour and the rhythms of renewal and decay in plants, we give meaning to the key moments in our existence, and avoid surrendering to paranoia in the face of our mortality and vulnerability to suffering. It is almost impossible to think of these biologically determined episodes – birth, growth sexual bonding, ageing, sickness and death, all areas of experience which are the special province of religious interpretation – without resorting to symbolism drawn from the life processes of other organic beings.

Ever since the eighteenth century, nature has been perceived as an alternative symbolic order to Christianity: in lieu of a dogma capable of authorising a credible explanation for existence and its purpose, nature could at least be revered as the supreme expression of those qualities we struggle to bring to our own lives: beauty, harmony and growth. And yet at the time when we have most need of its metaphorical resources, we suddenly discover that nature is failing us, or rather we are failing nature by destroying it. It is in this sense that I believe we can claim to have our own indispensable *cultural* need of conservation, which exists alongside our obvious material need, but requires more urgent recognition. Apart from all other consequences, the loss of each species or habitat from countryside amounts to a blow struck at our own identity.

The experience of loss, because it tends to foreshadow death, either of ourselves or those we love, is one of the hardest for us to bear; the longing to keep things as they stand is thus a reaction to our biological condition, and to some degree a denial of it. On the other hand, our desire to conserve does not only arise from our painful response to loss. The paradox of our nature is that we are both irrepressibly innovative and profoundly conservative: we are restless opportunists, for ever working to find new ways of improving our lot, yet at the same time we are ineluctably reliant on experience and tradition. Without an elaborately preserved tradition of skills, values, mores and paradigms of knowledge, society could not function and the individual could not fully develop his or her abilities.

In our society today this matrix of tradition has all but fallen apart: the notion of family as the fundamental core of social loyalty is no longer respected; ethical absolutes are derided; most forms of work no longer offer any creative exchange; religion is often the refuge of neurotics and fanatical crackpots; and the so-called liberal arts are disappearing into a cultural deep space invaded by nothing more nourishing to the imagination than the spectres of electronic entertainment. Under the circumstances, the need to preserve our wildlife and countryside is nothing short of imperative, for no other body of symbolic reference can fill as much of the void left by the collapse of this connective tradition as can rural nature.

While it is easy to scoff at the whimsicality and commercialism of rural nostalgia, it is also vital to acknowledge that this reaching-out to the countryside is an expression, however distorted, of a healthy desire to find some sense of meaning and relief in a world that seems increasingly bent on mindless annihilation. The countryside has come to stand as a complex symbol not only of what has already been lost from our society, both natural and man-made, but of everything that must at all costs be saved from destruction in the future. An uncongenial present no doubt always prompts a sense of loss and envy in relation to the past; certainly, the recent years of humiliating recession have induced an especially intense manifestation of these feelings. Moreover, it is only natural that we should look back to a seemingly richer past when the future promises nothing but a race to global extinction, the loss of history itself, between the two diabolical powers of nuclear and ecological destruction.

As an arch-symbol of growth and peace, the countryside stands opposed to these forces of death, and that in itself is a crucial argument for conservation. But the countryside also has an essential role to play in any planning for an improved future in which the spiritual and creative side of our nature is to be properly fulfilled. In this context, it becomes meaningful to talk of 'radical nostalgia'.

The word 'nostalgic' is commonly used to describe a sickly attitude to the past, a perversion of historical or biographical truth for the sake of cheap or gratuitous feelings, and nowadays it carries almost entirely pejorative connotations. Curiously enough, this usage does not conform with the dictionary definition of nostalgia, and it really refers to a specialised kind of sentimentality, for which a separate term does not exist in English. The word's original meaning is indicated by its etymology: the Greek *nostos*, meaning return home, and *algos*, meaning pain. Thus, it means home-sickness, or, to quote the full *O.E.D.* definition, 'a form of melancholia caused by prolonged absence from one's home or country'. No secondary definition is given in the dictionary to cover its current, despicable sense.

Of course, the 'home-sickness' of nostalgia is usually applied metaphorically to one's childhood or a period in the past coinciding with the childhood years of a middle-aged generation. The chief accusation brought against nostalgia is that it falsifies by sugaring the past on which it feeds: the boring, painful and dishonourable parts are all ruthlessly forgotten or sentimentalised, while the agreeable parts are grossly inflated, even imagined. Following from this is a second charge, that nostalgia is at bottom defeatist, and therefore in effect reactionary. Instead of spinning dreams of a better future, its response to present evils and discomforts is to surrender to them and seek consolation by escaping into a fallacious past. As I put it myself some years ago, in my book *Strange Land*, 'Although the past is the medium it haunts, nostalgia recognises no duty to history; to this extent it is a dishonest emotion.'

While I would still agree with this, I now believe that there is another dimension to nostalgia and that it should not be dismissed simply as a self-indulgent, escapist and pernicious failing. Whereas its account of history is patently untrue, and more ideological than it would pretend, it does none the less express a truth of its own, which reflects an authentic and deeply felt emotion. Its vision of the past, the home for which it pines, can be thought of more fruitfully as a metaphor, to which historiographic and biographical criteria do not apply.

Like many emotions, nostalgia is ambivalent. Our addiction to it is surely a symptom of our failure to make a satisfactory mode of life in the present, but perhaps it can also be seen as evidence of our desire to repair and revitalise our broken relations. The pastoral fantasy nostalgia has invented is after all an image of a world in which men and women feel at home with themselves, with each other and with nature, a world in which harmony reigns. It is an ideal, and an illusion, but one which gives comfort, for reality cannot be continuously endured head-on. The fact that it is conjured out of material remotely derived from rural history, and less remotely from certain persistent myths about the English countryside, does not detract from its value as a dream of a better, kinder, more connected way of life.

Our obsession with wildlife is no less ambivalent: in many respects it is unquestionably escapist, and yet even anthropomorphism can have its positive side. The inexhaustible creativity shown by plants and animals in response to the universal demands of existence, a creativity with which the legendary figure of 'the countryman' is identified, can be perceived as a symbol of the potentiality that resides in all of us. Achievements in nature can be interpreted as poetic models of both individual and social possibility, which if translated into human terms would transfigure our being. Nature, in other words, remains our richest storehouse of hope, and nostalgia, though it does not speak with a clear voice, or even one voice, is nevertheless an expression of that hope.

Cathedrals have also been the object of nostalgic fantasy, for they have been thought of as the products of purely communal effort, built by people whose shared belief in God inspired them to feats of engineering and decoration beyond the capability of a more fragmented community. This account contains its own sentimentality and shares in the mythology of the 'organic community', which is so attractive to ruralism. Yet, whatever the truth of their construction, cathedrals continue to represent to us a supreme flowering of human genius, testifying not so much to the power of Christianity, though that is indisputable, as to the power of the inspired human imagination. Our admiration, for Lincoln cathedral, or any other ecclesiastical building, is strictly aesthetic, but then it is the aesthetic impulse, more than any other, which today leads us to create visions of an alternative reality within the accepted, established one, just as the religious impulse did in previous centuries. Our secular sensibility can also respond with the same aesthetic radicalism to the living tissue of nature, seeing in its symbolism the prospect and promise of a redeemable future. In a world that seems inescapably destined for some horrific climacteric before the onset of a new dark age of sterility in nature and barbarism in man, the countryside, and all we associate with it may yet help to bring forth a new, life-loving humanity and secure our deliverance.

William Hazlitt showed his usual intuitive wisdom when he wrote in his essay, *On the Love of the Countryside*, of nature being 'a kind of universal home'. Presumably, we all want to attain some version of the 'content and mutual harmony' which he found in the countryside, and we certainly want to find our home in good order when we make our return. However, what must be conserved before anything else is the desire in ourselves for Home – for harmony, peace and love, for growth in nature and in our imaginative powers – because unless we keep this alive, we shall lose everything.

FEBRUARY

MAY

JULY

PAUL HILL

NOVEMBER

The Golden Age of Labour

BY JOHN BARRELL

'The past is a foreign country', said L. P. Hartley. This is never more true than when we try to look back to that golden age of our own pastoral past; to the Britain which had seemed so stable, so timeless and unchanging until the inventions of man and manufactory altered beyond recall both the face of town and country and the whole fabric of society.

I

More than in any other country of Europe, the enjoyment of the countryside and of country life in England seems to have been, for the last 400 years or so, a retrospective enjoyment: however much pleasure the English take in the contemplation of country life, it is a pleasure attenuated by the sense that, 20 or 50 or 100 years ago, it would have been greater still. Much of our enjoyment consists in the discovery of signs of a past age which have survived the encroachments – and that is what they seem to be – of the present; for in the understanding of most of us, the country is to the town as the past is to the present. No one is more aware of this than the advertising copywriter, whether he is selling beer, the advantages of moving to Milton Keynes or (as in the case of the paragraph I have just borrowed) a three-volume edition of Defoe's *Tour through the Whole Island of Great Britain*, bound in buckram, with pictorial slip-case and (for members of the National Trust) a free, 'full colour print of Robert Morden's 1695 map of England'. In fact, of course, Defoe is one of the least nostalgic of writers on the topography of Britain: the country he describes is not at all 'timeless and unchanging', and his main interest was to record with enthusiasm the signs of economic development. But whoever wrote that paragraph knew that *any* aspect of the rural past can be used as evidence against the present, and to suggest that the world we have lost was a golden world.

The form in which the Golden Age appears to us, however, changes continually, and at any one time there may be competing versions of it which serve the different interests in society; for though golden ages are almost always defined as periods in which, among other things, the social order was 'natural', before the emergence of political conflict, they are always defined politically, if only in the sense that what is 'natural' to one person or class is always 'political' to another. In most periods of history, however, one particular version of the Golden Age of rural society has been predominant; and in the last decade the dominant image seems to me to have been shifting forward slightly in time, from the era of Constable, where it had been located for a good few years, to a period beginning some time after the invention of photography, and ending with the invention – or widespread diffusion – of the combine harvester.

I use the word 'image' deliberately, for it is very much in terms of visual imagery, and of visual images that do not move, that this version of the Golden Age has been developed. Thus it has both prompted and been promoted by the publication, particularly in the last fifteen years or so, of countless books of old black-and-white photographs of this or that place as it used to be. The photographs are as often of urban as of rural life – of shopkeepers posing outside their shops, of almost empty streets unblurred by moving figures – but it is the images of the countryside that concern me here, which are (sometimes for technical reasons) equally static and frozen. Bearded old farm workers, in suits of worn corduroy or crumpled flannel, stand stock-still, ramrod-straight, arms by their sides, heads slightly tilted. Sometimes they clutch the instruments of their work. Sometimes, even, they appear to be working, their bending figures, as they stoop to mow or to bind, curiously sharp against the wind-tossed fuzz of corn. These authentic records of a better life have the power, it seems, to take most of the effort out of old-style rural employment. Much of the time was passed, apparently, in the intervals from labour, and labour itself was a picturesque affair, and mostly a matter of striking stately attitudes. The photographs always suggest the importance of work in this 'bygone' way of life, but always in such a way as to conceal its difficulty.

By that very process of concealment, however, they become able to reveal to us another aspect of rural work, one which would remain hidden from us had pre-1914 photographers been at first willing, and later able, more fully to capture the movement of figures: I am thinking of what we call (with however much embarrassment) the 'dignity' of labour. In the century before the invention of photography, the theory and practice of the visual arts had developed the notion that dignity is communicated to a figure by representing it in respose, or at least in an attitude that can be held – the point will be clear if we compare the carefully posed figures painted by an artist like Stubbs, with the hectic and certainly undignified energy that characterises the figures of Gillray or Rowlandson. This notion, still thoroughly influential on early photographers, made a virtue out of technical necessity, and gave them the opportunity to represent the limitations of their technology in the positive light of a particularly exalted mode of perception, one capable of discovering a dignity in movements which, had it been possible to capture them in all their swirl and energy, would have seemed much less than dignified.

So much valued was this mode of perception that it continued to influence the photography of labour long after the technological impediments to the representation of labour had been overcome. And to the extent that the connection of dignity and repose is still influential, early photographs of rural workers offer us, too, a notion of the dignity of labour: a dangerous notion, always, in so far as it can be offered as a compensation for low wages and long hours, or when it acts to obscure a sense of their own worth in those who cannot work; but an indispensable notion also, and more so now, in the context of the ruthless politics of the 1980s, than it has been for more than forty years. And, in that context, the image of the Golden Age I am considering has a paradoxical kind of virtue, the ability to communicate a moral value by a distortion of actuality.

Or rather, it would have such a virtue, if it could persuade us to look at the agricultural worker of the 1980s with the same respect as we look on the image of his predecessors – if it could persuade us, indeed, to look at him at all. If it fails to do so, this is partly because – and I am looking for reasons here within the phenomenology of the imagery itself, rather than in terms of the political interests that may promote it – of the supervention of another component of the Golden Age, by which all pre-industrial forms of manual work are coming to be understood as 'traditional skills' or as 'crafts', while the modern forms of work that have replaced them are just work or labour. This aspect of the Golden Age is clearly related to the revival of interest, largely middle-class, in various crafts such as pottery, hand-weaving, or whatever else can be carried on as a cottage industry, but the term 'craft' can now be found applied to all sorts of non-artisanal work, and to all kinds of old agrarian work in particular. In a representative collection of old photographs of my own county, it appears that rural 'crafts' included threshing with a flail, reaping, drilling wheat, cutting turf, loading it on to a barrow, and ditching. And the particular alchemy of the word is that, just like those old photographs, it takes all the sweat and most of the energy out of labour. 'Like all other trades and crafts', reads one of the series of Shire

Albums which has been influential in promoting this view of the past, 'the drovers developed their own folklore and superstitions and sang their own work songs and ballads as they rode or tramped with the cattle across the hills.'

The difficulty involved in ploughing, for example, was apparently of the kind represented only by the determination to keep the furrow straight – of the kind, that is, that can be overcome more by a knowledge of the 'craft' than by the expense of strength and stamina; the laying of hedges was an exercise of skill and patience, but not, it seems, of the particular kind of patience required to work in the cold, the wet, and the mud. My point is not that many such tasks didn't involve the exercise of great skill – they did, and the increasing habit of using the word 'craft' to describe them is an act of retrospective justice to workers whose skills were certainly undervalued when they were in demand. But the justice is retrospective only: modern agricultural workers are initiated, it seems, into no comparable crafts or mysteries, and if one function of the word is to dignify labour by emphasising skill and minimising effort, then to withhold the term from modern agricultural work is to deny that it has any dignity at all.

There may indeed be a certain political convenience in doing just that, and what it might be I shall consider later in this essay. For the moment I want simply to stress that work, however dignified by being represented as craft and not as labour, is an essential component of our modern, dominant image of the Golden Age. For it wasn't always so, and in fact, with a few exceptions here and there, the ideas of the Golden Age and of the work involved in agricultural production were for a long time treated as incompatible, and the more industrious the rural worker was believed to be, the more apparent it became that he had left the Golden Age behind. I want to consider now the process by which the Golden Age of Labour finally replaced the Golden Age of Leisure, for it is salutary sometimes to reflect upon the origins of the myths that are important to us, however unpleasant they may turn out to be.

II

In fact, of course, ideas don't have identifiable beginnings: a history of the Golden Age of Labour could be taken at least as far back as Virgil. Old ideas do, however, develop new applications, and to understand how it came about that our modern idea of the Golden Age is of an age of labour, the most convenient place to begin is in the eighteenth and early nineteenth centuries, when the representation of rural life in art and literature came to be perceived as a political, and not simply as an artistic or literary, issue. So I shall choose as my starting point the publication, in 1770, of Oliver Goldsmith's poem 'The Deserted Village'. The poem is one of the best known in our literature, and there's no need here to describe it in detail; but, briefly, it is concerned with the recent impark-ment of the village of 'Auburn', and the consequent eviction of its inhabitants.

Goldsmith's account of the life of the villagers before this catastrophe occurred does everything it can to minimise the importance of work as an element of rural life. He hardly mentions the labour his villagers perform except to show them not, actually, performing it — his interest is in the periods 'when toil remitting lent its turn to play', and so his images of the former inhabitants of Auburn are almost exclusively images of them relaxing — sitting beneath a hawthorn tree, dancing on the green, or drinking in the ale-house — and the easy-paced rhythm of the village life before it was destroyed apparently affected the poet as well, who describes how he used to 'loiter' on the green, and 'pause' to contemplate the landscape. This absence of labour in a village which, according to Goldsmith, enjoyed an almost perpetual summer, has led a number of commentators on the poem to dismiss it as an entirely unbelievable pastoral fiction, in which the poet, in his anxiety to elicit our sympathy for the suffering of the dispossessed villagers, has felt it necessary to conceal their involvement in all those dirty jobs which many eighteenth-century readers thought too ignoble to be described in the elevated language of poetry.

That is, indeed, exactly what Goldsmith has done, but not all that he has done. If we read carefully the opening description of the village, and compare it with other, similar descriptions in the poetry contemporary with it, we will be struck by the absence of one particular feature that in other poems we would almost invariably find there — the hall. There was, it seems, no great house in Auburn until after its imparkment, and the building of the hall was the occasion of the destruction of the village. The impression is that Auburn was once almost a little 'republic' of peasants (we shall meet that term again later), and it is confirmed soon afterwards by Goldsmith's identification of the way of life which had, until recently, been enjoyed at Auburn, with the myth of the egalitarian life of rural England as it had probably been enjoyed before the Norman Conquest and the imposition of the feudal system:

> A time there was, ere England's griefs began,
> When every rood of ground maintained its man;
> For him light labour spread her wholesome store,
> Just gave what life required, but gave no more.

England, it seems, may once have been what Auburn was until recently: a community of small independent freeholders who, unconcerned with the acquisition of luxuries, with no rent to pay, and with no responsibility to feed an urban population, had no incentive to produce anything surplus to their own immediate and very modest requirements. As a result, the cultivation of their land demanded from them only 'light labour': there was plenty of time to dance, or to sit around chatting and drinking beer. This development in the poem may seem to make it a yet more incredible fiction, but, by a process similar to the one we observed in the case of early photography, the distortion of actuality may have made possible the enunciation of an important moral truth.

In earlier pastoral poetry of the late seventeenth and early eighteenth centuries, the myth of a Golden Age of Leisure, similar to the one that Goldsmith has offered, is everywhere apparent, but with this crucial difference, that it was universally understood that the shepherds represented in pastoral poetry were not to be confused with (in Pope's phrase) shepherds 'as [they] at this day really are'. The 'shepherd's weeds' were either a disguise for courtiers, aristocrats, gentlefolk, or were worn by an entirely imaginary class of poets and graziers who had never existed in actuality, or they were the uniform of shepherds from a remote, usually Mediterranean Golden Age before the development of class and occupational difference, when 'the best of men follow'd the calling' (Pope again). But whatever the case, the shepherds of Pastoral were certainly never to be mistaken for the smallholders and agricultural workers of contemporary England, who were altogether too 'clownish' to appear in anything but burlesque versions of the genre; and the leisure enjoyed by the shepherds of Pastoral was understood to be in sharp contrast to the laborious tasks performed by the lower classes of English rural society.

But this separation between ideal and actuality, which was essential to the fictions of Pastoral if they were to have any slight degree of plausibility, in fact made them seem less and less plausible during the course of the eighteenth century. The economic expansion of a newly 'great' Britain, and of British agriculture in particular, seems to have generated a demand for a poetry of rural life more able to represent, and to promote, that expansion, and not least to emphasise the importance of labour if that expansion was to be maintained. The genre of poetry particularly adapted to perform this task, the Georgic, began to take on a greater importance than old-style rural Pastoral: it suggested that the Golden Age was the modern age, an age of industriousness, and it increasingly represented the workers in British agriculture as working, and as happy to be so. In a certain, obvious sense, this poetry was a good deal more 'realistic' than earlier Pastoral had been, but the function of this realism was not simply to *describe* more accurately the labours of the poor, but to *prescribe* them more accurately as well.

The rural workforce, that is, were represented as working not simply because that was, in fact, what most of the time they did, but also because that was what they should do, what it was their duty to do, if the capitalist agrarian and mercantile economy was to continue to flourish and develop. And as the century got older, and the problems of the proletarianisation and pauperisation of the lower classes of rural society became more evident to the polite, the duty of the poor to labour became increasingly insisted upon, in poetry, in painting, in sermons, and in social philosophy. Only by such means could the incomes of the rich be safeguarded, and the demands on the charity of the rich, enforced or voluntary, be kept within limits. The complaints of the poor were countered by the insistence that their condition was a 'natural' one: they were born to be labourers, and their duty was to perform that function as conscientiously as possible, and not to seek to change or escape it.

In this context, we can understand more clearly the significance of the representation of rural life in Auburn as a life of leisure, broken only by 'light labour'. For Goldsmith had mixed two aspects of the poetry of rural life in a compound whose potential volatility slowly became evident to a number of readers of the poem. To begin with, he had taken over the image of rural life as one of leisure (a leisure which could legitimately be enjoyed only by aristocrats and Arcadians), and he had taken over also the notion that the poetry of rural life should now be concerned with the representation of rural life in contemporary England. The result was a poem which could be read to suggest not that the poor had a duty to work, but that they had a right to leisure; and far from representing their condition as 'natural', it could be understood to be suggesting that, in the past, the rural economy had been so organised as to promote that right – and even, perhaps, to be hinting that it should be so organised again.

For various reasons, the volatile potential of the poem was not noticed until more than twenty years after its publication: the separation of Arcadian shepherd from rural worker was less complete in 1770 than it was later to become, so that Goldsmith's idle peasants may have been understood, when the poem was first published, more in terms of traditional pastoral fiction than of present (or *recently* past) actuality. A greater freedom of speculation on social and political topics was permissible in 1770 than in 1800; and the problems of poverty and of labour discipline in the country were perceived more acutely at the end of the century than when Goldsmith was writing. But when, in 1807, Crabbe

published 'The Parish Register', the dangerous implications of Goldsmith's poem were perfectly clear to him:

> Is there a place, save one the Poet sees,
> A land of love, of liberty and ease;
> Where labour wearies not, nor cares suppress
> Th' eternal flow of rustic happiness;
> Where no proud mansion frowns in awful state,
> Or keeps the sunshine from the cottage-gate;
> Where Young and Old, intent on pleasure, throng,
> And half man's life is holiday and song ?
> Vain search for scenes like these ! no view appears
> By sighs unruffled or unstain'd by tears;
> Since vice the world subdued and waters drown'd,
> *Auburn* and *Eden* can no more be found.

By the end of this passage, the generalised 'poet' of the first line has
been particularised as Goldsmith, and the charge that Crabbe brings
against him is not simply that he is nostalgic for a Golden Age of Leisure
that never existed, but that his nostalgia is touched by a delusive and
levelling radicalism.

As far as Crabbe was concerned, though we might well pity the
labourer's hard life, it was unwise and even fraudulent to invite him, as
Goldsmith seemed to have done, to see himself as anything other than a
labourer: he must simply reconcile himself to his lot. His condition is
not, however, hopeless – at least, not if, having accepted its
inevitability, he then seeks, not to change, of course, but to improve it.
For 'Toil, care and patience bless th' abstemious few', and the 'industrious swain', who is not taken in by the fraudulent pastoralism of
Goldsmith, could hope to find in Crabbe's parish a place in the sun, a
neat cottage where 'the sun's last ray/Smiles on the window and
prolongs the day'. All agricultural workers will be poor, it seems, but
the virtuous less poor than the rest.

Crabbe's attack on Goldsmith is only the most unguarded statement
of a general agreement among writers of the late eighteenth and early
nineteenth centuries that the Golden Age of Leisure was either a
dangerous fiction, or one unworthy of the poor, who deserve our
admiration more or less in direct proportion to the vigour with which
they embrace their identity as members of the *labouring* poor. Such
sentiments, in one form or another, are to be found in the poems of
William Cowper, for example, of Robert Southey, of a host of lesser
poets and, in a more thoughtful and complex way, in the writings of
Wordsworth. When the 'female vagrant', in Wordsworth's poem of that

name, finds herself destitute of food and shelter, her wants are relieved
by some gypsies, who describe their life to her in these terms:

> How kindly did they paint their vagrant ease !
> And their long holiday that feared not grief,
> For all belonged to all, and each was chief.
> No plough their sinews strained; on grating road
> No wain they drove, and yet, the yellow sheaf
> In every vale for their delight was stowed:
> For them, in nature's meads, the milky udder flowed.

The gypsies, by their own account, appear to enjoy the same life of
idleness as Goldsmith's 'bold peasantry' enjoyed, and they enjoy a
comparable social and economic equality as well, which was, in many
versions of it, a particular feature of golden age society. But as Crabbe
and a number of other contemporary writers make clear, this image of a
Golden Age of Leisure, and of equality, was being adopted, around
1800, as a politically radical image, not only of life as it once was, but of
life as it might be again, if the property of the rich could be confiscated. It
is appropriate, then, that the female vagrant should point out that the
actual − and the only possible − foundation of the 'long holiday'
enjoyed by the gypsies is theft, burglary, and poaching, for only by such
means could they get a living from the English countryside in the 1790s
(a place of growing insistence on labour discipline, of punitive game
laws, and of the accelerating enclosure of wastes and commons),
without resorting to the only legitimate alternative open to them, wage
labour.

The point in underlined by the fact that the lines I have quoted would
have been recognised by contemporary readers as an imitation of a
passage in James Thomson's immensely popular poem 'The Castle of
Indolence', in which the Wizard of Indolence attempts to persuade
whoever will listen to him that the Golden Age of Leisure can still be
enjoyed in eighteenth-century Britain. To such an extent is he successful that it requires vigorous intervention from the Knight of Industry to
get everyone back to work, and to restore the social order to its properly
harmonious, hierarchical, and natural form. The lines in Thomson are
in turn derived from the Sermon on the Mount: 'Behold the fowls of the
air; for they sow not, neither do they reap, nor gather into barns; yet
your heavenly Father feedeth them. Are ye not much better than they ?'
The best that can be said for this and the following verses is that they
had to be interpreted with great care and ingenuity if they were not to be
understood as questioning the attempts of agrarian capitalism to discipline its labour force, and Thomson and the female vagrant were

showing a sensible measure of discretion in choosing simply to discredit them.

For the most part, however, Wordsworth's attitude to the Golden Age of rural leisure, and to the necessity of dignity of labour, was a good deal more complex than those of his contemporaries. In Book VIII of *The Prelude*, he compares the 'smooth life' of shepherds he had seen near Goslar, in Germany, with the life of those in the lakeland fells. The account of the former, introduced, appropriately, by a series of references to the world of classical Pastoral, describes their life as one of 'unlaborious pleasure, with no task/More toilsome than to carve a beechen bowl'. There is no explicit suggestion, as there sometimes is in Wordsworth's poetry, that such an easy life is morally enervating, and to be rejected; and if it is compared unfavourably with the arduous and demanding life of the shepherds of Cumberland and Westmorland, this is only partly because the dignified poverty of the latter protects them from the dangers that attend a more comfortable life. Just as important are the severity of the weather and landscape, which presents the shepherd with a greater variety of challenges, to his skill as well as to his strength, and the particular distribution of land in the Lake District, by which many of the shepherds were (or appeared to be) freeholders, who were therefore free also to choose how best to dispose of their time and energy, the profits of which all accrued to themselves and their families. The discipline of labour was imposed on them by the only people with a right to impose it, themselves.

For the land in the lakeland dales, Wordsworth explains in his *Guide to the Lakes*, at least until 'within the last sixty years', had been owned and occupied by the members of 'a perfect Republic of Shepherds and Agriculturists, among whom the plough of each man was confined to the maintenance of his own family, or to the occasional accommodation of his neighbour'. Almost every feature of their lives 'exhibited a perfect equality' among them: none had more than 'two or three cows', and 'the chapel was the only edifice that presided over' their dwellings. But 'within the last sixty years' – a phrase repeated like a litany throughout Wordsworth's reflections on the society of the lakes – the decline of the outworker system in woollen manufactures, which provided an employment as important as agriculture to the maintenance of the 'estatemen', has led to the sale and engrossing of farms, which have fallen, or seem likely soon to fall, 'almost entirely into the possession of the gentry'. This new situation might have raised for Wordsworth the problem, by what moral authority can labour now be demanded and disciplined, if not by that of the freeholders who once both performed and profited from it? But this is a problem he does not discuss, and he concentrates instead on elegiac accounts of these freeholders and their

DAVID HOCKNEY *My Mother, Bolton Abbey, Yorkshire, November 1982*

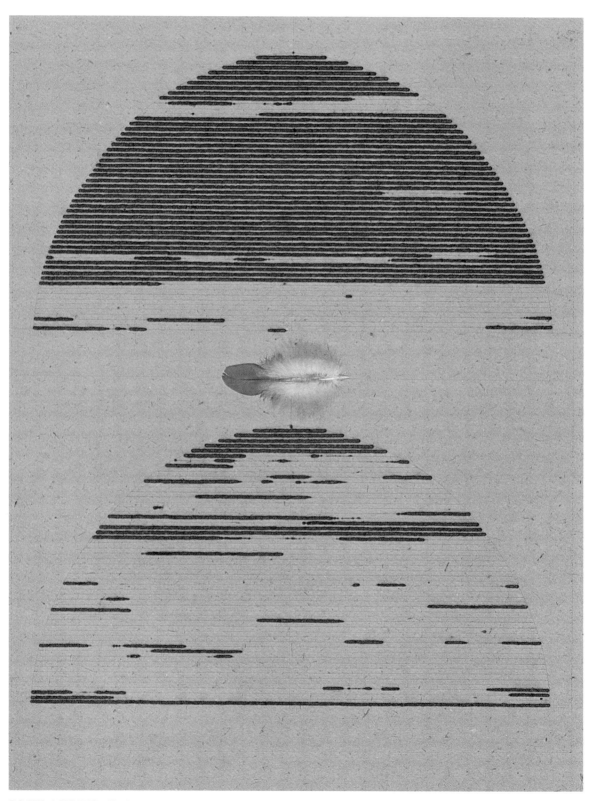

ROGER ACKLING *Cloud Drawing*

disappearance, which imply criticisms of the organisation of the contemporary rural economy that they do not enlarge upon.

If we look back on the phrases I have quoted from the *Guide*, we will see that Wordsworth has developed a notion of a Golden Age of Labour very similar in its structure to Goldsmith's Golden Age of Leisure, in its emphasis on equality, on the absence of symbols or figures of authority, on freeholding, and on the denunciation of luxury – a Golden Age, for Wordsworth, already in the past, and very different in terms of the social and political values it represents from the life represented by Crabbe in 'The Parish Register'. There is a difference of another kind between the attitudes to the poor evident in Crabbe's poem, which is concerned to insist on the duty to labour which the rural poor owe to themselves and to society, and in such poems by Wordsworth as 'The Female Vagrant', which are more concerned to defend the poor from the charge of indiscipline by showing that most of them have no choice but to be aware of that duty and that debt. But by routes however different, the poetry of Wordsworth and Crabbe alike has contributed to the formation of an image of the agricultural worker as repressive as it is (sometimes) benign. To those readers of Wordsworth, over the last 150 or so years, who have read his poetry in the context of the historical process that he hints at but does not spell out, his writing may have represented an attitude to rural labour very like that which I suggested earlier is dominant today – a regret for the passing of a lost ideal, and an unwillingness to consider what has succeeded it. It seems unlikely, however, that the detail of Wordsworth's views has communicated itself to many of his readers, if only because it is to be discovered more easily in his prose than in his poetry; and it is more likely that the general contribution of his poetry to the formation of our attitudes to rural labour has been, like Crabbe's, a good deal more simple. For the work of both writers has certainly reinforced an attitude to the representation of rural life which regards the failure to acknowledge the importance of work as an evasion of actuality.

So of course it is, which is not to say that there was not sometimes a moral and strategic value in that evasion; but the danger of this attitude to representation is that it treats the acknowledgment of the fact of labour as an authenticating mark of realism which, by exposing the image of leisurely rural life as artificial, endorses the counter-image – the rural life of labour – as natural. The idea of rural life that is thus naturalised is not a simple one – it is not an idea, simply of the importance of rural labour and of the necessity of its being performed, but of the dignity of that labour as inseparable from the poverty of those who perform it. This idea invites us to admire the fact that, as Wordsworth puts it, the 'manners' of workers in agriculture are

> ... severe and unadorned,
> The unluxuriant produce of a life
> Intent on little but substantial needs,
> Yet beautiful ...

– and it invites us to believe that the quality of such a life is a direct function of the exiguous quantity of its material rewards.

III

This idea of the necessary relation of rural work and poverty was not of course a new one – it can be traced back almost as far as we care to read. But its use in the literature around 1800 was different from earlier uses, for now it functioned not simply to promote a timeless ideal image of virtuous labour, by which the values of court or city could be measured, but as a statement of how things actually were, one which claimed to be based on a close observation and understanding of history and of the contemporary agricultural worker. The idea is now situated in a poetry which is self-consciously opposed to the fictions of Pastoral, and which asks to be read in specific contemporary contexts: the proletarianisation of rural labour, the problem of rural poverty, and the attempt to keep it under control by a firm insistence on the duty and discipline of labour.

But by the middle of the nineteenth century, the pressure of those contexts was being felt much less acutely. The main, if not the exclusive, concern of writers who exhibit a knowledge of contemporary social issues shifted to the workers in industry; it was they who seemed to carry the burden of England's economic progress, and who seemed capable of threatening it by indiscipline, idleness and revolt. By contrast, and in spite of the urgent attempts of a number of writers on 'the rural question' to arrest the process, the countryside came to be seen as a place whose characteristic was that it was empty of tension, and it became more clearly than ever before a place of the past. In this process, the idea of the rural life as a life of labour, essential to a realist literature, was retained, but at the same time it was distanced; and the image of the patient rural labourer became an image of a time when the quality of life had been more important than material reward. A new Golden Age of Labour was created, which was also a Golden Age of poverty.

As the countryside has come to occupy a smaller and smaller space in our view of the social, economic, and political condition of England, so this cultural inheritance, by which poverty was naturalised along with labour, has continued to influence our perceptions of rural life. It has certainly contributed to a continuing lack of concern about the continuing poverty of agricultural workers, and has thus to some extent acted to justify the economic policies, whether *laissez-faire* or interventionist, by which their earnings have been kept down. If, as I suggested earlier, the Golden Age of Labour is now most visibly embodied in such publications as books of old photographs and Shire Albums, the popularity of those publications is partly to be accounted for by the fact that they offer an image of rural labour more 'natural' than the countryside can offer today. It is more natural not simply because modern farmworkers work with machines – old stationary steam-engines, and even old tractors, seem to fit perfectly well into the image of a natural country life, as far as one can judge from the publications I have spoken of, and the large numbers attracted to rallies of such old machines. A more important component of the 'naturalness' of the Golden Age of Labour is that, by comparison with their modern counterparts (when we can see them at all), the practitioners of those old rural 'crafts', ditching and so on, were far more evidently poor, and their labour, therefore, so much more authentic and dignified. But since then, if there has been a decline in the dignity of agricultural work, that is because there has been an obvious increase in the rewards to the worker, who is now rather better-dressed than his black-and-white predecessor. No need to reflect, then, on the *relative* economic situation of workers in agriculture, to compare their apparent prosperity (when compared with those old photographs) with that of comparably skilled workers in other industries. It is common to hear complaints about the prosperity of farmers, but only rarely do we hear them about the poverty of farmworkers.

In those with a more direct interest in the countryside, the idea that it is natural for agricultural workers to be badly off may produce a more particular kind of unconcern for their well-being. It may combine, for example, with the idea of the countryside as the place of the past, to help justify the opposition to the building of council houses and small factories in villages, and to justify also the economic interests – a desire to keep rates low and house values high – that also prompt that opposition; with the result, when the opposition is successful, that (as the sociologist of rural life Howard Newby has pointed out) farmers have been insulated from competition in the local labour market, and that farm-workers who live in tied cottages have been inhibited from looking for more remunerative employment by the difficulties of changing their homes along with their jobs.

But the image of a Golden Age of labour has been particularly influential on the modern 'back-to-the-land' movement, the advocates of 'voluntary', and, as far as possible, self-sufficient, organic, unmechanised farming. That the nostalgic interest in old rural 'crafts' has been convenient to this movement is obvious enough, for the arguments for returning to the land have certainly been more persuasive, on themselves and on those they would proselytise, in the context of this nostalgia. But it is a nostalgia which, whatever the value of the images it offers of the past and of a potential future, seems inevitably to undervalue the skills of modern agricultural workers. 'Too many farm workers', writes one self-sufficient, 'spend too many days in a tractor cab and never touch the soil'; thus they never learn the 'ancient wisdom of nature', the 'secrets of the soil' that were known to their predecessors, and any secrets or wisdom they *do* learn – how to operate and maintain sophisticated machinery, or how to perform a wider range of tasks than those predecessors were called upon to understand – are a false acquisition, to be shunned like the fruit of the Tree of Knowledge. If for Tess of the D'Urbervilles in the age of steam, threshing was a job which made almost impossible demands on the stamina of those who fed the insatiable appetite of the machine, and endured its deafening noise and ceaseless shaking, for a modern self-sufficient it was 'an arduous . . . but joyful experience', 'abominably dusty . . . but the fun and excitement . . . made up for it all'. For this writer, the rot set in with the invention of the binder, 'which spoiled a lot of the fun' of harvest. And now that reaping and threshing are combined in a single operation, 'the harvest field is a boring affair of huge machines . . . driven round by dusty and noise-deafened men'. The implication of such a view of modern farm work is fairly clear: work which is denounced as boring cannot also be skilful, for to the back-to-the-land men the exercise of a skill is the greatest of pleasures; but as the only skills they acknowledge are the 'authentic' and 'traditional' rural skills, all modern forms of farm work must be unskilled, must be boring. It is worth pointing out that Newby, in his interviews of Suffolk farm-workers, found none who regretted 'the way in which mechanization has removed much of the physical effort and routine drudgery that used to be involved in working on a farm'; and that, however boring and lonely modern farm work might be, in particular during the weeks of ploughing, in general they regarded it as more varied, more skilled, and more responsible than it had been formerly. Such testimony only goes to prove, I suppose, to back-to-the-land men, that farm-workers must be liberated from the burdens of insensitivity and ignorance imposed on them by the processes of modernisation; but the insensitivity is not all on one side.

IV

I should like to conclude with some more general reflections on the dangers of the notion of a Golden Age of the rural past as it manifests itself in the writing of self-sufficients and conservationists. I can best sum these up in advance by suggesting that, though there may be a considerable value in representing images of a golden rural past as images of how life might be, once again, in a golden future, their use in this way seems often to be accompanied by a distaste for the kind of action – political action – which might do something to realise the possibility of that future; and that in any case such images tend to appeal to a nostalgic sentimentality in people of various persuasions, of a kind which cannot be relied upon to bring them together in any concerned political attempt to change the way the countryside is owned and managed.

An idea of the unwillingness of many advocates of conservation and self-sufficiency to consider the political dimension of their aspirations can be derived from the visions of the future they so frequently offer. It is not often a future that has to be worked for, or argued or campaigned for: it is too golden a future for that, and it just happens. According to one writer, 'when the cities can no longer be sustained and people come to their senses', the move back to the land, in search of the old wisdom, will . . . just happen. According to another, one day

> the huge and empty farms will be broken up again, and homesteads will grow up on them, and the land will become populous again and people will live as they are meant to live, close to Old Mother Nature, for surely this is the course suggested to us by that other Old Mother I have referred to many times in this book: Old Mother Common Sense.

A third writer dreams (and does at least acknowledge it as a fantasy) of a future perfect, a golden age re-established when farmers

> began leasing out their land in strips along lines that were scarcely distinguishable from the medieval open field system. The most eager tenants were health-food enthusiasts from north London and the Stour Valley, many of whom gave up the dole to tend their vast new allotments.

'The change', he says, 'happened quite quickly.' Various scenarios are proposed by which this change comes about: perhaps the C.A.P. will collapse and with it the price of land; or people will get increasingly bored with life in towns and cities, so that the trickle of families moving back to the land becomes (and without, it seems, much opposition from monopoly capital) a torrent. The most favoured scenario seems to be that one day soon the oil, for fertilisers and fuel, will run out. All of these futures have this in common, that an upheaval of some sort occurs, whether in the availability of natural resources, the cost of modern farming methods, or simply in the consciousness of city-dwellers, after which, as it were inevitably, large numbers are enabled, or obliged, to return to the land, each family to its ten-acre plot, where they discover the arduous delights of self-sufficiency or community living.

There's no space here to consider all these scenarios, so I will say a word only about the most popular. It is no doubt possible that reserves of oil will run out before any alternative, equally cheap and versatile, sources of energy are discovered, if ever they are. It is not a prospect I look forward to with quite the enthusiasm that many conservationists regard it with, not least because it seems more likely to lead to global war than to a peaceful redistribution of agricultural land. But suppose war is avoided. If and when the oil runs out, or becomes, before that, prohibitively expensive, it is almost impossible to predict what consequences this will have for the economic, social and political structure of Britain. But there are two predictions I would make with little hesitation. The first is that, short of a political revolution, the price and rent of land will not decline in real terms, for land will become no less valuable a commodity than it is now: so that whatever movement back to the land may be necessary to attempt to increase a drastically reduced food supply, it is far more likely to swell the numbers of an impoverished class of agricultural workers than of a class of small landowners and tenant farmers. The second is that, in so far as the possible futures of this country can be determined by its inhabitants, they will be determined by conflict among those able and willing to organise politically. The self-sufficient future will not just happen.

If I have little expectation that the British conservationist and back-to-the-land movements will be either able or willing to engage in concerted political activity, this is because they seem, for the most part, so unable or unwilling to do so now. The difficulties in the way of their doing so are of course extremely great. I would not be at all surprised if a poll showed that there was a large majority in favour of, say, the introduction of planning controls on farmers, and a reduction of certain kinds of subsidies to them, in the interests of conservation. I should be thoroughly surprised, however, if in the foreseeable future even a considerable minority regarded such a policy as anything but a very minor issue, of far less importance that the main issues in terms of which they decide their political affiliations. To attempt to mobilise, into a political movement, a generally diffused (and, at the level of its general diffusion, a thoroughly nostalgic) conservationist sentiment, would no doubt have the effect of exposing how weak that sentiment is. For whatever concern may be felt in Britain for the future of the countryside has been so much fostered by an appeal to the past, that it can't find expression in political terms: it is in the nature of rural nostalgia that, in referring back to a Golden Age, it refers back to an age before political conflict: its primary function, its primary appeal, and perhaps its primary value, is to offer an image of an apparently common past into which we can escape from the divisions of the present. Marion Shoard seems to have recognised the fragility of any general sentiment in favour of conservation that may exist, when, at the end of *The Theft of the Countryside*, she recommends action on a very largely *local* scale: for local politics can sometimes offer an illusion of collectivity of the kind offered also by the idea of a Golden Age: it can enable us, that is, to express a collective resentment at the local effect of policies which, at national level, divide us bitterly. How many who protest at local reductions of health and education services voted for the present government, and will vote for its return? How many who would protest locally at the clearing of a hedge, or the felling of a wood, would refuse to vote for parties whose agricultural policies promoted such actions?

The problem facing the conservation movement, in terms of presenting itself as a political movement, is thus considerable: its passive support is divided among all parties, and to attempt to mobilise much of that support into one party (as has been done in Germany) is to risk losing it altogether. If the conservation movement is to develop a political wing, more effective, more vocal and less polite than the Ecology Party, it may have no alternative but to identify, and concentrate on mobilising, a very small hard core of supporters who regard conservation (along with, no doubt, nuclear disarmament) as *the* crucial political issue – and thus, almost certainly, to alienate the great majority of its passive supporters. But because in Britain the myth of the Golden Age is no less a powerful component of the ideology of active conservationists than it is of their passive supporters, it seems to encourage, a reluctance on their part also to engage in political action: not simply because of the dangers of a (perhaps temporary) loss of passive goodwill, but because of the very nature of the Golden Age myth. That myth is of a 'natural' order, before politics, even before history: and as long as that remains our ideal, it seems as incapable of being realised by political action as it is of being realised without it.

PAUL HILL *Badger Set*

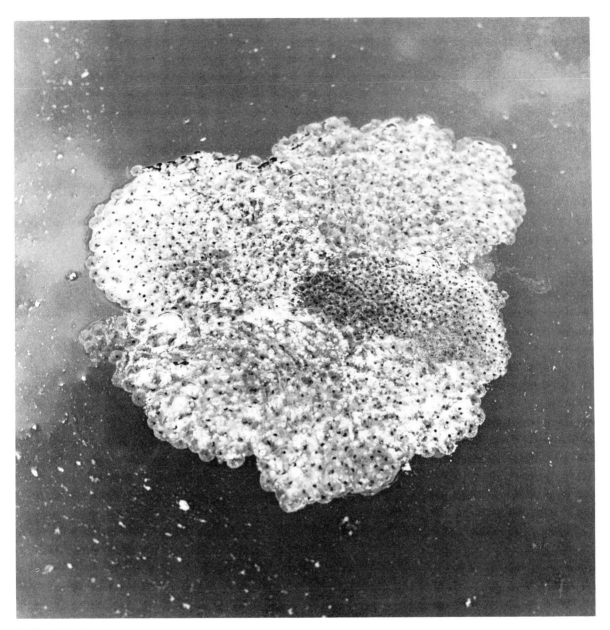

PAUL HILL *Frog Spawn*

A Place in
the Country

BY COLIN WARD

As a writer, I find that my continuing theme is the way people reshape
their own environment, and consequently their lives; breaking out of
the mould into which economic circumstances have cast them. So when
I look at the rural landscape I don't see it in terms of the imprint made
upon it by the vast landed estates and great houses, but in the light of
the activities of the people who scraped through life on the fringes of
control by landowners who were in fact the government, temporal and
spiritual, of the families who lived and died in their domain.

We have a great creative legend on the underside of British history
that at some time away in the past, the land was held by the people and
that every family had a right to the livelihood they could gain from their
portion of it. Gerard Winstanley and many others saw the Norman
Conquest as the moment of transition, but the rights of commoners and
cottagers, the people we would today call squatters, existed long before
then and persisted long afterwards. The process of enclosure, lasting
over many centuries, was an immense historical injustice directed by
the rich and powerful against the poor and needy. The excuse was, just
as it is in different circumstances today, that a very much more productive agricultural system, bringing benefits to all, would be the result of
putting control of the land into fewer and fewer hands. In any case, the
expanding industrial towns were crying out for the busy fingers of the
children of the poor.

Readers of *The Common Ground* will remember a marvellous fragment
from Cobbett in defence of the dispossessed: 'The cottagers', he said in
opposing a proposed enclosure,

> produced from their little bits, in food, for themselves, and in
> things to be sold at market, more than any neighbouring farm of
> 200 acres ... I learnt to hate a system that could lead English
> gentlemen to disregard matters like these! That could induce them

to tear up 'wastes' and sweep away occupiers like those I have described! Wastes indeed! Give a dog an ill name. Was Horton Heath a waste? Was it a 'waste' when a hundred, perhaps, of healthy boys and girls were playing there of a Sunday, instead of creeping about covered in filth in the alleys of a town?

The policy of 'improvements', coupled with the policy of getting all those stupid yokels off the land, brought the period of 'high farming', but it was shortlived and was followed by a decline which lasted, with a brief hiatus in the First World War, until 1939. In his contribution to the collection *The Victorian Countryside*, F. M. L. Thompson begins a paragraph with the sentence, 'The English countryside has probably never looked more prosperous than it did in the 1860s' and ends it with the lament that 'The countryside has seldom looked more dejected than at the turn of the present century; neglected and overgrown hedges, weed-infested meadows and pastures, decaying thatch, dilapidated buildings, untidy farmyards; everywhere examples of lack of attention, misfortune, or despair could be seen ... ' Anyone over sixty will remember this atmosphere of the broken-down picturesque as the characteristic rural landscape of their childhood. It was, of course, a haven for wildlife.

And paradoxically, when agriculture was at its lowest ebb, the mood of 'back to the land' and 'the simple life' arose. Jesse Collins won the Liberal Party to his slogan 'three acres and a cow' and the emerging socialist movement was similarly concerned with a revival of country life. Widely sold books of the 1890s such as William Morris's *News from Nowhere*, Peter Kropotkin's *Fields, Factories and Workshops* and Robert Blatchford's *Merrie England* (which sold a million copies in a few years), predicted a new marriage of town and country, whose most influential prophet was Ebenezer Howard, who in 1898 published his *Tomorrow: a Peaceful Path to Real Reform*, later reprinted many times as *Garden Cities of Tomorrow*.

Speaking at the newly founded London School of Economics in 1904, Howard declared that 'while the age in which we live is the age of the great closely-compacted, overcrowded city, there are already signs, for those who can read them, of a coming change so great and so momentous that the twentieth century will be known as the period of the great exodus, the return to the land ... ' But this return was not that of Cobbett's cottagers. It was an extension down the social hierarchy of a habit the rich had always taken for granted: that of living partly in town and partly in the country.

The railway companies, whose shareholders were often the land-owners en route, had made remote places accessible to the cities in their network of branch lines, and had a strong vested interest, not only in commuter travel, but also in generating traffic from the newly instituted bank holidays and the growing habit of half-day working on Saturdays. The weekend had been invented, and with it the weekend cottage and the weekend bungalow, free from urban constraints and the watchful eyes of elders and servants.

Among those devoted to plain living and high thinking, walking tours became popular, with a 'country book' in the rucksack: a volume of Borrow perhaps, or of Edward Carpenter, or Thoreau's *Walden*. When William Butler Yeats wrote his poem about the small cabin he would build and the nine bean-rows he would plant on the lake isle of Innisfree, he was inspired, not by any acquaintance with life in the west of Ireland, but by buying in Fleet Street a copy of Henry S. Salt's edition of Thoreau's book.

Gypsy caravans were eagerly sought after and cycle tours, as well as 'cycle-camping', became popular with the invention of the pneumatic tyre. In the 1890s the infant socialist movement in the cities was linked with the cult of fresh air and exercise. The Clarion Scouts combined propaganda with pleasure in bicycle excursions into unknown country with their saddlebags stuffed with copies of Robert Blatchford's weekly *Clarion*. A decade later when Baden-Powell wrote *Scouting for Boys*, spontaneous groups of scouts all over the country preceded any central organisation. The idea of 'the country' was linked with that of moral and physical well-being, not surprisingly, since the urban scourge of tuberculosis was thought to be held at bay by the fresh air cure.

Meanwhile the livelihood of those who actually depended on the land became ever more precarious. Agricultural depression, already discernible as improvements in shipping brought cheap imports in the 1870s and hastened by a series of wet summers and poor harvests, became the belated subject of a Royal Commission in 1893. An assistant commissioner, appointed to enquire into the desperate situation in the heavy clay lands of south-east Essex, reported that thirteen per cent of the farmland in this area had gone out of cultivation between 1880 and 1893 and that much more was to follow. There were continual farm sales in the area, usually by order of the liquidators in bankruptcy or 'under distress for rent'. The only incomers were immigrant Scots hoping to convert from arable to dairy farming.

The usual purchasers, at knock-down prices, when buyers were to be found, were speculators who, either on their own account or as investment agents for others, were content to exploit whatever market could be developed over time for subdivided portions of this land. The dominant individual was Frederick Francis Ramuz, mayor of Southend, whose firm The Land Company, apart from its seaside properties, acquired vast holdings, representing at least a third of many south Essex parishes. He tried to release it on the market to speculative builders in large lots, but customers were few. But if land could not be sold *en bloc*, some of it could at least be disposed of as individual plots, typically with a frontage of twenty feet and a depth of, say 100 feet, on a notional grid of roads, pegged out amongst the scrub and thistles. This was the birth of the landscape known to planners as 'plotlands'.

Techniques were developed of advertising auctions in pubs and corner shops in the East End of London, wooing potential buyers with free railway tickets and food and drink served in a marquee as the plots were auctioned. The festive atmosphere of these 'champagne auctions' was vividly remembered by many east London families who went for a cheap outing to the country and came home, flushed and weary, as property owners for a few pounds. Often the impressively printed deed to the land was put in a drawer and forgotten, but equally often the family went, first to camp, then to build and finally to live on its plot or its accumulation of plots.

The advertising campaigns of The Land Company sought to attract every kind of back-to-the-land aspirant. 'Toiling, rejoicing, onward he goes,/ He has land of his own and fears no foes.' says the Company's 1906 catalogue. And it also persuades its reader that 'Land is the basis for all wealth. Even an acre leads to independence.' Anxious not to dismay those who only aspired to a plot for weekends and holidays, it also includes an article on 'The Ideal Summer Holiday' urging readers that there were preferable alternatives to seaside resorts, and that 'a piece of land with a small bungalow on it would be the ideal solution'. The family man was encouraged to think of the pleasure of seeing his 'wife and little ones enjoying themselves revelling in the fresh air, feeding on healthy country produce. It would be without doubt a home from home.'

The Land Company's example was quickly followed. Ramuz had rowed his sons across Canvey Island during one of the periodic floods and had concluded that this was not a site for him, but another speculator, Frederick Hester, attempted the same kind of development there and was soon bankrupt. In 1914 the price of a single Canvey plot was eleven shillings and sixpence. Much later, in the 1930s, Frank Stedman promoted the development of Jaywick Sands, farther up the Essex coast. Among the supporters of his and other ventures in the Essex coast and country was the revered Labour politician from Poplar, George Lansbury, who, like many other East Enders at the end of the last century, was himself a rural immigrant. He completely understood and respected his fellow citizens' aspirations for a taste of country life and, when leader of the Labour Party in 1934, declared, 'I just long to see a start made on this job of reclaiming, recreating rural England.'

The agricultural decline which made land a glut on the market was followed by the highly effective legislation of the Liberal government early in this century which, after the deaths of so many sons and heirs of landowning families in the First World War, put land on the market which had been held by the same families for centuries. Howard Newby, in his book *Green and Pleasant Land?*, comments that 'It is plausible to regard Lloyd George's measures as having been decisive. They produced a trickle of land sales between 1910 and 1914 which became a deluge once the First World War was completed. In four years between 1918 and 1922 England, in the words of a famous *Times* leader of the day, "changed hands". One quarter of the area of England was bought and sold in this hectic period of transaction, a disposal of land which was unprecedented since the dissolution of the monasteries in the sixteenth century.'

Many of the large-scale purchasers were those who had been enriched by the war, fulfilling *their* aspirations for a place in the country, but they also included estate agents hoping to profit from dividing their purchases into plots to meet the yearnings of humbler urban dwellers to rebuild their lives in rural surroundings. They seem to us today to have been cynical adventurers, exploiting, for example, the gullibility of those ex-servicemen, thankful to have survived, who sank their gratuities into schemes for raising poultry or chickens, or even mink or coypu for the fur trade, and were cruelly disappointed.

But when Dennis Hardy and I went around the plotland districts questioning the survivors among the earliest inhabitants, we found that every one of the entrepreneurs has his defenders, just because they provided opportunities to move into the country for people who were far below the income levels where the ability to do this was taken for granted. Take, for example, Charles Neville, the developer of Peacehaven, where the Sussex Downs meet the sea. Mrs Sayers has lived at Peacehaven for sixty years. Her husband had been severely gassed in the First World War, and their doctor in London advised a more bracing, upland climate. So they applied to estate agents in the Surrey hills for houses there, but found that everything available was far beyond their reach. At this time, thanks to the publicity campaigning of Charles Neville, every London tram ticket had on its obverse an advertisement for Peacehaven as 'the Garden City by the Sea'. Mr and Mrs Sayers inquired, and bought three adjacent plots at £50 apiece. They got title to the land in 1921, built their bungalow in 1922, and in 1923 they opened their branch post office and grocery store. They never looked back.

Many of the coastal plotland sites were simply 'discovered' by their early colonists. Shoreham Beach is said to have been started one summer in the 1880s when a camper pitched his tent on the lonely expanse of shingle, returning to put up a hut in the following year. Pagham Beach on the Selsey peninsula was first colonised by the young men of the cycle camping club of the Congregational Church in Guildford, joined by the families of a taxidermist from Croydon and a shopkeeper from Bognor. This close-knit little group for many a summer fetched fresh water from a well dug for them by a local fisherman, and milk and eggs from Church Farm, swam and sailed, gathered driftwood and mushrooms, heard corncrakes and nightjars by night and watched plovers and redshanks by day. They intermarried and some of them lived there for many decades. (One of them, Dorothy French, wrote *The Flora of Pagham Harbour*, published in 1962 by the Bognor Natural Science Society.)

By 1939 the plotland landscape, usually a gridiron of grassy tracks, sparsely filled with bungalows made from army huts, railway coaches and even old tramcars, shanties, sheds, shacks and chalets, was to be found in pockets across the North Downs, along the Hampshire plain, and in the Thames Valley at riverside spots such as Penton Hook, Marlow Bottom and Purley Park. They were interspersed among the holiday resorts on the coast of East and West Sussex at places such as Pett Level and Camber Sands, and most notoriously of all, at Peacehaven. They crept up the east coast from Kent to Lincolnshire, and were clustered inland all across south Essex.

They have several common characteristics. They are invariably on marginal land. An invisible line across Essex divides the plotland belt on the heavy clay which was known to farmers as three-horse land, and which went out of cultivation earliest in the agricultural depression, from the lighter land where farming remained viable. The other Essex plotlands are on vulnerable coastal sites (as was tragically proved in the great floods of 1953), while many others are on estuarial marshland or on riverside sites like those in the Thames Valley, also liable to flooding. Or they are on acid heathland or chalky uplands. Even Peacehaven is built on an area of the South Downs where the ancient sheep pasture had been replaced by a tough wiry grass as a result of ploughing in the Napoleonic wars and the First World War, and which was consequently among the soonest to be abandoned as grazing.

Another characteristic of all the plotland areas is for the holiday home to remain in the same family for generations and to become the retirement home of its owners. What seems to the outside observer to be inconvenient, sub-standard and far from the shops, is for *them* loaded with memories of happy summer days when the children were small. Linked with this is a final common attribute: the tendency, unless deliberate obstacles are put in the way of the residents, for these humble homes to upgrade themselves over time. Extensions, the addition of bathrooms, partial or total rebuilding, the provision of mains services and the making-up of roads are part of the continuous improvement process in any old settlement that has not been economically undermined or subjected to 'planners' blight'.

If you read the pre-war literature of planning and conservation, you are made aware of the intense horror that was felt by all right-thinking (that is, privileged) people at the desecration of the landscape they thought they saw happening everywhere. Dean Inge, a celebrated publicist of the period, coined the phrase 'bungaloid growth' with its implications that some kind of cancer was creeping over the face of the Home Counties. Howard Marshall, in the compendium *Britain and the Beast*, published in 1937, declared that 'a gimcrack civilisation crawls like a giant slug over the country, leaving a foul trail of slime behind it'. One cannot help feeling in retrospect that part of this disgust was ordinary snobbish misanthropy. The wrong sort of people were getting a place in the sun.

Of all new developments the plotlands were the most vulnerable. They failed to comply with the building by-laws, they could be held to be a menace to public health, their rateable value was negligible and their owners were not people with an influential voice in public affairs. In the post-war years, armed with the most comprehensive planning powers in the world, what have the authorities done about them? In those areas now designated as Green Belt the ideal has sometimes been to eliminate them totally and to return the land, if not to agriculture, then to public recreational use. In most places such a policy has failed and has simply resulted in empty scrubby wasteland in between plots still occupied by obstinate people who fought public inquiries and won. In some places it has succeeded. At Havering Park in Essex, the G.L.C. has eliminated all plotland dwellings to make a country park, and the same has happened at Langdon Hills, celebrated, as an example of the way nature re-asserts itself, in Oliver Rackham's study of *Ancient Woodlands* (1980).

Near by, the new town of Basildon was designated to make some kind of urban entity out of the Pitsea–Laindon area which the authorities claimed was a 'vast rural slum'. In many other parts of the South-East, planning authorities have tried to freeze developments by refusing all applications for permission for improvements, refusals which again have often been reversed on appeal. In other places they have permitted selective development, aimed at filling the gaps. There, and more particularly where the authorities have adopted a policy of benign neglect, or of positively encouraging the upgrading of houses and services, the plotlands have worked their way up in the world, as site values have shot up. The little houses, now that their gardens are mature, nest in their foliage far less obtrusively than their newer, larger neighbours. Even their asbestos-cement roof tiles, described as 'a monstrous rash of salmon-pink' in the 1930s, have now, through attracting moss and lichens, become the colour and texture of Cotswold stone.

What struck us most of all about the plotlanders has been their enormous attachment to their homes, their defensive independence and their strong community bonds. The residents of Jaywick Sands, for example, have for fifty years provided and paid for their own street lighting, and organised their own daily emptiers of Elsan closets, known locally as 'the Bisto kids', and who have become just a memory with the building of a sewer.

Our overwhelming impression has been of the number of plotland dwellers, poor residents from the inner London boroughs, starting with pathetically little, who have over the years turned their own labour into capital, with no help from building societies, local councils or anyone else. Mrs Granger, who put down the ten per cent deposit on her plot with a borrowed pound, and raised a family in what was, to her, idyllic Essex, remarked to us, 'I feel so sorry for young couples these days, who don't get the kind of chance we had.'

That the same kind of aspirations still exist can be seen from the 'leisure plot' rackets of recent years where speculators sell plots without planning permission to gullible purchasers who discover that there is nothing they can legally do with their land. And the irony is that, by comparison with agri-business and its destructive power, these humble human incursions have been positive sanctuaries for flora and fauna. 'Plotlands', Oliver Rackham remarks, 'are of value for wildlife because of their varied structure and freedom from agricultural pressures.'

Today, when we have been bulldozed into acquiescence in the fact that large-scale joblessness is going to be a feature of British society for as far into the future as we can guess, there must be large numbers of families who dream of a place in the country simply because employment no longer holds them to the town, and because they believe they could put up some kind of dwelling which could be improved over the years and could meet at least some of their own needs. Their dreams must remain dreams not just because of the rigidity of our building and planning legislation, though that is the first obstacle, but simply because of the astronomical price of land. A building plot of a third of an acre with planning permission for one house is on the market where I live in west Suffolk at £15,000, and the 75-acre farm down our lane was sold at auction in July 1983 at £3,175 an acre. We are very far from the days at the turn of the century when farm land was sold at prices below its agricultural value. Planning permission itself can turn the modern farmer from a millionaire into a billionaire. Apart from corrupting the very purposes of land use planning, it ensures that poor people can no longer make for themselves a place in the country.

John Seymour is, among other things, a writer whose modest success arises just because his books cater for those yearnings for just a little independence in the countryside and he has a vision which echoes Cobbett's defence of the cottagers. He knows a man who farms ten thousand acres with three men and some contractors, growing barley for the subsidy. And he reflects,

> Cut that land (exhausted as it is) up into a thousand plots of ten acres each, give each plot to a family trained to use it, and within ten years the production coming from it would be enormous . . . The motorist wouldn't have the satisfaction of looking out over a vast treeless, hedgeless prairie of indifferent barley – but he could get out of his car and wander through a seemingly huge area of diverse countryside, orchards, young tree plantations, a myriad of small plots of land growing a multiplicity of different crops, farm animals galore, and hundreds of happy and healthy children . . .

ROBIN TANNER *The Fritillary Fields*

ROBIN TANNER *March*

Between Country and City

BY RAYMOND WILLIAMS

I wrote *The Country and the City* in the late 1960s and early 1970s. Looking at it again, the other day, I was surprised to find how many things had happened, in both country and city, in those few intervening years. It is true that the main tendencies I had identified seemed strongly confirmed. I do not mean only that there has been an intensifying crisis in the cities, and especially in the inner cities, though that record of a mounting pressure on housing and services, of financial emergencies and in some extreme cases of actual riots and burning, is evidently grave. Nor do I mean only that there have been some important changes in the country districts: the further rapid development of agribusiness and high-input arable farming; the rapid relative increase in the importance of the agricultural sector in the national economy, especially since joining the European Community; and the continuing growth of country settlement and rural work of new kinds. But my central case in *The Country and the City* was that these two apparently opposite and separate projections – country and city – were in fact indissolubly linked, within the general and crisis-ridden development of a capitalist economy, which had itself produced this division in its modern forms. With the increasing development of a more fully organised agrarian capitalism, ever more closely linked with the general money market, this is clearly even more true now than then.

Yet this was always the underlying social, economic and historical analysis. What I was more immediately concerned with was the set of human responses, in everyday attitudes and activities but also in art and writing and ideas, to these always practical facts and developments. Here again I found much to confirm what I had argued. There was a continuing flood of sentimental and selectively nostalgic versions of country life. Identification of the values of rural society with the very different values of certain dominant and privileged mansions seemed even more strong; indeed these mansions were now often defined, flatly, as 'our heritage'. I say 'mansions' rather than 'country houses' because that ordinary term is part of a very revealing ideological confusion. These places of the landed aristocracy but now much more of the rich of all kinds, including notably the leaders of City finance and of urban industry, are 'country houses' in necessary relation to their 'town houses' or apartments. The real country houses are those of the people who find their diverse livelihoods *in* the country. The presumptive 'country house' is, by contrast, the formal expression of the double base – in city and country alike – of a class based on linked property, profit and money. A more modest and economically different version of a comparable double base is the 'country cottage' of those who mainly earn their livelihood in salaried employment and professional fees in the cities. There is a wide variation of scale, in both kinds, but it is always necessary to distinguish 'the country' as a place of first livelihood – interlinked, as it always must be, with the most general movements of the economy as a whole – and 'the country' as a place of rest, withdrawal, alternative enjoyment and consumption, for those whose first livelihood is elsewhere.

Yet while that distinction is clear and firm, there is no simple corresponding distinction in attitudes to 'the country' or in the 'country' images that we make and exchange. There are, it is true, some obvious general differences, notably in accounts of rural work, which vary according to how often and on what terms – above all, for whom – it is done. But in the increasing interaction of 'country' and 'city' several interesting changes in more general attitudes seem now to be happening, some of them in complex ways. It is these I will now try to define, at least provisionally, as a contribution to an ever more widely-based argument.

The first and most obvious change, which has been developing for many years but is now at a critical stage, relates precisely to the rapid increase in agribusiness, and specifically to the practices of high-input arable farming and new forms of intensive animal and poultry rearing. In a historical perspective these new methods and techniques are evidently the result of the application of industrial methods to traditional farming practices. They are thus a prime case of the interaction of 'country' and 'city' within a single industrial-capitalist economy, just as the closely associated changes in land ownership, agricultural finance and modes of capitalisation are elements of the operation of a single money market. It is then not surprising that there should be some familiar but also some unfamiliar kinds of opposition to them. In cities in arable areas, but perhaps even more in country towns and villages, there is intense and often angry opposition to such effects as straw-burning and crop-spray drift, which have markedly increased. In a more general way there is strongly organised opposition to conditions of intensive animal and poultry rearing which are seen as cruel.

This overlaps in one direction with intense opposition to most forms of the exploitation and even use of animals, and of course with strong objections to older forms of country sport such as hunting. But it overlaps in another direction with a much more general ecological case. Straw-burning is seen as not only polluting but typically wasteful. Crop-spraying, even when there is no drift, is seen as in at least some instances a characteristic example of profitable production taking priority over both public health and the natural environment as a whole. Selective breeding of some plants and animals is seen as diminishing the necessary genetic range, and this is related to the underlying dependence of these varieties on heavy use of imported fertilisers and feedstuffs, itself necessarily connected, not only in the long but even in the short run, with the facts of finite natural resources, renewable and non-renewable, and their now biased distribution in favour of the old rich economies. Thus there are several new kinds of antagonism between what are no longer simple 'country' and 'city' positions, but between and across changing versions of both.

This already complex situation is made even more complex by the fact, unlooked-for even a generation ago, that agriculture is now the most successful sector of a generally failing economy. The time is past when a powerful and influential contrast could be made between busy and thriving industrial areas and a depressed and neglected agriculture. Moreover, and greatly to the long-term advantage of the whole society, the proportion of food raised within the country has increased remarkably, and could be still further increased, with important effects on the viability – and in extreme cases the survival chances – of this heavily populated island. It is common to reply to criticism of the new methods and techniques with the facts of this genuine advantage. What is then replayed within agriculture is the old argument, from the nineteenth century onwards, between the advantages of increased production and the full social, human and natural effects of its processes.

But this has been, from the beginning, a much more difficult argument than it is usually made to seem. The producers, in majority, deploy their powerful statistics of supply and demand, and dismiss most objections as sentimental or at best marginal. This is clearly expressed in that ideological term 'by-product', which is an attempt to separate out the often unwanted but usually predictable and even necessary results of a whole productive process, keeping only the favourable outputs as real 'products'. On the other side, many objectors to these processes are indeed only objecting to the inconvenience of any production, if it happens to blow their way. There is a long tradition of *rentier* objection to physical productive processes of all kinds, though its profits are regularly taken and used to finance other styles of life. There is some continuation of these attitudes among many who are not strictly *rentiers* (people living on incomes from invested money and property) but who, finding their own livelihood elsewhere, are intolerant of other people at work, especially in those country areas which they have chosen for withdrawal and rest. While the argument is confined to exchanges between these two large groups – statistical producers and *rentiers*/weekenders – there is plenty of heat but little light. The real arguments are at once more discriminating and more general.

Thus it is not reasonable, in my view, to pick out a few obviously damaging agricultural applications of science and technology and suppose oneself to have proved some general case. Every particular technique and method needs specific assessment. I am myself persuaded that very-high-input arable farming, with its expensive reliance on heavy fertiliser, energy and pesticide applications, and with its necessary relation to varieties selected for these conditions, leading to some consequent neglect of other possible (including new) varieties, is unsustainable in the long term, given probable developments in both world economics and world ecology. I am similarly persuaded that intensive animal and poultry breeding on imported feedstuffs or on the deliberate surpluses of high-input grain production is wrong both in terms of world food needs – where the surpluses of meat, grain and dairy products in the old rich countries coexist with widespread basic starvation in the growing populations of the poor majority of the world – and in terms of any sustainable economy in our own land. But there are shadings to put on even these conclusions, and in other cases there are significant and valuable real gains, especially in scientific agriculture, as from improved grasses and improved breeds of sheep – which I have been watching fairly closely.

Underlying all these problems of intensive production there is an increasing actual pressure of a financial rather than an economic kind. The huge involvement of agriculture in high-interest debt and credit is usually a truer cause of the most frantic attempts to increase production at any environmental cost than the causes more often assigned, of merely cruel or greedy exploitation. This is not to say that there is no cruelty, no greed, but these can be better distinguished when this much more general pressure is defined and traced to its sources in a specific kind of money-market economy. Moreover this is something that could be changed, with the provision of longer-term and lower-interest credits for more generally agreed kinds and levels of production: reforms which would have to carry with them the acceptance of realistic prices for food, realistic interest on savings, and some dietary changes –

especially in sugar, meat and dairy products – if a general and long-term policy were to have a chance of holding.

Why do most of us not now think in these ways? The superficial divisions of country and city – and specifically, now, of 'agriculture' and 'the rest' – push in to prevent us. This latter division, between 'agriculture' and 'the rest', is especially significant and interesting. For what has happened, at one level, is a misleading simple identification of 'the country' with agriculture. This is better than identifying it with 'country houses', but it is still misleading. A rural economy has never been solely an agricultural economy. Indeed it is only as a consequence of the Industrial Revolution that the idea (though never the full practice) of rural economy and society has been limited to agriculture. It is obvious that food production will always be central in any rural economy, as indeed in any stable whole economy. But this does not mean that a more complex and diverse economy and society cannot or should not develop beyond this base. All rural economies and societies of the past have been more than agricultural, they have included, because that was their natural place, a wide diversity of crafts and trades. The unbalanced development of cities and industrial towns, through the periods of centralisation of state power, concentration of the money market, and large-scale factory production, drained the rural economy of much of its work and, with that, its relative autonomy.

Yet all these developments are now moving, or are capable of being moved, the other way. There is a powerful demand for the decentralisation of state power. There are early opportunities for altering the conditions of the money market, in the now critical circumstances of local government finance and development capital: a range of possible initiatives for more local resource audits, financing and control. Meanwhile there is a firm trend away from factory processes requiring the physical concentration of large numbers of workers, and towards smaller and more specialised workplaces, which with the advantages of new energy and communications technologies can be more diversely sited, including in country areas.

At such a time it is especially necessary to broaden the arguments about rural economy and society from the simple specialisation to agriculture. Beyond even the environmental and resource effects of high-input farming is the effect of the reduction of human work on the land, through mechanisation and automation, with damaging results not only for rural employment prospects of the traditional kind, but for the cities which are no longer the thriving centres to which displaced workers can go. It is here that the structure of modern capitalist agriculture has complex and even contradictory effects. The revitalising effects of a profitable agriculture are real, in many areas, but its political base in the whole society is uncertain and even precarious, given the present scale of subsidies and arranged markets. If it is at the same time, as in the arable areas, actually reducing the broader rural economy and society, it will soon find that it has few friends. It could be overwhelmed at any time by a shallow urban consumerism, pushing its way back, however shortsightedly, into a global free market. Hatred for the Common Agricultural Policy is already intense, and its political outcome – reduction or cancellation – could be disastrous for our rural economy. Yet if profitable production and market criteria are the only norms, as in capitalist agriculture itself, there is no principled way of resisting their global extension. The only sustainable objective of a Common Agricultural Policy is – as some French ministers have correctly stated – the maintenance of a viable rural economy *and* society. If capitalist agriculture is concerned only with itself, and not with rural society as a whole, in a necessary and changing balance with urban and metropolitan society, it has little long-term future and virtually no political defences.

This has several effects on our ways of thinking about the future of rural economies. First, it is necessary to oppose the current drive to get rid of what are called 'small inefficient producers'. This drive is powered by an unholy combination of large agrarian capitalists and the urban Left. It is one of the miseries, indeed crimes, of agrarian capitalism, throughout its history, that it has reduced the spread and diversity of landholding and repeatedly made so many of its neighbours redundant. The cruel fact about contemporary redundancy, by comparison with earlier periods in which the cruelties were of a different kind, is that there is now almost literally nowhere to go: not the old Empire; not the new lands; not the expanding factory towns.

Yet in these new conditions the number of farms in Britain has declined from a pre-1914 figure of 400,000 to some 200,000 today. The pressure to reduce this number yet further comes from a whole range of political and economic bodies which disagree about almost everything else. The identification of efficiency is almost wholly in capitalist terms, as return on capital. Real returns on land use need to be quite differently assessed, not only by extension from the immediate operation to the true full costs in the economy as a whole, but also by extension to an accounting of the full social costs, including the costs of maintaining growing numbers of the displaced and unemployed and the usually overloooked costs of the crisis of the cities to which so many of them gravitate.

This is a worldwide phenomenon, much more serious in many other countries than in Britain, but its shape is already discernible here. What is called environmentalism resists pollution and the destruction of habitats by high-input large-scale farming. Ecology, in its usual forms, resists in terms of the unbalanced and often reckless use of non-renewable resources. Agrarian capitalism answers both with its own version of the priorities of profitable production. What is then necessary is a new kind of political ecology, based in but surpassing these earlier cases, which can trace the processes to the economic and social structures which develop and are strengthened by them, and which can reasonably propose alternative kinds of economic and social organisation.

Thus efficiency must never be reduced to a monetary criterion, or to a simple criterion by gross commodities. Efficiency is the production of a stable economy, an equitable society and a fertile world. Every local measurement is important but the full accounting has to be in these broad terms. Ironically, in all such real accounting, the maintenance and development of rural economies and rural settlements comes out as a high priority. All those who are really committed to them have a central interest in such wider accounting, and in resisting the kinds of calculation, derived from urbanism and industrialism, which have become specific to capitalist agriculture and especially to money-market agribusiness.

Among its many other uses, this perspective helps us to understand a growing contemporary tendency which still awaits its full analysis. There has been a good deal of scattered comment on the movement of a new kind of people into country areas: not just the retired and the commuters, which is an older phenomenon, but a wide range of active people in a diversity of occupations. Some of this has been disparagingly described as the descent of the drop-outs, and there have indeed been many odd encounters between these new arrivals and an older rural population. Yet it seems in reality to be a very mixed phenomenon. Some of course have 'dropped into' forms of farming and smallholding, including some experimental forms. But others are simply taking advantage of independence of location for their particular kinds of work, finding the physical country a major attraction and able, in part, to settle in it because of the relative depopulation caused by earlier phases of industry and agriculture. If we look at this tendency in terms of a whole rural society, rather than of a rural economy limited to agriculture, the judgment seems to alter.

I noted down recently the first occupations of my neighbours within five miles of my house in the Black Mountains. This wasn't a proper statistical survey, just a series of informed impressions. The largest single group of the economically active are of course farmers; most of them sheep-farmers. Just beyond these are the growing number of small contractors: hedge-cutters, tree-fellers, shearers, earth-movers, and (travelling because little grain is grown there) harvesters. Then there are the carriers, of animals and of straw. There are butchers and in one case a sausage-and-pie maker in a new small factory unit. There is the usual range of trades: jobbing builders, electricians, plumbers, plasterers, carpenters. There are the council roadmen. There is a septic tank emptier. Then there are the doctor, the teachers, the school bus drivers, the parson, the police, the publicans, the shopkeepers, the postmen, the garage and petrol station people. All these already show the actual diversity of a working rural society.

But it is the rest of the list that shows the change: weavers and knitters; potters; cabinet-maker; pine-furniture maker; booksellers; book illustrator; antique-clock restorer; antique dealers; painter and gallery owner; writers; sculptor; restaurateurs; glass engraver; stained-glass maker. The majority of all these are comparatively recent immigrants, but consider how much they are, taken as a whole, restoring a genuine fabric of rural society. There are some problems of integration and settlement, but at least in the pastoral areas, with their natural beauty, there is some real movement towards a more diverse and more balanced society. For look also at the move from the other direction. Several of the sheep-farmers double as pony-trekking providers, a rapidly increasing activity. There has been an equally rapid development of farmhouse bed-and-breakfasts, holiday cottage letting and, along quite another line, of farm shops and of growing pick-your-own fruit and vegetables (including potatoes). There is even the beginning of a system of shares in breeding sheep. Some of this is directly related to the attraction of such districts to tourists. Some, again, is part of that pattern of part-time country living which can have depressing effects when many houses and cottages are shut up for the winter. But, taking it all in all, this movement has very interesting implications for the future of a balanced rural society.

It is important to look at some continuities and changes in images of the country in the context of this kind of development. They tell a strange, mixed story. On the one hand there is a continuation of the false or weak pastoral and landscape images, as can be seen in some of the painting and writing and in some pottery. On the other hand the weavers and knitters and furniture-makers are working with the grain of the actual rural economy, and bringing to it qualities of design and, even in reproductions, of workmanship which had been thought to have been exiled to the towns. It is the same with country knowledge and lore. There is a distinct strain of the merely quaint and also of the highly irrational and unhistorical, including the ley-line, medical-magic and supernatural tendencies,. In the Black Mountains this seems perverse, since the real history and prehistory are so very much more interesting and surprising. Yet the only real local anger I have seen was

against a few isolated cases of cannabis-growing and a more organised
camp to celebrate the 'liberty cap' fungi: pitched, as it happened, on a
neolithic site.

Yet it would be false to make this odd tendency the dominant
element. On the contrary the major element is undoubtedly the recovery, exploration and propagation of kinds of natural knowledge, some
strengthened by modern learning and science, which were in part
drained out of the surviving rural population in the period of urban and
industrial dominance. For every cranky or overstated case, as at times
with some of the descriptions of medical herbs, there are twenty cases of
genuine practical knowledge, interacting with the best of the surviving
rural economy: in the wholefoods, the honeys, the culinary herbs, the
fuels, the jams and cordials. As this floods into print and into shops it
can be seen as mere fashion, but in general it is a healthy practical
recovery of the skills and resources of the land. Moreover it is reaching
back into the cities and suburbs, providing a different and better base
for urban attitudes to the country.

Necessarily, however, these are marginal uses and forms of production. The commitment to an industrial and then imperial social
order has occurred in much more than the head. It is now literally on the
ground and in the air, not only in its massive physical and social
embodiments but above all in its crowded population, which has for at
least a century gone beyond the possibilities of any acceptable model of
natural subsistence. Thus there are deep current contradictions. First,
between the true necessities of production as such, industrial and
agricultural, and the inherited and monetarily imposed patterns of
production which obscure but then make others unreasonably deny
these absolute necessities. Second, between the country areas as necessary places of production, in either mode, and the inherited and
culturally imposed patterns of rural enjoyment, placing access to the
'unspoiled' as primary, in the long dream of a simple Rural England
which could export, to the colonies, a large part of its rural working
population. There are good ways forward beyond each of these contradictions, but much of the cultural and intellectual argument is still held,
confusingly, within them.

I have, for example, watched the problem of access in two very
different areas: one Eastern arable; one Western pastoral. The three
fields behind the house in which I was living when I wrote *The Country
and the City* have been cleared into one, and the old ponds drained. A
council signpost still indicates a footpath that used to run beside a
hawthorn hedge but is now across the middle of the large field. If you
have the nerve or indifference to walk across growing corn you can still
always use it, but country-bred I found I could only walk it in autumn

and winter: the respect for crops is still too strong, though I saw clearly enough what had happened. Then in the Black Mountains I admired the arrangements for access to the open tops, with so many miles of attractive hill-walking: the car parks, the picnic sites, the signposts. Yet I have watched, only this summer, a car arrive at the edge of a mountain full of grazing sheep, and three large dogs immediately released and of course chasing and terrifying them. A young farmer neighbour told me that much of his cut winter firewood had been stolen from a stack by his gate, but that he had only lost his temper when the newly-made timber gate had also been stolen. There are also more frequent reports of the theft and butchering of sheep and cattle. In the actual country community you can leave anything open around the place, without the least chance of theft or damage by your neighbours.

Again, once or twice a year, a notice is put through our doors that there is to be an overnight car 'rally' by an urban club: no rally but a timed race in the dark along the narrow twisting lanes where all year it is necessary to reverse or manoeuvre if another vehicle is met. There are procedures for objection and complaint, but the cool advice to keep animals off the roads, as if they were dogs on Guy Fawkes night, is a voice from another world. It is intolerable, I believe, that offences and indifferences of this kind are unnoticed or underplayed within a general position which has its own strong examples: of the destruction of habitats and earthworks, including many that have been listed; of resistance and obstruction on real rights of way; and of organised prejudice against National Parks and even some minimal planning regulations.

None of these complex matters can be resolved within the simplifying images of a polarised 'country' and 'city'. I would take the naming of 'wilderness' – a cultural import from the United States – as an example. It is indeed important that some 'wild' places should be kept open and within the forms of natural growth. The acid blanket-peat uplands are those I know best and most value. Yet these, as I have seen them over many years, are entirely compatible with extensive sheep-farming. Some of them would be more inaccessible without it. When I see the amount of hedging and ditching that goes on in our valley I know what would happen if, for their own reasons, the sheep-farmers were not doing or paying for it. There is not much wilderness in this anciently worked island, and most of it is a man-made facsimile of the real thing, but we might find there was too much for most tastes if this kind of tending stopped. When I see the amount of work on urban parks and gardens, publicly paid for as a matter of course, I wonder at the common urban blindness to all this work that actually produces and preserves much of the 'nature' that visitors come to see. If there were not farmers on these uplands, with the hill-sheep subsidy and guaranteed prices, there would have to be paid wardens if much accessible country were to be left. Indeed I have often thought that some direct part-time payment of that kind would be the fairest kind of settlement on rights of way and important sites.

On the other hand I know that there are sharp and perhaps absolute differences, in these matters, between the pastoral and the arable areas, and especially the arable areas in their current phase of high-input mechanised farming. The linkage between grain surpluses and intensive livestock feeding, in those areas, has to be contrasted with the natural benefits of sensible grassland improvement for pastoral livestock-rearing of a radically different kind. It is a matter, always, for specific judgments, as when I find myself a friend of bracken above a thousand feet and an enemy below that contour. Yet when I once mentioned grassland improvement as an investment priority, to an eminent socialist friend, he looked at me as if he thought I had gone mad.

The deepest problems we have now to understand and resolve are in these real relations of nature and livelihood. I argued in *Towards 2000* that the central change we have to make is in the received and dominant concept of the earth and its life forms as raw material for generalised production. That change means, necessarily, ending large-scale capitalist farming, with its linked processes of high land costs, high interest-bearing capitalisation, high-input cashcrop production. But in the equally necessary perspective of what I called in *The Country and the City* an apparently unmediated nature – the living world of rivers and mountains, of trees and flowers and animals and birds – it is important to avoid a crude contrast between 'nature' and 'production', and to seek the practical terms of the idea which should supersede both: the idea of 'livelihood', within, and yet active within, a better understood physical world and all truly necessary physical processes.

Both industrial and agrarian capitalism have overridden this idea of livelihood, putting generalised production and profit above it. Yet the dominant tendencies in socialism have mainly shared the same emphases, altering only the distribution of profit. The most hopeful social and political movement of our time is the very different and now emergent 'green socialism', within which ecology and economics can become, as they should be, a single science and source of values, leading on to a new politics of equitable livelihood. There is still very much to be done, in clarifying and extending this movement and in defining it, practically and specifically, in the many diverse places, requiring diverse solutions and resolutions, where it must take root and grow. But here, at least, is a sense of direction, born in the experiences between city and country and looking to move beyond both to a new social and natural order.

Biographical Notes

ROGER ACKLING says of his own work: 'The earth, the sky and people – I am part of them and try to record their spirit and presence. As many have for centuries I want to offer back into the world affirmation of what is wonderful.

'My work is physically made by burning with the energy from the sun. I focus light with the help of a small lens which I hold in my hand. I keep still and clear my mind of thoughts.

'Early photographers used a similar method, their invention was the photographic plate; the positive and negative process of recording and duplicating.

'Instead of chemical papers, I use found natural materials, wood and bone. My images are not duplicates and do not belong to the world of science.

'I work on the surface but am aware that the spirit is often hidden within like a shadow in the darkness.'

Roger Ackling's simple way of using the sun and the clouds to mark the surface of natural things reflects his own passive and profound relationship with nature. He has worked and exhibited in Japan as well as in Britain and Europe.

NORMAN ACKROYD was born in Leeds in 1938. He studied at Leeds College of Art and the Royal College of Art. His early work showed a preoccupation with places, but since 1970 he has become increasingly absorbed by landscape. He is especially intrigued by the relationship between water and sky. Etching, he feels, is a wonderful and mysterious way of drawing. His way of working is described in *Artists in Print*, a B.B.C. book which followed a television series and mixed exhibition at the I.C.A. Recent books of his etchings include *A Cumberland Journey: Etchings from a Journey around Southern Cumbria*, 1981 and *Itchen Water: Etchings and Poems* with Jeremy Hooker, 1982.

He was a prize winner at the British International Print Biennale in 1972 and 1982 and has exhibited widely in Britain and the U.S.A. He has produced several large etched murals. He lives in London and plays for Lord Gnome's XI in the Home Counties. He is happy to draw on location when the cricket is rained off.

CONRAD ATKINSON was born in Cumbria in 1940. He studied at the Colleges of Art in Carlisle and Liverpool and the Royal Academy School in London, finishing in 1965. He has exhibited and lectured in Europe, the U.S.A. and Australia.

In 1984 he wrote that his current work 'seeks to stretch out a basis for a cultural practice which will re-examine our received notions of such apparently "traditional" and unquestioned ideas about subjects such as landscape. From a different aspect it examines and attempts to expose those practical organisations which structure our consciousness whilst claiming to be simply mechanisms of progress. This involves examining multinational corporations as well as the media to uncover the blizzard of images and meanings constantly inflicted upon us. It also involves the arms industry and pictures of war . . .'

Conrad Atkinson has explored these ideas in his controversial works on Northern Ireland, Thalidomide victims, industrial disease and hunger. His concern for Cumbria, its workers, its poets and its plight emerges in works such as 'Strike at Brannans 1972', 'Iron Ore 1977' and 'Cumbria for Wordsworth/for Shelley 1978–1980'.

A comprehensive view of his work was taken in the book *Conrad Atkinson: Picturing the System* by Lucy Lippard *et al.*, 1981. More recent writings, lectures and works were published under the title of *Writings* in 1984.

He lives in London and is Arts Advisor to the G.L.C. and during 1984 was Artist in Residence in the Borough of Lewisham, London.

JOHN BARRELL is a Fellow of King's College Cambridge, and a historian of English literature and art. He has published *The Idea of Landscape and the Sense of Place* (1972), an approach to the poetry of John Clare; *The Dark Side of the Landscape* (1980), an examination of how the rural poor are represented in English landscape painting; and, most recently, *An Equal, Wide Survey* (1983), on the organisation of society in eighteenth-century England. He is currently working on a study of serious painting in England, from Reynolds to Hazlitt.

JOHN BERGER, born in London in 1926, is well known as a novelist, essayist, screenwriter, documentary writer and art critic. His many innovative books include *About Looking, Ways of Seeing, Art and Revolution, The Success and Failure of Picasso, Another Way of Telling, Pig Earth* and the novel *G.* which won the Booker Prize, the James Tait Black Memorial Prize and the Guardian Fiction Prize in 1972. His latest book is *And Our Faces, My Heart, Brief as Photos*.

MICHAEL BERKELEY was born in 1948 and is the eldest son of the composer Sir Lennox Berkeley. He was a chorister at Westminster Cathedral and subsequently studied at the Royal Academy of Music and with Richard Rodney Bennett. From 1974 to 1979 he was a B.B.C. announcer on Radio 3 and is now a regular contributor to radio and television.

In 1977 Michael Berkeley was awarded the Guinness Prize for composition for his 'Meditations for Strings' and in 1979 he was appointed Associate Composer to the Scottish Chamber Orchestra. His music has been heard all over the world and has been performed by artists such as Julian Bream, André Previn, George Malcolm, Robert Cohen, Raymond Leppard, the Gabrieli String Quartet, the Philip Jones Brass Ensemble and the Nash Ensemble. He has written orchestral works for the English Chamber Orchestra, Royal Liverpool Philharmonic Orchestra and the Philharmonia Orchestra. In 1983 the London Symphony Orchestra and Chorus conducted by Richard Hickox gave the first performance of Berkeley's Oratorio 'Or Shall We Die?' for which Ian McEwan wrote the words. This work has been filmed by Richard Eyre and recorded by E.M.I.

Michael Berkeley's music is published by Oxford University Press.

JOHN BLAKEMORE lives in Derby and lectures in photography at the Derby Lonsdale College. He studied at Coventry College of Art.

He says of his work: 'The landscape photograph is narrowly defined, a stretch of beach, a wooded hillside, a short length of river valley, areas which in some way speak to me, and which I visit again and again; to learn to see, to allow the possibility of communion, of understanding. My photography is built around this ritual intimacy yet, paradoxically, I do not see my photographs as concerned with place in a physical, a geographical sense. What I try to evoke is the dynamic of landscape, its spiritual and physical energy, its fundamental mystery. The photograph provides an intense delineation of reality, but the camera also transforms what it sees. I seek to produce images which function both as fact and as metaphor, reflecting both the external world and my own inner response to, and connection with, it.'

His work has been exhibited widely in Britain and Europe and he has shown in group exhibitions in the U.S.A. and Australia.

An Arts Council monograph on John Blakemore was produced in 1977.

EDWARD BLISHEN was born in 1920 and worked as a teacher for some years before turning to full-time freelance writing and broadcasting in 1959. He has written several books about the pains and pleasures of teaching, including *Roaring Boys* and *Uncommon Entrance*, and a number of volumes of autobiography, the most recent of which is *A Second Skin*. For thirteen years he conducted a programme for African writers on the B.B.C.'s African Service. In 1979 he was awarded the Society of Authors' Travelling Scholarship and in 1981, with *Shaky Relations*, he won the J.R. Ackerley Prize for Autobiography. He is married, with two sons, and lives near Barnet.

RONALD BLYTHE was born in Suffolk and much of his work reflects East Anglian culture and scenery. *Akenfield*, first published in 1969, is, among other things, a compression of all that he has seen and heard in Suffolk since his childhood. He has written stories, history and screenplays. His study of Britain between the wars, *The Age of Illusion*, has just been issued by Oxford University Press in their Modern Classics series. He has edited and introduced the work of Thomas Hardy, Jane Austen and William Hazlitt, and is currently working on a book titled *Divine Landscapes*.

LEONIE CALDECOTT was born in London in 1956, and educated at the French Lycée and Hertford College, Oxford, where she read French and Philosophy. Since graduating in 1978, she has worked mainly as a freelance journalist, with a special interest in women's issues, nuclear technology, the peace movement, ecology and spirituality. She has written for numerous papers and magazines, including the *Guardian*, the *Sunday Times, New Society, Time Out, Over 21* and *Good Housekeeping*. In 1982 she won the Catherine Pakenham Memorial Award for young women journalists. She has contributed to several collections of writing, including *Keeping the Peace*, 1983 and *Walking on the Water*, 1983. She is co-editor, with Stephanie Leland of Women for Life on Earth, of *Reclaim the Earth*, 1983, an anthology of women's writing on 'green' issues. Her book *Women of Our Century* was published in the spring of 1984 to coincide with the B.B.C. television series of the same name, in which she also participated. She is currently working on a book about women and Christianity, *Leave the Apple to Eve*.

STEPHEN DALTON was born in 1937 in Surrey. He studied photography in the early 1960s under Professor Margaret Harker at the Regent Street Polytechnic (now the Polytechnic of Central London).

He has received many awards for his extraordinary skill in high speed photography – the most coveted being the Royal Photographic Society's Silver Progress Medal in 1978. His books include *Borne on the Wind: the Extraordinary World of Insect Flight*, 1975; *Caught in Motion: High Speed Nature Photography*, 1982 and *Split Second: High Speed Photography*, 1983.

Stephen Dalton lives in Ardingly, Sussex.

CHRIS DRURY was born in Sri Lanka in 1948. He studied at Camberwell School of Art, which he left in 1970.

His work has always explored connections with the earth: 'I have gone out and touched the earth physically walking through the wilderness at home and abroad and have come back to discover, through the medium of sculpture, an echoing wilderness within myself.'

During 1983 his shows included 'Medicine Wheel' at the Coracle Press, who published his book of the same name, the Third World Wilderness Congress at Findhorn, Scotland, and the 'British Art, New Directions' show in New York.

Chris Drury lives in Lewes, Sussex.

JOHN FOWLES lives in Lyme Regis, Dorset and since 1963 has been a full-time writer. He has written several novels: *The Collector, The Magus, The French Lieutenant's Woman, Daniel Martin* and *Mantissa*; a novella and collection of short stories, *The Ebony Tower*; and *The Aristos* (philosophy). He has also written many works of non-fiction including *Shipwreck, Islands, The Tree* and *The Enigma of Stonehenge*. In addition he has edited John Aubrey's *Monumenta Britannica*.

DAME ELISABETH FRINK was born in Suffolk in 1930. She studied at Guildford Art School and Chelsea School of Art, and taught at Chelsea School of Art, St

Martin's College of Art and the Royal College of Art.

Since 1973 Elisabeth Frink has lived and worked in Dorset, where she keeps horses and frequently rides.

Her sculptures are best seen in the landscape and her beautiful garden provides an ideal setting for her work.

In 1979 she said: 'The very best I can hope to achieve is the feel of a man running or the movement of an animal in the landscape. Working in a landscape has become very important to me. I think my sculptures are about what a human being or an animal feels like, not what they necessarily look like. I use anatomy to create the essence of human and animal forms and their freedom of spirit.'

Elisabeth Frink's work is shown world-wide. In 1982 she received the D.B.E. Books on the artist include *The Art of Elisabeth Frink*, introduced by Edwin Mullins, 1972, and *Elisabeth Frink: Sculpture*, 1984.

HAMISH FULTON was born in 1946 in London. He studied sculpture at St Martin's School of Art in London, but his work since the late 1960s has been dominated by the photograph combined with words. Influenced by the culture of the American Indian, Zen Buddhism and by nature, his work demands direct experience through walking, the emptying of the mind and immersion in time and distance. Many works have been created in the exotic wilderness areas of North and South America, the Himalayas and Japan. He says: 'The site is important, but the walk itself is more important. Although I sometimes travel to make my artworks, most of them are done in England. Kent, in particular, has a very unspectacular landscape which allows my real concerns to surface without an exotic overlay.'

Hamish Fulton has participated in commissions and exhibitions all over the world. His publications include *Hollow Lane*, 1971; *Skyline Ridge*, 1975; *Nine Works 1969–73*, 1975; *Road and Paths*, 1978 and *Song of the Skylark*, 1982.

Ironically the man with the motto 'no walk, no work' broke his leg in the summer of 1983, dashing hopes of doing a special work for this book, but we are happy to include works of his own choice from Kent.

FAY GODWIN has no formal photographic training but became interested in photography in the mid-1960s while photographing her young children.

Her work has been widely exhibited in the U.K. and the British Council is touring a world-wide exhibition from 1984.

So much of her published work is of landscape that it is easy to forget that she enjoys portrait photography and has a strong eye for farce and wry situations, as shown in *Bison at Chalk Farm*, 1982. Her other books include *The Drovers' Roads of Wales* with Shirley Toulson, 1977; *Islands* with John Fowles, 1978; *Remains of Elmet* with Ted Hughes, 1979; *The Saxon Shore Way* with Alan Sillitoe, 1984; and *Landscapes* with an essay by John Fowles, 1984. During 1982 and 1983 her major work has been in photographing National Trust properties in Wessex and a book of this work will be published in 1984.

Fay Godwin lives in Kentish Town, London.

ANDY GOLDSWORTHY was born in 1956. He studied at Bradford Art College and Preston Polytechnic in the mid-1970s and began working outside within walking distance of wherever he was living in Leeds, Ilkley, Morecambe and Bentham. He now lives in Brough in Cumbria.

His work ranges from the bold manipulation of large stones and ice to the gentle and exquisite arrangement of leaves and feathers. No sense of permanence or intrusion pervades his works, but they often evoke surprise, humour and wonder on a grand or small scale.

He says: 'I explore and try to understand through my art, my own and the earth's nature. My art is a meeting point between the two. The earth is the source of all things, it sustains my art and gives me the reason to create. Without a strong relationship with that source my art would become meaningless ... I have become aware of how nature is in a stage of change and that change is the key to understanding. I want my art to be sensitive and alert to the changes in materials, seasons and weather ... Sometimes a work is at its best when most threatened by the weather. A balanced rock is given enormous tension and force by a wind that might cause it to collapse. I have worked with colourful leaves, delicate grasses and feathers made extra vivid by a dark rain and leaden sky that cast no shadow. Had it rained the work would have become mud splattered and washed away.'

Photographs, notes and drawings are usually all that remain of Andy Goldsworthy's work and these have been shown in London and the major British galleries.

FRASER HARRISON was born in 1944 at Stackpole near Pembroke. He was educated at Shrewsbury and Trinity Hall, Cambridge. He then worked for a number of publishing houses, including Sidgwick and Jackson where he was the editor for five years. In 1975 he left London for Suffolk and lives there now with his wife and two children. His first book was an anthology of *The Yellow Book*, his next was *The Dark Angel*, a study of Victorian sexuality, and in 1982 he published *Strange Land: The Country's Myth and Reality*. He has published short stories and is a regular contributor to the *Literary Review*. He is currently working on a second book about the countryside and the cultural importance of conservation.

PAUL HEMPTON was born in Yorkshire in 1946. He studied at Goldsmiths College and the Royal College of Art from 1964 to 1971. He has participated in many one-man and group exhibitions in the U.K., Europe and Latin America.

Silbury Hill has had a profound influence on Paul Hempton and is a recurring theme in his work, appearing in different forms in many of his paintings.

In 1982 he said of his work: 'One of the strongest driving forces behind my desire to make paintings comes from looking at landscape – the earth, the sky – the matter in it, and the witnessing of the laws of nature that govern it – its process, pace, rhythm, light, colour. I observe these elements in order to re-order them – to use them as vehicles for ideas that are not necessarily connected with the landscape – to construct metaphors. I am really after an equivalent for an internal state of being, an interpretation of the relationship within ourselves between the physical and the spiritual.'

In 1983 his work was shown at the exhibition 'Landscape' at Bury Art Gallery, the Gulbenkian Print Prize-winners Touring Show, at the Ian Birksted Gallery in London, Bath Arts Fair, and Basle Arts Fair, Switzerland. Paul Hempton lives in Minchinhampton, Gloucestershire.

PAUL HILL was born in Shropshire in 1941 and began work in the border area as a reporter in 1959. He moved on to become a freelance photographer, self-taught, working for many of the national newspapers between 1965 and 1974. He then taught at Trent Polytechnic in Nottingham running the Creative Photography course there in the late 1970s. In 1976 he founded the Photographers' Place, a workshop and study centre in Bradbourne, Derbyshire. This, visiting lectureships and his own photography now take all his time.

He has exhibited widely in the U.K., Europe, the U.S.A. and Japan. He has written articles for many of the leading photographic journals and written two books: *Dialogue with Photography* with Thomas Cooper, 1979 and *Approaching Photography*, 1982.

'I believe that landscape photography is about the *land* – the stuff under your feet. My interest is in what goes on *on* and *in* the land and how the elements and seasons affect it, how man manipulates it and how the flora and fauna mark it. I am mostly concerned with trying to understand what is around me in my non-urban environment, not with making commercially acceptable "views". I did this enough when I earned my living in publishing . . . I got fed up with trying to make photographs of the picturesque that confirmed an idea of pastoral bliss and romantic escapism.' (Paul Hill, 'A Personal Approach to Landscape', *S.L.R. Camera*, September 1983.)

His four seasons series of photographs in this book show Winn Brook, Bradbourne in Derbyshire.

JOHN HILLIARD was born in Lancaster in 1945. He studied sculpture at St Martin's School of Art and then moved on to photography which he teaches part time at Brighton Polytechnic. He lives in south London.

His exhibitions in Britain, Europe, Japan and America have not been confined to landscape: 'Windswept moors, doting lovers, military hardware or banana beef steak might all equally come up for consideration – but only as secondary devices.' (1977) 'My use of landscape subject matter, although it characterises perhaps half of my total output, is by no means consistent – indeed, these works made on Arran during the summer of 1983 are located within a period of otherwise unrelievedly urban activity. It is, in fact, a consideration of some aspect of the language of photography that usually triggers the work, and the picture elements are prescribed by that interest. In the end, however, there is an intended rapport between process and image, a reciprocal bond, a meeting point between photography of nature and the nature of photography, an acknowledgment of their mutually and respectively inherent features. Besides, it's a pleasure to work outdoors.' (1984)

DAVID HOCKNEY was born in Bradford in 1937. He studied at Bradford School of Art and the Royal College of Art and has lectured in many American and British universities. He lives in Los Angeles.

Hockney's paintings are internationally collected and exhibited. Recently he has been concentrating on the medium of photography. In a letter to a friend in 1983 he said: 'For many years I have been aware of the photographic flaw. Its lack of time and therefore of life ... as the exposure time got less and less the image would appear more and more frozen, i.e. time stopped – an impossibility, making the picture merely a glance and our looking time at it far *more* than the time in the picture. This can only be overcome by the still life or the empty street of Atget etc., or of course a photograph of a flat surface, a drawing or a painting. Now surely it's no accident that within a few years of the popularising of photography, Cubism was invented. I think Picasso and Braque saw this flaw and therefore the other flaw of the window ... a wall distancing us from what is seen – we are not involved.' (Taken from the catalogue to the exhibition 'Hockney's Photographs', sponsored by the Arts Council of Great Britain, 1983.)

Hockney's collages of photographs are an attempt to capture time and life. Many of his 'joiners', as he calls them, are of domestic scenes and others are of landscapes.

Books on or by Hockney include *David Hockney* by David Hockney, 1976; *David Hockney Photographs*, 1982 and *China Diary* with Stephen Spender, 1982.

JOHN HUBBARD was born in Connecticut in 1931. He studied at Harvard – English Literature with Art History, particularly Far Eastern Art. After being based in Japan during the Korean War he studied at the Art Students' League in New York City, and eventually settled in Dorset, England in 1961 after extensive travels in Europe.

'I have lived the greater part of my life in the country and spend a lot of my time walking, looking and drawing. I draw to sharpen my eye, and to fix an image on to my unconscious mind and to seek a counter-balance to an abstract brush stroke's tendency to become too generalised and repetitious ... The walking, the looking, the drawing all serve to awaken my ideas and suggest starting points, but the actual act of making the painting, pushing it and being pushed by it, is at least equally important. For me this is how one arrives at the unexpected, how one reveals what has been there all along. While there are certainly echoes of abstract expressionism here, I have been more profoundly influenced by the classical Chinese Landscape school, both poets and painters.'

John Hubbard's paintings have been shown in Europe and South America and he has also designed decor and costumes for ballet, including the backdrop for the Royal Ballet's *Midsummer* in 1984.

SIRKKA-LIISA KONTTINEN was born in Finland in 1948. After a brief time at Helsinki University and film school in London she has worked as a member of Amber Associates based in Newcastle upon Tyne. Since 1969 Amber has built a creative relationship with the local working-class communities which has resulted in films and touring exhibitions. In 1976 the group set up the Side Gallery, which is now recognised as one of the most radical photographic galleries in Britain.

Sirkka-Liisa Konttinen has done freelance work for Finnish and English magazines, television and film. Her larger projects have included photographing fairground sideshows, holiday-making on England's north-eastern beaches and a major twelve-year documentation of Byker – a close-knit working-class community in Newcastle whose homes have since been demolished and the area completely re-fashioned. Although primarily made for the local population, these photographs have travelled as far as America and China. Two films, *Keeping Time* (1982) and *Byker* (1983), have been shown on television and Jonathan Cape published a book of text and photographs entitled *Byker* in 1983.

PETER LEVI, a classical scholar, archaeologist and poet, was born in 1931. He has published many volumes of poetry, the latest of which is *The Echoing Green*. His other prose works include *John Clare and Thomas Hardy, The Noise Made by Poems*, and travel-books about Greece and Afghanistan. He translated Pausanias, *Guide to Greece*, and is the editor of Johnson's *A Journey to the Western Islands of Scotland* and Boswell's *The Journey of a Tour to the Hebrides*. He lives in Oxford where he has recently been elected Professor of Poetry.

JORGE LEWINSKI was born in Poland of Ukranian parents. He arrived in Britain in 1942 and after studying at London University worked in business until 1967. In 1960 he began to photograph artists and to contribute to newspapers and magazines. By 1968 he was a full-time professional photographer and teacher of photography at the London College of Printing. He has exhibited in America and Britain and has collaborated on many books including *Byron's Greece* with Lady Longford, 1975; *Writers' Britain* with Margaret Drabble, 1979; *James Joyce's Odyssey* with Frank Delaney, 1981 and *The Shell Guide to Photographing Britain*, 1982. He is currently working on *Architecture of Southern Britain* with John Julius Norwich and *The Shell Guide to the Archaeology of Britain* with Jacquetta Hawkes. He lives in London.

RICHARD LONG was born in Bristol in 1945 and still lives there. He studied at St Martin's School of Art in London in the late 1960s. Since 1968 he has had over eighty one-man exhibitions based usually upon walks and works made in Britain, Europe, North and South America, Africa, Japan, Nepal and Australia. His work, built upon lines and circles, has been influential on many people.

'The source of my work is nature. I use it with respect and freedom. I use materials, ideas, movement and time to express a whole view of my art in the world. I hope to make images and ideas which resonate in the imagination, which mark the earth and the mind. In the mid-1960s the language and ambition of art was due for renewal. I felt art had barely recognised the natural landscapes which cover this planet, or had used the experiences these places could offer. Starting on my own doorstep and later spreading, part of my work has been to try and engage this potential. I see it as abstract art laid down in the real spaces of the world. It is not romantic; I use the world as I find it. My work is simple and practical . . . I like the idea of using the land without possessing it . . . My work has become a simple metaphor of life. A figure walking down his road, making his mark. It is an affirmation of my human scale and senses: how far I walk, what stones I pick up, my particular experiences. Nature has more effect on me than I on it. I am content with the vocabulary of universal and common means: walking, placing, stones, sticks, water, circles, lines, days, nights, roads.' ('Words after the Fact', Richard Long, 1982, from *Touchstones* Arnolfini, Bristol, 1983.)

His many books include: *Rivers and Stones*, 1978; *Richard Long*, 1979; *Twelve Works*, 1981; *Touchstones*, 1983; *Countless Stones*, 1983 and *Sixteen Works*, 1984.

RICHARD MABEY lives in the Chilterns, and is a writer and broadcaster with a special interest in landscape and the countryside. His best known books are *Food for Free, The Unofficial Countryside, The Flowering of Britain* (the last made into an acclaimed B.B.C. documentary film) and *The Common Ground*, an inquiry into the philosophy and practice of conservation. He has edited and introduced the work of Gilbert White and Richard Jefferies, and a selection of his essays and journalism was published in 1983 as *In a Green Shade*.

As well as owning and managing a community woodland in the Chilterns he is active in green politics, and in 1982 was appointed to the Nature Conservancy Council.

He is currently working on a biography of Gilbert White, and in 1983 was awarded a Leverhulme Trust award for this work, and to continue research into the portrayal of landscape in literature.

JAMIE McCULLOUGH is a Scot, a sculptor and many other things. In 1976 while strolling over a canal bridge in inner London, he had the idea of reshaping and recovering a derelict patch of land near Paddington. His vision, collaborative hard work, organisation and fundraising led to the creation of Meanwhile Gardens – a place created with and by the local community for play and relaxation. It has an open air theatre, bike and skateboard track, sand pit, trees, flowers and nature areas. His engaging and frank description of its creation makes fascinating reading in *Meanwhile Gardens*, published by the Gulbenkian Foundation in 1978. Over the last three years he has lived an itinerant life. With the support of the Forestry Commission in south-west England he spent eighteen months creating 'Beginners' Way' – a magical and mysterious walk through a forest. He continued work in the forests of the south-west until 1983, searching for a way of electronically capturing the sound of the trees, recording 'portraits' of individual trees in the wind and working towards a 'concert of trees'.

ALEXANDER MACKENZIE was born in Liverpool in 1923. After war service he studied at Liverpool College of Art and in 1951 moved to Cornwall where he met Ben Nicholson, Peter Lanyon and John Wells. His work owes much to place, and the Yorkshire Dales as well as Cornwall have been of great inspiration.

'Mackenzie's paintings are not overtly descriptive and neither are they totally abstract. His understanding of geography and geology is as important as his aesthetic judgment. The line of a rock fault is tellingly simplified to give the sensation of a hillside and a mass of colour can read as a field shape ... A sharp movement of line again suggests stone walls or sheep paths. The resolution of these observations into a painting is assisted by the vertical picture plane of the Cubists. This enables Mackenzie to exploit his love of being above his landscape. He is able to transmit the surprise of height and the evolutionary urge of man to fly. It also brings the thrill of weather, which is the twin element in landscape.' (John Halkes, Newlyn Orion Gallery Catalogue, 1980.)

He has exhibited widely, particularly in Britain and Europe. He lives in Saltash, Cornwall.

DAVID G. MEASURES was born in 1937 in Warwickshire. He studied at the mid-Warwickshire School of Art and the Slade School of Fine Art, and has taught at the Lancaster School of Art, Nottingham College of Art and Goldsmiths College of Art. He now lives in Southwell and teaches in the Fine Arts Department of Nottingham Polytechnic.

David G. Measures has been a life-long naturalist. He spends hours in the field observing wildlife, making drawings and taking notes. *Bright Wings of Summer*, published by Cassell in 1976, was the culmination of seven years' work largely drawn from seven notebooks about the natural history of the butterflies which he observed on a local disused railway line. To paint a fast-moving butterfly, Measures uses his fingers rather than a brush. A local copse is now the focus of his close observations.

He has exhibited throughout Britain as both artist and natural historian. A selection of his field sketch-books was toured by the Arts Council in 1984.

BEL MOONEY was born in 1946, educated at grammar schools, and gained a first class honours degree in English from University College London. After that she pursued a successful career as feature writer, newspaper columnist and television interviewer. She has published *The Year of the Child: Portraits of British Children*; a children's book, *Liza's Yellow Boat*; a novel, *The Windsurf Boy*; and a collection of articles, *Differences of Opinion*. She is married with two children.

HENRY MOORE was born in Yorkshire in 1898, the son of a miner. After service in the First World War he studied at Leeds School of Art and the Royal College of Art. He was an official War Artist from 1940 to 1942.

In 1983, the year of his 85th birthday, more than thirty exhibitions of his work were showing throughout the world.

Of the many books written about him, *Henry Moore: Sculptures in Landscape*, with an essay by Stephen Spender, published in 1978, explores Moore's love of placing his work in the landscape: 'The sky is one of the things I like most about "sculpture with nature", there is no background better than the sky because you are contrasting solid form with its opposite space.'

'Sheep Piece' (1971/2) stands in a field next to Moore's extensive garden in Hertfordshire. The sheep have polished a band of gold around the sculpture and have beaten a track between it and their watertrough. Henry Moore enjoys their amicability towards his work – their scale enhancing its presence.

Among the many books written about or by him are *Henry Moore's Sheep Sketchbooks*, with Sir Kenneth Clark, 1980 and *Animals*, a book of animal drawings covering sixty years, 1983.

DAVID NASH was born in Surrey in 1945 and studied in the mid-1960s in Brighton and Kingston Colleges of Art. Since 1967 he has lived and worked in Blaenau Ffestiniog in North Wales. He has worked, taught and exhibited in many parts of the world, most recently in the U.S.A., Holland and Japan. A comprehensive book about his work, *Sixty Seasons*, was published for the exhibition at the Third Eye Centre, Glasgow in 1983.

Nash's work, mainly in wood and some in stone, has become increasingly subtle and often transient. It always reflects his care and sensitivity to the land. He has recently said: 'I am not interested in an object dominating a space, I prefer near invisibility. It's there if it is known about, or if it is recognised, but it can be passed by unnoticed.'

'Sheep Spaces' and 'Sod Swap' are observations of just that idea; the latter has been renamed 'Turf Exchange' and now reposes amongst the refined grass of Kenwood Kitchen Garden on Hampstead Heath in London, thanks to the G.L.C.

NORMAN NICHOLSON was born in 1914 at Millom, Cumbria and educated at local schools. At the age of sixteen, a breakdown in health forced him to leave school and spend two years at a sanatorium in the New Forest, after which he returned to the house in Millom where he still lives.

He has published seven volumes of poetry, four verse-plays and a number of books on the topography and literary history of the Lake District and Cumbria. His first book of verse, *Five Rivers*, 1944, was the first book ever to be awarded the Heinemann Prize. Since then he has received a Cholmondeley Award (1967), a Society of Authors' Travel Grant (1973) and the Queen's Gold Medal for Poetry (1977). Manchester University and the Open University have each honoured him with a degree and, in 1980, he received a Doctorate from Liverpool University. He was married in 1956 but has been a widower since 1982.

DAVID POWNALL was born in Liverpool in 1938. After Keele University he followed a career in the motor industry and on the Zambian Copper Belt before turning to full-time writing. He has published many poems, short stories and seven books, including *Between Ribble and Lune*. His most recent novel is *Beloved Latitudes*. His plays, from *Livingstone and Sechele* to *Master Class* (recently performed at the Old Vic, London), add yet another dimension to his diversity as playwright and novelist. He is also a founder of the Paines Plough Theatre Company.

JAMES RAVILIOUS was born in 1939 in Eastbourne, the second son of the artist Eric Ravilious. After studying at St Martin's School of Art he taught drawing and painting at Hammersmith College of Further Education. His full-time involvement with photography began in 1972 when he became photographer to the Beaford Centre in North Devon.

The Beaford Archive comprises 4,500 photographs of the area taken between the mid-eighteenth and mid-nineteenth centuries. These have been collected from local sources and rephotographed. The new part of the archive consists of photographs and other material gathered by James Ravilious.

The Heart of the Country by James Ravilious with his wife, Robin, (published in 1980), includes some of these photographs. It offers a rare insight into the life, work and landscape of the people as change forces itself upon the traditions of North Devon. 'The greatest changes have occurred in agriculture . . . Nevertheless, it is a curious characteristic of this area that the changed and unchanged continue to co-exist, almost as if unaware of each other.'

His most recent freelance work has been to collaborate with Frank Delaney on *Betjeman's Country*, published in 1983.

ROBIN TANNER was born in Bristol in 1904. He studied at Goldsmiths College in the 1920s and began full-time teaching there at the same time as attending evening etching classes. He moved to Wiltshire in 1929. Through his pioneering work in teaching and as an inspector of schools, he became influential in art education.

In 1939 *Wiltshire Village*, written by his wife Heather and illustrated with his etchings, documented unconsciously the many facets of a small locality about to undergo a radical change. The book was republished in 1978. The Tanners's next publication, *Woodland Plants*, appeared in 1981 – the result of many years' work, finally completed during retirement.

Greatly influenced by Samuel Palmer and with an indefatigable commitment to the countryside, Robin Tanner has closely observed a few square miles of Wiltshire for more than fifty years. He has recorded 'a vision of the ideal world that could be ours, had we but the will and courage to work for it'. (*The Etcher's Craft*, R. Tanner, Friends of Bristol Art Gallery, 1980.) Complete collections of the etcher's work are held by Bristol City Art Gallery and by the Ashmolean Museum, Oxford.

KIM TAPLIN was born in 1943 and has lived in Oxfordshire for the last twenty years, compensating for a shifting, suburban childhood. She has been, among other things, a parish clerk, and is assistant secretary of the Oxford Fieldpaths Society. Her writing includes essays, reviews, poetry and a book, *The English Path*, about the place of footpaths in English life and literature. She is a frequent contributor to the *Countryman*.

COLIN WARD was born in 1924 in Essex and worked for many years in architectural practice and teaching before turning to full-time writing. He edited *Anarchy* during the 1960s and *BEE* (the Bulletin of Environmental Education) during the 1970s. His books include *Anarchy in Action, Tenants Take Over* and *The Child in the City*. His chapter in this book is based on the research into the 'plotlands' which he undertook with Dennis Hardy, with whom he has written a forthcoming book entitled *Arcadia for All: The Legacy of a Makeshift Landscape*. He lives near Kersey in Suffolk.

FAY WELDON was born in Worcestershire but spent her early childhood in New Zealand. Since the late 1960s she has been a highly-acclaimed novelist, short-story writer and scriptwriter. Her novels include *Down Among the Women, Little Sisters* and *Praxis*, which was shortlisted for the 1979 Booker Prize. Her most recent novel is *The Life and Loves of a She-Devil*. In 1983 she spent five months in Australia, where she was invited to the Adelaide Festival and then became writer-in-residence at Sydney's Institute of Technology. She now divides her time between London and Somerset.

RAYMOND WILLIAMS was born in 1921 at the Welsh border village of Pandy. He was educated at Abergavenny Grammar School and at Trinity College, Cambridge. After the Second World War, in which he served as an anti-tank captain in the Guards Armoured Division, he became an adult education tutor in the Oxford University Delegacy for Extra-Mural Studies until 1961, when he was elected Fellow of Jesus College, Cambridge. He was later appointed University Professor of Drama. In 1947 he edited *Politics and Letters* and during the 1960s was editor of the *New Thinker's Library*. In 1968 he edited the *May Day Manifesto*.

Raymond Williams's many books include: *Culture and Society, The Long Revolution, Communications, Towards 2000* and *Television, Technology and Cultural Form; Drama in Performance, Modern Tragedy* and *Drama from Ibsen to Brecht; The English Novel from Dickens to Lawrence, Orwell* and *The Country and the City; Politics and Letters* (interviews) and *Problems in Materialism and Culture* (selected essays); and four novels – *The Volunteers*, and the Welsh trilogy of *Border Country, Second Generation* and *The Fight for Manod*. Two of his plays, *A Letter from the Country* and *Public Inquiry*, have been performed on B.B.C. Television.

He was married in 1942, has three children, and divides his time between Cambridge and Wales.

Acknowledgments

We owe thanks to a large number of people for giving us help and the courage to transform an idea into this book. We should especially like to thank:

Ronald Blythe for getting us started; Michael Clifford and the Board of Directors of Common Ground – Roger Deakin, Robin Grove-White and Robert Hutchison – for their constant help and advice; Sue Davies, Director of the Photographers' Gallery and Alister Warman, late of the Arts Council, now Director of the Serpentine Gallery; John Halkes, Director of the Newlyn Orion Gallery, Penzance, for his help and enthusiasm and for organising an exhibition of the art work from this book; and everyone at Jonathan Cape for their faith, enthusiasm and generosity throughout.

Most of all we wish to thank Richard Mabey for the way he has shaped the book, his forbearance and his generosity to Common Ground, and all the writers and artists who have influenced our perceptions, and who have so kindly and thoughtfully given their time and often much more and for making us feel at ease in a new environment. We thank them all for generously agreeing that some of the proceeds from the sale of this book should go to Common Ground.

Susan Clifford & Angela King
Common Ground

Common Ground

'Our belief is that conservation should begin at the local level and with the commonplace to help a much wider section of the community maintain its contact with the natural world. Our intention is to give inspiration and courage to people to conserve their local surroundings — their village ponds, historic barns and bluebell woods. As a means to this end we intend to provide links between the arts and the conservation of landscapes and nature. We are convinced that it is time for the arts with all their emotional force and power of persuasion to help justify and strengthen the resolve of people to speak out for what they find valuable in the world about them.'

Common Ground acts as a catalyst or agency promoting ideas and bringing different groups of people and ideas together. *Second Nature* is, we hope, the first of a series of anthologies drawing together ideas and people from the arts. In addition we are involved in promoting practical action at the parish/local level. *Holding Your Ground*, a handbook offering straightforward advice on how to conserve local wildlife, landscape, vernacular buildings and ancient monuments is to be published by Temple Smith in January 1985.

The New Milestones Project is encouraging a new generation of village and countryside sculptures involving artists and craftspeople with local communities in celebration of their locality.

Common Ground has no membership; it is a small limited company and charity, relying on grants and donations to continue its work.

Common Ground
21 Ospringe Road
London NW5

Picture Credits

The editors and publishers wish to thank the following for granting permission to reproduce the works listed below: Roger Ackling, for 'Cloud Drawing' (© Roger Ackling 1983) on p. 188; Norman Ackroyd, for 'Sutton Mandeville – Walter's Path' (© Norman Ackroyd 1983) on p. 12, 'Westmere Evening' (© Norman Ackroyd 1980) on p. 13 and 'Summer Daybreak – Crockey Hill' (© Norman Ackroyd 1982) on p. 14; Conrad Atkinson, for 'Plutonium Landscape' (© Conrad Atkinson 1980) on p. 152; John Blakemore, for 'Wind Series, Ambergate, Derbyshire, 1981' (© John Blakemore 1981) on pp. 94–5; Stephen Dalton, for 'Swallow Drinking' (© Stephen Dalton 1984) on p. 116 and 'Carder Bee' (© Stephen Dalton 1984) on p. 117; Chris Drury, for 'Medicine Wheel' (© Chris Drury 1983) on pp. 44–5; Elisabeth Frink, for 'Dog, 1980' (© Elisabeth Frink 1980) on p. 103 and 'Barn Owl, 1974' (© Elisabeth Frink 1974) on p. 104; Hamish Fulton, for 'A Hollow Lane on the North Downs' (© Hamish Fulton 1971) on p. 132, 'No Horizons' (© Hamish Fulton 1976) on p. 133 and 'Barking Dogs' (© Hamish Fulton 1978) on pp. 134–5; Fay Godwin, for 'Peak District, Derbyshire' (© Fay Godwin 1984) on p. 54 and 'near Haystacks, Cumbria' (© Fay Godwin 1984) on p. 55; Andy Goldsworthy, for 'Bracken Leaves' (© Andy Goldsworthy 1982) and 'Sycamore Leaves' (© Andy Goldsworthy 1977) on p. 80, 'Ice Stacks' and 'Ice Arch' (both © Andy Goldsworthy 1982) on p. 81 and 'Snowball in Trees' (© Andy Goldsworthy 1982) on p. 82; Paul Hempton, for 'Stone Staff and Triangle (No. 13), 1983' (© Paul Hempton 1983) on p. 154; Paul Hill for 'February, 1983', 'May, 1983', 'July, 1983' and 'November, 1983' (all © Paul Hill 1984) on pp. 173–6, 'Badger Set, 1983' (© Paul Hill 1984) on p. 195 and 'Frog Spawn, 1983' (© Paul Hill 1984) on p. 196; John Hilliard for 'Revelation, 1983' (© John Hilliard 1984) on p. 63, 'Isle of Arran, 1983' (© John Hilliard 1984) on pp. 64–5 and 'Vision, 1983' (© John Hilliard 1984) on p. 66; David Hockney for 'My Mother, Bolton Abbey, Yorkshire, November 1982' (© David Hockney 1982) on p. 187; John Hubbard, for 'Abbotsbury Gardens, 1982' (© John Hubbard 1982) on p. 74 and 'The Sunken Lane' (© John Hubbard 1982) on p. 79; Sirkka-Liisa Konttinen, for 'Harry, St Peter's Allotment, 1973' (© Amber Associates 1983) and 'Kids with Collected Junk near Byker Bridge, 1971' (© Amber Associates 1983) on p. 35; Jorge Lewinski, for 'Laugharne by Dylan Thomas's House' and 'Walter Scott's Tower' (both © Jorge Lewinski 1984) on p. 153; Richard Long, for 'Childhood Ground Abiding Places, 1983' and 'Avon Gorge Water Drawing, 1983' (both © Richard Long 1983) on pp. 90 and 91, 'A Line in England, 1977' (© Richard Long 1977) on p. 92 and 'Low Water Circle Walk, 1980' (© Richard Long 1980) on p. 93; Jamie McCullough, for 'Beginners' Way' (photographs © Peter Thomas 1984) on pp. 146–7; Alexander MacKenzie, for 'Farndale, 1983' and 'Grange, Cumbria, 1983' (both © Alexander MacKenzie 1983) on p. 150 and 'Lee Moor Variations' (© Alexander Mackenzie 1983) on p. 151; David G. Measures, for 'from Sketchbooks 1976–83' (© David G. Measures 1976–83) on pp. 105–113, 'Hare, 1982' (© David G. Measures 1982) and 'Lapwings on Stubble, 1978' (© David G. Measures 1978) on p. 115 and 'Night of Total Eclipse, 1982' (© David G. Measures 1982) on p. 118; Henry Moore, for 'Sheep Grazing in Long Grass (No. 1), 1981' (© The Henry Moore Foundation 1981) on p. 148 and 'Henry Moore and Sheep Piece' (photograph © Jorge Lewinski 1984) on p. 149; David Nash, for 'Sheep Spaces' (© David Nash 1983) on p. 46, 'Sod Swap' (© David Nash 1983) on p. 47 and 'Wet Stones' (© David Nash 1983) on p. 48; James Ravilious, for 'Lost Sheep', 'In the Heat of May' and 'Sheep at Upcott' (all © Beaford Archive 1984) on pp. 25, 26 and 27; Robin Tanner, for 'March, 1982' (© Robin Tanner 1982) on p. 208 and 'The Fritillary Fields, 1983' (© Robin Tanner 1983) on p. 207.